Alike

AND

DIFFERENT

The Clinical and Educational Uses
of Orff-Schulwerk

SECOND EDITION

Carol Hampton Bitcon

Barcelona
PUBLISHERS

This second edition is published and distributed by Barcelona Publishers, 4 White Brook Road, Lower Village, Gilsum, NH 03448.

ISBN: 1-891278-09-6

First Barcelona Publishers printing July 2000

10   9   8   7   6   5   4   3   2   1

Copyeditor: Katharine O'Moore-Klopf of *KOK Edit*
Cover design and layout copyright © 2000 by Frank McShane

Printed in the U.S.A.

I Dedicate This Book to Me

I am—a product of my ever-changing environment.
I am—a result of those who loved, nourished, and trusted me.
It is through relationships, exploration, diversity, and discovery,
all of which have been gifted to me—that *I am*.

Those whom I thank, know—for they are loved.
Those whom I thank, know—for they are respected.
Those whom I thank, know—for they are a part of me,
as I am a part of them.

I rejoice in my heritage, for it is me.
I rejoice that I am allowed to be me,
although to be what I am is not always what I relish.

I dedicate this book to me,
For it *is* me—today and tomorrow.

Carol Hampton Bitcon . . .

- Grew up in Menlo Park, California, in a warm, supportive environment that reinforced diversity and a sense of humor.
- Teaches university and college workshops; attended San Mateo College, San Francisco Conservatory of Music; and received a bachelor's degree in music from the University of the Pacific and a master's degree in counseling psychology from Chapman University.
- Is a Registered Music Therapist and filled an administrative position as program director for the Adolescent/Social Development Program at the Fairview Developmental Center for the Learning Disabled in Costa Mesa, California.
- Completed classes while participating in research, clinical work, and play.
- Was married to John Bitcon and two children, Ron and Shari, with him.
- Has traveled extensively and is respected for her clinical and administrative work.
- Has adapted Orff-Schulwerk concepts to clinical and educational programs emphasizing success and diversity in music, dance, drama, poetry, and art.
- Has the highest respect for simplicity and for the complex results of co-authorship.

Since the first edition of *Alike and Different* was published, Carol has gone through a variety of life changes while maintaining her professional standing. John died early in 1994, leaving her prepared to move forward. She still teaches, assists people trying to achieve personal growth, writes, and struggles to recover from a bout with *Escherichia coli* in 1998, which required many weeks of work with a rehabilitation specialist. Her current address is 3446 Magnolia Boulevard, West Seattle, Washington 98199.

Carol Hampton Bitcon

ACKNOWLEDGMENTS

My thanks to

- The staff of the Adolescent Social Development Program at the Fairview Developmental Center for the Learning Disabled, Costa Mesa, California, who have endured, suffered, supported, laughed, and sighed with me. It's been an arduous journey for us all.
- My parents, Wade and Edith Hampton, for their love and support, and my husband John and children Shari and Ron, for their encouragement.
- The Department of Mental Hygiene, now known as the Department of Health, for the training and resources it provided.
- Those who showed me that being a civil servant has many bright sides.
- Those who have developed projects used in this book.
- Dr. Anthony N. Toto for his support and encouragement, since adaptation of Orff-Schulwerk was just a germ of an idea, through many expenditures for instruments, many hours of training, many strange sounds during meetings, and many meetings that were overtaken by gongs, chanting, and spontaneous laughter. You see, Dr. Toto knew that an institution does not have to be dull and routine; he knew that every person has unique qualities worthy of consideration. His management style and leadership was in fact open-ended, providing for exploration, diversity, and discovery. Is that not Orff-Schulwerk? Thank you, Dr. Toto!

Alike and different,
Alike and different.
We are both
Alike and different.

CONTENTS

FOREWORD

I had promised myself the pleasure of writing this book for 3 years. Writing is quite different than lecturing. I find it so easy to talk, a venue without much criticism of my words, but writing cries for rewriting and more effective, exciting ways of stating what I mean. An additional problem with writing is that many of the materials used in this book were developed by students and associates or drawn from written material that I cannot credit because Orff-Schulwerk is a process of sharing, drawing on stimuli relative to your own internal rhythms. Often, the material is changed in the process; the original is forgotten as the changing material is used by many and passed on, with the originators going without recognition. I hope those who originated some of the material in this book are rewarded by its inclusion—in altered form—here.

The resources, insight, and philosophy in this book were shaped by clinical and educational experience as teacher, observer, and, perhaps most influential, participant. I may come across as disoriented at times, dropping in quick thoughts, but take these and shape them to your own role development and they may become a part of your repertoire, without your realizing it. Just jump right in!

I am often asked, "Where do I buy that kit you're using?" "Where do you buy the resources?" "Will you give me your kit to copy so I, too, can be an Orff-Schulwerk specialist?" These very questions are what, for a long while, kept me from writing: the resources are useless without knowledge of how to use them or experience in developing and adapting your own material and then seeking out new ideas to integrate into your own style of work/play. These resources are useless when taken out of context and without some thought of where and how they can be expanded on. I allude to expansion possibilities in some of the examples in this book, hoping to prompt you into developing additional ideas. It is always stimulating and productive to work with someone who critiques or builds on ideas, a process that creates an open, functional product.

I ask you now to learn from this book, consider the resources as starting points, expand on and change them, use them, and let them go, casting aside your purpose, letting them develop as a product of group co-authorship. Internalize the material, decide how you will present it and how you will feed it, and then remain open to the "aha!" experiences of Orff-Schulwerk.

It's great to have open-ended ideas and plans for special effects—a resource of rhythms, tricks, cute sayings, and movements—but it's really wonderful when the resources in the book are merely resources and your material is what you and those working with you develop, explore, and celebrate with *joy*. When the material comes from participants and you allow it to develop, providing guidance and dynamic resources, *then* you are there—you are participating in Orff-Schulwerk!

Carol Hampton Bitcon

Chapter 1

INTRODUCTION

CARL ORFF AND HIS SCHULWERK

Carl Orff[1] was born in Munich on July 10, 1895. In his long career as a composer, he was never a detached artist. During his lifetime (he died in 1982), he became one of Germany's greatest living composers, creating such major works as *Carmina burana, Prometheus,* and *Cantuli carmina,* to mention just a few.

Coming from a Bavarian farming family, Orff demonstrated an early and extraordinary interest in fairy tales, myths, and especially puppet shows. For his shows, he constructed his own stages and wrote his own plays and his own music. As a child, he already preferred percussion and piano; the rhythmic element was more important than the melodic.

Orff was, strictly speaking, his own teacher: there were no teachers for what was important to him. Only when he had finished his *Carmina burana* in 1936 did the 40-year-old write to his publisher: "Here begin my 'Collected Works'!" Carl Orff continued then with a series of compositions that seem contrasting in nature but are so only on the surface. "Music alone has never been my singular concern, but rather a spiritual statement" was how Orff justified his choice of subject matter.

Orff's preoccupation with Shakespearean theater began when he was a young student with Otto Falckenberg at the Munich Kammerspiele. In the 1920s in Munich, Orff encountered dance instructress Dorothea Gunther. She had opened her own school that combined gymnastic elements with dance gestures and movements that corresponded to a natural feeling for the body. From the beginning, Orff wrote "gesticulative" music, music that mirrored and awakened movements both in a spiritual and a physical sense. "Music

---

[1] Having reviewed Carl Orff's biography and numerous articles in trying to pull ideas together, I found some of the most informative materials on a record jacket written by Walter Panocsky on the album *Musicalisches Hausbuck,* released by Harmonia Mundi in 1973, Stereo KHB 20374.

from movements—dance from music" was the motto of Gunther's school.

Martha Wampler[2] wrote that

> His Schulwerk, translated "School-Work," was already making an impact on educational thought before the 1937 Premiere of his "Carmina Burana." . . . Orff's elemental style was rejected for many years. Rooted in both his artistic and educational life was Orff's spiritual attitude. This spiritual attitude would return men's minds and hearts to elemental, first impulses of human expression. Orff felt that all art forms should be integrated in the important formative years. Instead of using a standard theoretical teaching method, everything in the child's experience, music, movement, speech, should be combined to provide raw material for his or her own creative efforts.

Orff[3] based his philosophy on the premise that because children learn to speak before they learn to read and write, it follows that they should have a "musical language" with which they feel comfortable before being required to perform the more difficult tasks of playing a traditional instrument or studying music theory. Therefore, "music for children," as Orff has developed it, is elemental in the literal sense of that word. It deals with the elements, the basic groundwork from which more complex ideas grow. Children learn to feel rhythms, hear melodies, and put their own feelings into those rhythms and melodies before they are required to read and write music.

Both speech and movement are instinctive—we use them from birth. But they are more than this: they are rhythmic. If we can adopt these functions, which we have performed done so naturally for so long, to our teaching pedagogy, it makes our learning of musical skills easier and more certain.

This unique music educational work in its present form has been developing since the World War II. The original idea of the creative, educational power of music is realized in that it is already found in Plato's ancient world of ideas. With Schulwerk, Orff brought back us

---

[2]Orff-Schulwerk, *A Celebration of Lifelong Learning*, vol. XXVII, March 5, 1973, University of California, Los Angeles.

[3]Johnson, S. E. P. *The Journal*. New York: Rochester Early Learning Association.

back to what has been obscured by 2,000 years of socialization: the development of the consciousness through the elementary forces of rhythms and sounds in conjunction with the magic word. This development is intended to begin in the child and continue with the maturing of the individual. Orff-Schulwerk is lifelong learning.

Orff developed a special instrumentation for his Schulwerk based, above all, on rhythm instruments, xylophones of all sizes, glockenspiels, kettle drums, tambourines, tambours, hand bells, and triangles. In the Schulwerk process, melody instruments, especially recorder and deep strings, are gradually added. The element of rhythm remains the basis of music-making, growing from word and verse texts purposely taken from old language traditions, such as children's rhymes and magic sayings, prayers, fairy-tale verses, and folk songs. The words are returned to their magical origins: pictures are transformed into music and music into movement so that the imagination is stimulated and nourished and can unfold in its own spectrum of sound. In his Schulwerk, Orff not only returned to an elementary world of sound but also demonstrated, through creatively comprehended and interpreted history, routes to a new communion with objects of the spiritual world through movement.

The play pieces of the Schulwerk are not to be understood as final, unchangeable compositions but rather as models that can be imitated, transformed, and further developed by each individual. The are no boundaries for imagination: in a short period of time, Schulwerk has conquered foreign lands and continents.

In July 1961 at the Academy for Music and the Arts in the Mozarteum in Salzburg, a center and seminar for Orff's Schulwerk was established. The center is for teacher training and further research in view of the unforeseen way in which the practice of Schulwerk has spread throughout Europe and other continents. Orff collaborated with Gunild Keetman in developing the institute. At the institute, training in movement is as important a factor as any other aspect of Schulwerk. There are English-language classes given at the institute, which has relocated out of the main part of Salzburg to the quiet countryside where nature's beauty enhances joyful learning.

Carl Orff said in an interview, "I never imagined that my educational effort would win understanding and acceptance so quickly and so widely. When I was writing Schulwerk, I had merely the intention of providing my Bavarian homeland with a useful and practical course in elementary musical education. But these ideas have spread so much in the last ten years that now Schulwerk is being taught in over twenty languages."

Shortly before he turned 81, Orff received an honorary degree from the University of Regensburg in Germany. When he was presented with the degree, it was stated that no other composer living in Bavaria since Richard Wagner and Richard Strauss enjoyed such undisputed world recognition and stature as did Carl Orff.

If you have the opportunity to work with Gertrud Orff, who frequently travels to the United States, or with Martha Wampler, you can get additional information concerning Carl Orff.

WHAT IS ORFF-SCHULWERK?

One of the best resources I have found for describing Orff-Schulwerk is the *Orff-Schulwerk Design for Creativity*, a report to the U.S. Office of Education of ESEA Title III Project, Bellflower Unified School District, Bellflower, California, 1968.

Some of the following concepts are taken from the work, as they relate to my own work, but there are many additional concepts that might interest readers. I have used *participant* and *individual* instead of *child* because Orff-Schulwerk involves lifelong learning, even though the project was written for schoolchildren. Martha Wampler, Gertrud Orff, and Margit Cromueller-Smith were instrumental in developing the project, pulling in many resources for evaluations, organizing seminars, and then compiling the publication. This particular section of this chapter draws on their resources.

Orff-Schulwerk is a creative process that involves every participant through participation in the process. In addition to music, concerns itself with the complexities of the body, the spirit, and the deepest feelings common to all humankind. In short, it is concerned with all possible forms of communication.

Improvisation is main facet of Orff-Schulwerk. Individual awareness of the active process becomes a self-motivating power in performance; thus, Orff-Schulwerk is self-expression. Orff-Schulwerk involves rhythmic education: rhythm is first a mental activity and then is manifested in sound and movement. Orff-Schulwerk, then, facilitates participants' innate predisposition toward self-expression, a broad basis on which much other work can be built.

As individuals participate in the group process, feedback is immediate through acceptance; contributions are frequently modified in spontaneous co-authorship. Individuals' contributions to the group vary according to their level of involvement and inner range of resources. Individuals' feelings of making a contribution will vary according to their success at group participation, including self-expression. Reinforcement of individuals' belief in themselves and their ability to express themselves cannot be handled by telling them they are right or wrong. Their unique contributions should receive consideration each time, and the criteria by which their ideas are accepted or modified should in terms they can perceive, such as through listening, looking, empathizing with others, and modifying others' work as it relates to their own. Successful facilitation of the group process will provide immediate feedback. The growth of dependable spontaneity among participants in Orff-Schulwerk activities is first perceived by participants in their ability to sustain a germ idea throughout many improvisory contributions. If the invention of a given idea destroys the parameters selected by the group, then its effectiveness is lost and the participant has shown his or her lack of dependability. At that point, the individual can perceive the appropriateness, or lack thereof, of his or her contribution. Usually, a group interaction in process of modifying an individual improvisation is not a damaging experience. The group can sustain an error through honest reflection of the unfitting response. (See "Clinical Orff-Schulwerk" below.) The role of the teacher/clinician determines the results of the experience. The inventor can continue his or her search in the atmosphere of total participation; with every stage of development, the group becomes more engaged in finding the most varied inventions in terms of ideas, so that constant reinforcing of appropriateness occurs with the widest possible interpretation of the idea.

Orff-Schulwerk is an experience in elemental music. Carl Orff defined *elemental* as pertaining to the elements, primeval, rudimentary, treating of first principles. Elemental music, then, is never music alone but music in unity with movement, dance, and speech. It is music that one makes oneself, in which one takes part not as a listener but as a participant. It is unsophisticated, employs no big architectural structures, and uses small sequence forms, ostinato and rondo. Elemental music is of the earth—natural, physical, within the range of everyone to learn it and to experience it.

Orff-Schulwerk is concerned with participants' learning the power of creativity to affect innovation in cooperation with others. The Orff-Schulwerk instructor integrates social skills—namely, behaviors that allow participants to interact with the group and, in a special sense, as co-authors of group compositions—with elemental musical forms.

Beginning with the circle, Orff-Schulwerk activity is based on concerted responses in imitation of the solo inventor who occupies the middle of the circle. Such a design develops the echo or imitation form, the question–answer form, and simple solo–tutti compositions of contrasting bodies of sound. The solo may become a group of soloists and instruments may be added into the same design. Leadership and participation in meaningful ensemble play become social skills as well as musical skills in the design of creativity, in this case the circle.

Learning how to participate within these forms grows out of unforced experiences that naturally follow the group design, such as a circle, and that fall into the play patterns of elemental composition:

- Imitation or echo
- Extension by question–answer responding
- Invention of opposites
- Invention of contrasts
- Invention of ostinato accompaniment
- Simple solo

Play patterns are the forms known as

- Rondo, composed of imitation and contrast
- Solo–tutti, composed of echo or question–answer
- Three-part, composed of similarity and contrast
- Recitative, composed of solo invention

In Orff-Schulwerk, participants are working and manipulating real sounds and real space designs, but creative action must depend on ideas. Reflection, then, is important before activity; it is also important to follow the activity to internalize experience and symbolically represent it.

The rondo form (*A, B, A, C, A, D,* and so on) is frequently used in the beginning of Orff-Schulwerk because

- It provides a strongly recognizable structure for elements of sound (tonal, verbal, rhythmic) into which every given part has a particular place and function.
- It provides natural opportunities for individual creation that occur organically in the structure of the whole.

- It provides by its process of repetition an unforced and musical basis for teaching skills; instrumental, vocal, or movement techniques can be worked and reworked in every recurrent *A* theme.
- It allows for maximum variety of responses within a balanced rondo form and therefore works well in group teaching in which original and individual participation must be expedited.

The rondo form is used extensively in the clinical application sections of this book, so perhaps stop now to reread and absorb.

(Yes, teacher! I'll do that right now.)
(Good student! You'll go far if you can reread and then experience diversity of thought—and your own process.)

The Orff-Schulwerk instrumentarium is a specially designed body of instruments with elemental characteristics of sound and physical manner of performance. In Orff-Schulwerk, spontaneity is supported by valuing discovery because divergent thought is safe in an atmosphere relatively free of convergent expectations. The use of melodic and accompaniment instruments increases, but technique is never a crucial matter and no participant is penalized for ineptness or lack of coordination. On the contrary, the specialized instruments of Orff-Schulwerk have such a pleasing sound and nonabrasive tone that any contribution is acceptable.

Orff-Schulwerk can be expressed as the processes of

- *Improvisation,* which is a natural activity in Orff-Schulwerk because Orff-Schulwerk is concerned with growth in quality of improvisation and in increasing dependability of spontaneity. Developing improvisation skills is more than an exercise, but it should involve growing awareness of appropriateness and structural elements.
- *Selectivity,* which is basic to the artistic experience. Participants, as co-authors, select from an array of improvisations those works, gestures, or movements and rhythms they want to save and formalize.

- *Fulfillment* of a given idea for composition, which is often in itself improvisatory. Filling out in Orff-Schulwerk means both social and artistic growth.
- *Closure,* which is necessary to aesthetic experience. Orff-Schulwerk is both an aesthetic and an intellectual experience. Therefore, because intellect requires continuing motivation, the most effective kind of closure is open-ended. Orff-Schulwerk is like a germ itself. It can wake you, follow you, or cause finger-tapping in least expected surroundings. The need to turn something over and over in the mind—for Orff-Schulwerk, the rhythms, words, or gestures and movements that evolve in the process of composition—is an inherent tension in any artistic endeavor or invention.

CLINICAL ORFF-SCHULWERK

My interest in the clinical applications of Orff-Schulwerk began at the Fairview Developmental Center for the Learning Disabled in Costa Mesa, California. There I encountered extensive challenges as a clinician. Innovative adaptive programs were needed for the more independent clients; in fact, a new client population was developing. Meanwhile, less dependent clients were placed in protective environments in the community or at other facilities, meaning clinicians were faced with developing programming for more severely limited individuals who certainly needed programming and had the right to programming. Accordingly, clinicians used any resource possibly appropriate for meeting the needs of these individuals in a humanizing, healthy environment. Many resources were developed and many techniques were tried, some with success and others without much success. Support from the Department of Mental Hygiene (now the Department of Health) was available in the form of training funds and resources to be used to better meet programming objectives.

During this stage of trial-and-error searching, members of the rehabilitation services staff attended an Orff-Schulwerk symposium in May 1968 in Los Angeles. The symposium's emphasis was on Orff-Schulwerk for grades kindergarten through 5; there was an exciting presentation of the qualifications for creativity. I was most impressed with the description of the various traits of creativity. As I listened, I became intrigued with the similarity of those traits to many traits possessed by the developmentally disabled and I wondered about the level of creativity of those with limited intelligence. At that conference, I met Gertrud Orff, Martha Wampler, and Margit Cromueller-Smith. I returned to Fairview to talk with the staff and find funds for training the staff in Orff-Schulwerk. There were funds available for training and for bringing consultants into the facility. Gertrud had already provided a demonstration workshop, with the Western Regional Music Therapy Association, at Fairview, and Martha Wampler signed a contract to come to Fairview to provide a series of workshops for the clinical staff. The staff was then presented with the challenge of adapting the Orff-Schulwerk training to the needs of the clients at Fairview. The dynamics of working together as a staff would have warranted the training without ever moving on to direct programming for the clients in Orff-Schulwerk.

Dr. Anthony N. Toto, Fairview's medical director, became interested in the new modality being developed, earmarking funds for the instruments and allowing the hours needed for staff to further develop the clinical use of Orff-Schulwerk. As we experienced success and the program grew, I wrote a training proposal for the Department of Mental Hygiene and was granted funding to provide training in the community and at other state facilities so others could use and adapt new clinical skills. We were soon successful with many clients with varying disabilities. The strange name *Orff-Schulwerk* began to confer a bit of status once people knew what it meant. Members of the finance section in the state system would visit Fairview, ask what this strange expenditure was, be invited to visit a session, and, before the day was over and at the insistence of the clients, sit on the floor in a circle and participate with the group. Each group member, old and new, experienced success.

VARIATIONS IN CLINICAL
ORFF-SCHULWERK

As you expose yourself to different teachers, clinicians, musicians, and nonmusicians in working with Orff-Schulwerk, you will have a different experience each time. Orff-Schulwerk truly is a seed that grows in many ways, and as the seed finds welcome soil, it cuddles, fosters additional growth, expands, and then moves on, leaving enough behind to flower on its own. Each experience influences the shape of this seed and rewards one's openness to learning and experiencing.

I've had students say they had seen another therapist and hadn't done Orff-Schulwerk because they would have had to read music or they didn't experience success or the therapist was serious, quiet, and nonstimulating. I am always disappointed when such criticism is directed toward others because of the teaching experience I have offered. It is not success for me when I visit a classroom or demonstration session in which one of my students is leading and hear myself emulated. Certainly, I could feel complimented, and in some ways I am, but such an experience means that I have failed to assist that individual in exploring his or her own uniqueness in teaching and in relating and that I have made that student dependent on my style. Teachers and clinicians must expose themselves to a variety of situations; participate fully and then evaluate what has happened, what has been effective, and what was or was not useful; and internalize these experiences to develop an individual style that will continually be subject to change. I have incorporated a page entitled "Leader Goose" in this book that details an experience I had when I turned off to a new experience and watched with closed-mindedness and criticism. I lost out because the session grew to exciting dimensions without my participation. After that, I made a commitment to allowing other people the chance to lead, to stop placing myself in a position of control from which I could stop or encourage events according to my level of comfort.

The criteria for Orff-Schulwerk depend on the people participating in the session, but success depends on the leader's sensitivity and resourcefulness. Clinical Orff-Schulwerk places heavy emphasis on the process rather than the product, so that success is implicit. There are four vital requirements that must be met to ensure desirable results with Orff-Schulwerk in clinical settings:

- **Success must be implicit in the session.** Granted, success may not always be immediate, but it must reward any approximation of participation. As participants become more sophisticated, so will their contributions. It's amazing how both adults and children can be so hesitant to participate in a group setting until they perceive the environment as positive and then increasingly take on more risk.
- **Open-ended material should be presented to whatever degree possible.** There may be a requirement for a specific response, but then expansion on that response is allowed. For individuals with extremely limited ability to participate, the material presented might at first be very controlled, requiring little—if any—expansion on a theme. This control will lessen as the participants understand the process and are better able to participate. Sometimes with applied learning, repetitious material is presented that on the surface seems controlled but that on review of the needs and the progress of the group is found to have a surprising degree of openness relative to group members' abilities.
- **Materials used must be appropriate to the abilities of the individuals in the group.** The leader's skill and the resources available to him or her will guide him or her in selecting appropriate materials.
- **Adaptability, flexibility, sensitivity, knowledge of disabilities and therapeutic needs, a sense of humor, and a regard for personal dignity must be employed.**

The preintellectual approach to music, movement, communications, silence, dramatics, mime, and art provides an excellent resource for any participant, whether with or without problems. Drawing on all of these resources with the sophistication of simplicity (which takes great skill) provides ready tools for functional programming (programming with applied purpose) and joyous celebration. Both verbal and nonverbal participants can work and celebrate together, as can the mentally limited and the mentally gifted. The deaf can expand their ideas on instruments, as can the blind, the aged, the disturbed, the palsied, the depressed, the inappropriate, the painfully introverted, and those who act out. All can and do celebrate together.

Visiting school programs for the disabled can be an eye-opening experience. Frequently, the special classes are in temporary buildings off in a corner of the school away from the others and the labels *retardos, dummies,* and *freaks* are readily used on the playground against disabled students. Orff-Schulwerk, which is preintellectual and can be totally nonverbal, provides a great opportunity for children with a variety of skills to work together, modeling the leader in reinforcing and respecting each individual as a unique person with special qualities that only the wise will discover . . . and even sharing real names. Suddenly the "retardo" becomes Jane or Bill or the child who is learning to whistle or play the kazoo—the child "we" are helping to talk or smile or move. A pretty big change in attitude? It sure is! The success children have in helping others is going to be the success of those being helped.

As a sixth-grader, my daughter took skills she had learned teaching and working with me and shared them with a few friends who had participated at some sessions my friends and I had provided at her grade school. Together they developed a project and worked with kindergarten children in the classroom. At first the kindergarten teacher was patronizing, but suddenly she wanted to know more. What she did with what she learned, I do not know, but an opportunity for teacher and students to share was there. My daughter and her friends thought about the playground structured activities presented to the kindergarten children and adapted activities to meet the younger children's needs in a most appropriate manner, each of the older girls contributing ideas and success. They encountered some difficult obstacles, such as presenting an activity that was not structured enough and very physical, a fire drill in the middle of the unstructured activity, an uncomfortable teacher who continually interfered by making the children go back to the instruments and "play better," and one little girl who asked them "What are you going to do with all those damn instruments?" and shocked the sixth-grade girls into giggles.

So you see, there really are no set requirements regarding participants' abilities. The responsibility for success is really that of the leader, who must carefully group, interact, reinforce, select materials, and be ready to develop resources on the spot. The leader needs an ability to draw from minimal responses and nurture them responses to develop that which will contribute to a composition of excitement, ownership, and fulfillment. The signs of success and closure will be sighs, grins, deep breathing, joy, and each participant's knowledge that *"I am."*

Chapter 2

NAMES

I am. I am Carol. I have a possession that all others have. Whether institutionalized or limited in intellect or not, I still have a name. Sometimes my name is spoken softly, sometimes harshly, sometimes with anger, often with love. But I *am* Carol.

Names are probably used in every group process and almost always initial activities because in sharing and learning others' names, we begin our relationships on common ground. If we are to move forward and discover how unique we are, we need to make a statement about our selves and know who else is contributing to the statement. Sometimes we have the same name as someone else, but then our discovery is how we two are alike and how we are different. It's not hard to make a name unique regardless of its similarity to someone else's name. Looking for a singular trait and finding something special about same names is just one step forward in determining uniqueness. It can be fun to look at those with the same name and determine what's different about them. At a later date, the differences will be clearer, and it's interesting to remember, when the differences have become so obvious, what it was like when the search was on for those differences.

I am going to give you a big variety of name activities. You will learn which ones accomplish what you want or feel comfortable to you. There are all sorts of ways of approaching names, so I hope you add to the activities presented in this chapter. There are also a few other name activities in different sections of the book.

(1)
I've got a name
And it sounds like this!
I've got a name
And it sounds like this.

For activity 1, develop a comfortable rhythm for the chant. Rubbing legs, hitting the floor, snapping the fingers, and clapping hands all add to the variety . . . as does silence.

(2)
Name game,
Name game,
Let's play
A name game.

Dr. Bette Davis developed activity 2 and presented it at a workshop on creative practices. I use a *patchen* on the words and *snap, snap* with my left hand and then my right hand. I keep going with the *patchen, patchen* (left thigh, right thigh), left-hand *snap*, right-hand *snap* through the activity and then stop:

Name game [snap, snap],
Name game [snap, snap],
Let's play [snap, snap]
A name game [snap, snap].

You'll need to separate the theme (*A*) from the response (*B, C, D,* and so on) or you'll get a cheerleader routine in which the response is controlled by the *A* part of the activity and must meet the rhythm requirement of part *A*. Initially that might be a good idea until participants are comfortable. Sometimes, however, you want to put the control on the response, have movement within a certain period of time, or emphasize phrasing. It gets very boring if you maintain the theme through the responses too often. The group will try to keep it going just because they get comfortable with the rhythm and do not want to lose it.

I believe Genola developed activity 3 at Stockton State Hospital in California when she wanted a relaxed name review with the participants revealing something about themselves and discovering alikeness, such as coming from other states or having visited someone's state of birth. I believe she was using the activity with older mentally handicapped individuals who needed the socialization skills of being aware of each other and relating to current real issues. Even if I have misremembered the type of group she was working with, this activity would still have worked with such a group.

(3)
Who are you
And where
Were you born?

(4)
Names go up;
Names go down.
Show us how
Your name sounds.

For activity 4, I raise my arms high, snapping my fingers, and then drop them low for the *down*, raising my voice far up and then dropping it far down. Inflection is the emphasis in this activity, although *up* and *down* can inadvertently be learned. Get a high stretch; it loosens the group up for more activities to follow.

(5)
You have a name,
Rum-a-tum-tum.
I have a name,
Rum-a-tum-tum.
Now play your name
On the drum!

(6)
I am your neighbor.
How do you do?
I am _____ .
Who are you?

As our able instructor, Martha Wampler brought activity 7 to our early training sessions at Fairview when the rehabilitation therapists received intensive training in Orff-Schulwerk. That certainly was a special time in our lives. With Martha's guidance and philosophy of learning through discovery, we all grew rapidly.

(7)
Round and round and
Round in the game.
Around in the circle
Is to know your name.

For activity 7, make circular movements with your arms, entire body, and parts of your body, again stretching. Discover what round things are in the room. Sometimes I play with round sounds after this activity if the group is ready to play.

(8)
I've got a name and
You do, too!
My name's _____ .
Who are you?

I developed activity 8 after working with Grace Nash with her activity "Have a Happy Day." I use the same "Have a Happy Day" rhythms that she developed, and I appreciate her sharing. The rhythm is

Patchen, patchen [both hands to both thighs],
Clap, clap [both hands together],
Patchen, patchen,
Snap, snap [both hands snapping in the air].

Work on it! After you get the rhythm going, add the chant and name and then keep the rhythm going. One group member turns to the adjacent person and gives his or her name, and then that person picks up the chant and turns to the next person and gives his or her name—and so on until all have had a turn.

(9)
Leader: *Good morning!* [Clap, clap, clap.]
Group: *Good morning!* [Clap, clap, clap.]
Leader: *Good morning!* [Stamp, stamp, stamp.]
Group: *Good morning!* [Stamp, stamp, stamp.]
Leader: *Who are you?* [Points to a participant.]
Group: *Who are you?* [Points to same participant.]

Activity 9 is a call–response activity. When someone is pointed at, he or she says his or her name and the group states it back. When the person feels comfortable, interesting rhythms can be added to his or her name and the group will respond with imitation of the rhythm. This activity gets the group active, although if you are too exuberant, the group will moan loudly.

(10)
Name game, name game.
What's your name and
What's your game?

(11)
I've got a name
It belongs to me.

(12)
Names, names,
We've all got names.
Say your name;
We'll say the same.

Again, more intricate patterns of rhythm and body sounds can be offered and imitated.

(13)
Tell us your name—
What you like to be called.
Tell us your name
And play it loud!

(14)
I've got a long name
Full of many sounds
My whole name is _____ .
Now on the drum I'll pound!

Activity 14 can be effective with regressed individuals who have pride in their total name and should be reminded of that pride.

(15)
I have a great name.
Listen to it loud:
[Response:] _____ .
I have a great name.
Listen to it soft.
[Response:] _____ .

(16)
Rhyming names,
Rhyming names.
What rhymes? [Clap, clap.]
What rhymes? [Snap, snap.]
What rhymes with your name?

The playground names that children make up to taunt children and nicknames that stay for a long time can be fun if voluntarily revealed but painful if revealed by someone else. After all names have been developed with a rhyming name in activity 16, quickly go around the circle and have the real name and rhyme name stated all the way around. Everyone has a silly teasing name and everyone has a real name.

(17)
Name machine—
Jerk, jerk, jerk.
Feed it your name
And make it work!

With activity 17, take turns being a machine that goes to someone in the circle who feeds a name to the machine and then watches the machine process it. The "name feeder" trades with the "machine" and goes to someone else.

(18)
Spring, spring—
A happy sound.
Sing your name
And pass it around.

For activity 18, make up a happy, springing tune and then encourage the names to be sung and have others sing the name with free chanting. Perhaps I would sing, "Carol, I am Carol!" and the next voice would sing, "Carol, she is Carol" with me or in countermelody, building the name on around the circle.

(19)
Hey, children, who's in town?
Everybody stop and look around.
Hey, children, who's in town?
Tell us your name and then sit down.

For activity 19, the group stands and each person has a turn giving a name and then sitting down. The activity ends when the last person still standing sits down.

(20)
To the beat-beat-beat of the tom-tom,
We're glad you came.
To the beat-beat-beat of the tom-tom,
Tell us your name.

If I left out the next activity, I would never live it down. The chant is one of the first activities we used at Fairview, and we also taught it to people at other facilities. It became most common to be walking somewhere in another country and hear "Name, name, what's your name?" done with a slurry nasal voice. Anytime someone mentioned Orff-Schulwerk or I was at a conference table, I would hear it resounding. I haven't used it for a long time, but it is good.

(21)
Name, name,
What's your name?
Name, name,
What's your name?

With activity 21, I would hit the floor on each side of me and then snap my fingers with both hands.

(22)
Shake hands.
How do you do?
I am _____ .
Who are you ?

(23)
My name is _____ .
How do you do?
My name is _____ .
What shall I call you?

Activity 24 is used with spelling or just giving a name. If you have a setup for shadow play, use a rear projected light and have the person spelling his or her name stand in front of the projector and spell the name with body letters. You can still spell the name with body letters in a circle, but it is not as rewarding to the person doing the spelling because body shapes cannot be seen or corrected. A student brought this activity from her daughter's cheerleading exercises. Think of the typical cheer and put the sounds with it.

(24)

N-A-M-E your name, your name.
N-A-M-E—spell us [or give us] your name!
Rah!

Enunciate each letter spelled. If you chant slowly, you will get more extended movement.

There are a few naming activities, like activity 25, that suggest that participants might want to be called something else or be someone else.

(25)

Doobie, doobie,
Doobie, dee.
Tell us who
You'd like to be.

Put pantomime with activity 25. Sometimes it is very hard for participants to answer; this activity often elicits the response "Me" because of the rhyme or, of course, because people are pleased with themselves.

(26)

Friends and neighbors,
Whoopeeeeee dooooooo!
Tell us who
Is next to you!

For activity 26, I encourage participants to tell something about the person next to them. What have they learned in sessions? Give a few minutes for a quick check with neighbors so something can be shared when it's time to do the activity.

(27)
Fee, fi, fo, fum,
Tell us which state
You're from, you're from.
Fee, fi, fo, fum,
Tell us which state you're from!

(28)
Call: [Echo]
Response: [Echo]
Call: [Echo game]
Response: [Echo game]
Call: [Echo name]
Response: [Echo name]

For activity 28, have the names sung or called, with an echo response.

Chapter 3

INSTRUMENTS

INSTRUMENTS ARE
WHERE YOU FIND THEM

The instruments used in Orff-Schulwerk can be elegant, sensitive, handmade, resourceful, or even just one's own body. I have heard beautiful music from the instrumentarium endorsed by Carl Orff and from others that are similar. I also have attended sessions where plastic trash cans, handmade instruments, and a bouncing ball have been used. Simple sounds can be combined to create a complex sound. Simplicity is the focus of this book because one simple thing combined with another simple thing becomes something more sophisticated that when handled with sensitivity allows exploration and discovery. Explore sounds, quality, rhythms, and sound resources, listening to others and the sounds around you. As you play with sounds discovered in a room, encourage others to bring in different sounds. A friend of mine at Fairview, Rose, mentioned to me that she had found a great instrument. It was a large chair holder on wheels. The bars hanging out for the chairs made an interesting sound when strummed. Better yet, the feel of the sound was very exciting and perfect for sensory deprived people. I didn't run right out and try the chair holder, but one day when attending a play in the auditorium, I found myself next to a few of the racks and happened to strum them. They *are* great!

INSTRUMENT SELECTION

Instrument quality is paramount in Orff-Schulwerk. There is no substitute for an instrument that can endure loud, heavy sounds and fragile, tender sounds and provide an opportunity for beautiful music to be made!

Toy instruments are horrible to work with once you have used quality instruments. Until you have used quality instruments, you may not understand the value of the expenditure. Please allow yourself the exposure. Xylophones, glockenspiels, and metallophones all have tuned bars that can be easily removed and scales that can be redesigned. A banged, unresponsive toy is of little value in making music.

Parents of my clients have been willing to assist with the purchase of quality instruments by holding bake sales and raffles. They are so thrilled when their children are actually participating in music-making. I sometimes go to a classroom and provide a demonstration for parents' night. That way, both parents and school administrators can hear what teachers are striving to acquire. When the financial people at Fairview came to visit Orff-Schulwerk sessions, they immediately were impressed with the use of the instruments and the respect the most difficult clients gave to the instruments. Frequently they were invited to join the circle and were turned on to their own music. When working with adults, I find they frequently first preempt their playing by saying that they have never been successful on an instrument and then suddenly, they want to play and they experience a new success.

My own use of instruments varies. I do not carry very fragile instruments when traveling or if I do not know the group. Once a group is established, I then risk taking in fragile, lovely instruments for exploration and new sensory input. I love to use instruments that have a nice feel.

For drums, I prefer the skin heads to the plastic ones simply because they have more texture when one slides one's hands across the surface and they have clear, oily-feeling sections that allow shadow play. The plastic heads certainly serve a purpose when one is working in air conditioning and moving from the cool air to extreme heat, and some of the plastic heads do have some texture.

Take care in selecting your instruments. Try their sounds and feel them and be influenced by those that give the most pleasure. I use a number of percussive instruments that I find in local music stores or while traveling. While in Europe, I picked up a large variety of bells that I have since enjoyed using in many ways. When visiting import shops, keep your eyes and ears open and fingers searching for lurking instruments to add to your collection. You need a basic complement of controlled instruments; then you can introduce some of the more diverse accent instruments. *But beware the rhythm band sound!* That is not what we are seeking in Orff-Schulwerk. We want form and diversity, matching sounds, and expansion on rhythms that come out of the natural process of the group. Still, instruments from rhythm band sets certainly can be integrated with the other instruments. Each of the types of instruments I use is described in this chapter.

ADAPT INSTRUMENTS
TO THE PERFORMER

I have a real complaint about the sticks/mallets used in many sessions. Toy instruments have interesting mallets. The instruments are designed for small children, so the size of the striking surface and the stick that must be grasped by little or poorly developed hands makes it impossible to control the instrument and get the sounds desired. Toothpick-size handles are hardly appropriate, yet some of the nicely balanced mallets with good-quality sound still are too small for special needs. Build the sticks up. Because it is very easy to do this, it is sloppiness on your part if you do not take the time to adapt mallets or sticks for the needs of the participants. When an instructor must struggle to help a participant make a solid sound or to help the participant raise a hand and drop it on a surface and then the stick flies out of the hand or wobbles uncontrollably, the joy of the experience is frequently lost. Why expend so much energy for such unsatisfying results? Adapt the instrument for the participant's needs.

Cotton with tape over it works well for adapting sticks and mallets. I use Aire-cast, an easy-to-use professional casting material, to mold a hand grip on the sticks. Surgical tubing is easily wrapped under the casting so that the tubing can be tied around the hand, leaving more surface area on the stick for play. Aire-cast looks like gauze. You unroll it, then dip it into acetone and wrap it around whatever you are adapting. If you grasp the gauze while it is drying, you'll leave an impression of your grip. Once the casting is dry, it can go through a dishwasher, making it excellent for adapting eating utensils, too.

Placement of an instrument is also important for many of the same reasons as for the correct size of the mallets. The instrument should be at the correct height, should be the correct distance away from the performer, and, if necessary, should be held at an angle if that is the only way to get the best tone. Two people can work with a performer (one behind and the other in front) who has an inability to grasp or limited range of motion. The one behind can help lift the elbow, leaving the wrist to work, or can just prompt the performer to lift his or her arm and can assist. Sometimes encouraging an adaptive posture or lifting a head will help produce sound. It is necessary, as mentioned before, to be able to work effectively with others who assist in leading the groups.

You may want to put the instruments on a table or mount them on legs. I prefer having the instruments directly on the floor. Different textured floors produce different sounds.

Be sure that mallets are the correct mallets for the instrument being used. Otherwise, heavy mallets will go through skin heads or the lovely tones of the instrument will be distorted by being struck by the wrong type of surface. The tone quality desired should be explored by trying out different mallets; once you find a good match, place the chosen mallets with their respective instruments. Sometimes I use two different colored mallets so that right and left sides can be emphasized. I think two mallets should always be presented to performers playing drums or tone bar instruments so that they are encouraged to use both sides of their body in performing. Many times, an individual with laterality problems is asked to use two sticks and he or she immediately puts both sticks in one hand. The same person might also strike at a surface and completely miss it. If this happens, work from behind and prompt both of the performer's hands into striking. The performer's joy will be your delight, as will the sound resulting from the performer's usually inactive side. Moving the drum away from the player—by even a few inches—while prompting him or her to stay in the same spot by putting pressure on the elbows or shoulders will increase the performer's chances of success in striking the instrument. Many times I have been surprised by those who can or cannot hold a stick in both hands and strike a surface.

SPECIAL CONSIDERATIONS
WITH PARTICULAR INSTRUMENTS

Because glockenspiels are less expensive than other tone bar instruments, they are more often purchased. However, a glockenspiel's striking surface is very difficult to hit and it is hard to discern specific sounds with this instrument. Before you buy an instrument, please think carefully about what playing it will require of the performer. Lower-pitched instruments have wider striking surfaces. At the same time, a variety of sounds is needed, so glockenspiels should be included in your instrumentarium. Encourage those who have the best eye–hand coordination to use glockenspiels if they are available and be sure they are located in the best position in relationship to the body so participants can get the most effective sounds with minimal struggle.

Instruments that need to be blown obviously must be played by someone who can control his or her breathing and knows something about the instrument. The recorder is lovely, but it does require skill. The kazoo or melodica is probably the easiest to use if there is no particular skill available.

Beware of the eager beaver who wants to play the drum. The timpani can control and destroy a composition quicker than can any other instruments except maybe a hanging gong. When a drum is explored thoroughly for loud and soft, quick and slow sounds, then— and only then—would I suggest considering the use of the drum in composition. Adults lose their cool over drums, making it hard to remove the sticks or ask them if they can hear others' music. With musicians, the drum can present a few distasteful problems. For example, many drummers do not handle lovely, organic co-authorship very well. If you luck out and have a sensitive drummer who isn't trying to win a best-drummer contest, you'll have supportive, sensitive leadership. Sometimes presenting timpani without the mallets is very wise. When working with children, I station myself behind the drummer, prompt him or her to play softly, reinforce any variety in presentation, and whisper, "Can you hear the others?"

The gong likewise presents difficulties. I seldom encourage its use until the group has advanced in dynamics and musical exploration. That is when the instrument can contribute very appealing effects. Explore the gong's possibilities through the duration of sounds, some quick and some long.

When performers use the pentatonic scale, many times the mallets are dropped down between the missing tone bars and the wood of the instrument is used as part of the performance. Sometimes I am asked how to play an instrument and I demonstrate the variety of sounds that can be accomplished and leave the performer to decide what will be used. I do this because I personally do not enjoy having instruments taken from my hands and my presentation corrected. I know that I can learn the correct way, but I do not want my efforts diminished, because I am exploring and discovering. I learn by observing others; eventually I determine how I will use the instrument at any particular time. There is certainly a time for learning about music; I just typically do not make that a priority in my sessions. If that learning occurs, great! I am interested in the process, not the end product. However, I must state again that the end product does not go unnoticed.

SPECIAL CONSIDERATIONS
FOR PERFORMERS

When someone is initiating a rhythm and might need help, I station myself across the circle from that person and provide some type of body movement in sync with his or her beat. This can help hold a composition together.

Presentation of drumsticks and mallets to a participant is an obvious sign of turn-taking. When the participant hands them back, it is because closure is well established. The sticks can then be handed on to those who are attending and behaving well while others are playing, so that the sticks/mallets become a reinforcement of appropriate behavior.

People who have trouble getting up and down from the floor frequently lean on the instrument instead of on the floor to push themselves up. Just encourage them to remove their hand from the instrument and help them up, putting them through the motions of leaning on the floor to push their bodies upward.

When presenting the claves, be sure you have a matched set. One shorter than the other makes the player struggle as if one arm is longer than the other. I was in a position as an instructor at the University of California, Los Angeles to accompany a male and a female participant improvising movement while instruments accompanied. The group was small and each instrument became a vital part of the process. I quickly grabbed a pair of claves but I didn't notice that they didn't match. I didn't really realize the problems presented by the mismatch until I tried the claves. As I attended to the dancers and established my part in the composition, I kept striking one clave against the other and missing. I finally stopped and looked at my hands, wondering what was wrong with me. One stick was about an inch and a half shorter than the other and I had to watch carefully to strike one against the other, which decreased my spontaneity.

RESPECT THE INSTRUMENTS

When the instruments are respected by staff and are carefully presented as surprises or magical tools, participants pick up this respect. I have seldom seen very limited individuals misuse the instruments. Some common problems that do occur are sticks being popped into the mouth, being bent, or being used to flip the tone bars off the instruments. If someone is hitting the instrument too hard or too near the end, I get behind the person and gently prompt him or her to move the arms forward, pulling the elbows out. If someone is deliberately trying to make the tone bars fly, I remove that person from his or her turn; sometimes I remove the instrument because it is easier!

When carrying instruments into a group, I try to make it a special presentation. I like to have the instruments in a closet or behind a screen and then ceremoniously present them, with immediately establishes respect for them. You may want to discourage helping hands. The large bass xylophone is always one of the most favorite instruments. Its heaviness makes it hard to carry, so it is likely that any group participants with sensorimotor problems trying to do so will slam the instrument to the floor because of a lack of depth perception. Other instruments are dropped also, but I feel compelled to mention the bass xylophone because it makes such a loud sound when this happens, which makes one feel more like crying than with any of the other instruments.

Pegs easily get bent on tone bar instruments, which produces a vibration or dead sound. Straightening them improves the tone. The rubber tubing on these instruments rots over time, but it can be easily replaced.

The heads of timpani, tambours, and tambourines will endure very heavy blows as long as the hide does not have holes. If you stack your instruments so that the screws go into the heads, you will soon end up with small holes in the heads that explode when struck. Also, if you do not loosen the heads of the skin instruments when playing them—and then assist performers in tightening the heads of all sizes that can be adjusted—you will find that the frames warp. I have a few circles that look like Easter eggs because I was sloppy when in haste.

Instruments should be kept in good repair. I use an Afuche/cabasa that has long strands of metal beads wrapped around a corrugated circle of metal on wood. If the handle comes unscrewed, the whole instrument falls apart and the beads dump into performers' laps or all over the floor. That is a horrible experience for people who think they've broken the instrument. It is my responsibility to see that the screw is tightened before I hand out the instrument. Likewise, if an instrument needs to be handled a certain way, it is my responsibility to explain, before I hand over the instrument, how it should be used so that the performer can succeed. This doesn't mean, however, that I insist that instruments or mallets be held the "correct" way. I understand the value of technique, but when I am working with people with special needs, I think it is more important to encourage exploration and discovery as to the most effective sound and the most effective way of getting it. I merely demonstrate how I use mallets and hold instruments so that participants have to chance to model me.

Treasure whatever instruments you are using. Your attitude toward the instruments will be quickly observed and modeled. Be resourceful. Remember: there are many activities in this book (not to mention those waiting in your head to be discovered) that use the simplest—perhaps even no—instruments, so you do not have an excuse for not initiating Orff-Schulwerk because of a lack of resources. Don't lay that lack of instrument trip on me!

A SUGGESTED INSTRUMENTARIUM

A standard group of instruments I use for a group of 15 to 30 participants includes the following:

- Four tunable tambours
- Two tambourines
- Two tunable timpani (two different ranges)
- One bass xylophone
- One bass metallophone
- One alto xylophone
- One alto metallophone
- One alto glockenspiel
- One hanging gong
- Bells (a variety)
- Claves
- Wood blocks
- One triangle
- One cymbal and stick
- Cabasa/Afuche
- Recorder
- Maracas

- Finger cymbals
- Guiro
- Castanets

In addition, I carry a bag full of special instruments, which typically include the following:

- Two-tone bells
- A variety of bells
- A kalimba/thumb piano
- Bamboo shaker
- Flexitone
- Gourd
- Shaker
- Squeeze drum
- Appalachian Dancing Man (instructions for making one are at the end of this chapter.)
- Kazoos
- Melodica
- Any other things that catch my eye

As I've traveled, experienced student projects, and attended conferences, I've seen many adaptive instruments. Here are some of them:

- Nose harp
- Sand in a tube
- Washboard bongos
- Song flute
- Balloon stick beaters (about 15 to 20, tied together and taped; slap them on the floor to make sounds)
- Ball drinking glasses (with or without water)
- Different lengths of metal pipe
- Music boxes
- Gourds
- Coconut shells
- Buttons on string
- Combs with cellophane
- Harmonicas
- Dishpan (used as a gong)
- Ear chime (piece of metal hanging from string that is hung over the ear; it is struck with another piece of metal)

- Metronome
- Ticking clock
- Typewriter
- Door spring on wood
- Coffee cans with different contents inside (decorated by children)
- Papier mâché instruments
- Footstool
- Trash can
- Bells on elastic
- Water gourds (wooden salad bowls floating upside down in a tub of water and struck with a mallet)
- Bamboo planter (A University of California, Los Angeles student took a woven bamboo planter, cut it open, laid it on the floor, and used it as a xylophone. She also separated the pieces and made sets of bamboo sticks to use as claves and sticks for playing the planter instrument.)
- Steel drum
- Chopsticks
- Spoons
- Rocks (struck against each other)
- Washtub base with broom and string
- Bladder from a ball, filled with rocks
- Bottle caps nailed to sticks
- Sandpaper on blocks of wood
- Metal bent into a triangle and struck by large nail
- Kitchen tools
- Wood shaped like a guitar, with a sandpaper circle in center that was scratched with a pick or sandpaper disc
- Film cans with objects in them
- Metal cigar boxes with sand in them

The most obvious resource for sounds is the body. The book *Where the Sidewalk Ends* by Shel Silverstein has a great poem called "Ourchestra" about using belly, nose, and clapping hands instead of drum, horn, cymbals, respectively. The poem concludes that

> . . . Though there may be orchestras
> That sound a little better
> With their fancy shiny instruments
> That cost an awful lot—
> Hey, we're making music twice as good

By playing what we've got![1]

The pictures are great, as is the rest of the book. I recommend it.

When I am teaching a particular sequence of notes on tone bar instruments, I remove the notes that will not be used so that there is greater likelihood for success. For example, if a pattern using the first and third steps of the scale of C is desired, then I remove the remainder of the notes. Other instruments to be used in the same performance may have other tone bars removed, allowing easy development of a composition with the combination of notes remaining on each instrument. The extreme concentration on the face of performers who are playing those two notes methodically can be amusing. It is not uncommon to see performers so engrossed that their tongues are hanging out and they are breathing very deeply. This is all part of the involvement and joy of co-authorship, with each person contributing.

---

[1] Silverstein. S. (1974). Ourchestra. In *Where the sidewalk ends* (p. 23). New York: Harper & Row.

APPALACHIAN DANCING MAN

Like so many other American folk toys, the Appalachian Dancing Man was a demonstration toy—a toy intended to amuse children but not necessarily one they played with. Just as there is music to listen to and music to play, there are some toys to play with and some toys to watch.

The Dancing Man is a wooden doll with jointed arms and legs that can do an amazingly realistic tap dance to any music you sing or play. In many ways, it's actually a rhythm instrument. Working it takes practice.

Construction

Materials	Tools
• ¼-inch-thick wood scrap	• Coping saw
• 1-inch thick wood scrap	• Drill
• Wooden dowel	• Screwdriver
• Wood screws	• Sandpaper
• Drawer knob or thread spool	• Glue
• Tracing or writing paper	• Pencil

Making the Dancing Man does require some careful cutting and fitting of parts, so unless you're handy yourself, get someone who is good at making things to help you out. Follow Figure 3-1 (page 36) for the shape of the body parts, but you don't have to be exact; you might want to add your own design touches. Be sure to make two arms and two legs. Draw all the parts on tracing paper and cut them out to use as templates.

With just a little bit of glue, stick the arm and leg templates onto a piece of ¼-inch-thick wood (or hard cardboard), then cut out the shapes with a coping saw. Stick the paper doll body template on a 1-inch scrap of wood and then cut out the shape. Drill holes (a little larger than the screws you're going to use) in the arms and legs at those places marked with a circle on the templates. Sand smooth the sides and edges of all the parts. Sand off the tracing paper. Then drill a hole about halfway through the center of the body part. The hole should be just big enough to fit the long wooden dowel tightly. Find a big drawer knob or empty thread spool to use for a head.

Assemble all the parts as shown in Figure 3–2 (page 37) using small and short wood screws through the drilled holes and into the places marked with a cross on Figure 3–2. Don't tighten the screws all the way—the arms and legs should swing quite freely. The long dowel should be glued in place.

The dancing paddle, shown in Figure 3–3 (page 37), is made from another piece of ¼-inch wood about 5 inches wide and 20 or more inches long. It is not attached to the doll; see below for how to use it.

You might want to decorate the doll.

Dancing

Play a tape or CD or sing a song—something with a fast rhythm. Sit on one end of the dancing paddle on a hard surface like a bench, table edge, or metal or wooden chair. Keep time to the music by hitting the other end of the paddle with your hand or thumb. Hold the Dancing Man by the dowel so he is just above the paddle, then watch him go! The vibration of the paddle as it hits the doll's feet is what makes him dance. You can do some dancing tricks by holding the doll in various positions above the paddle—sitting, on his knees, or tilted to lean on one leg.

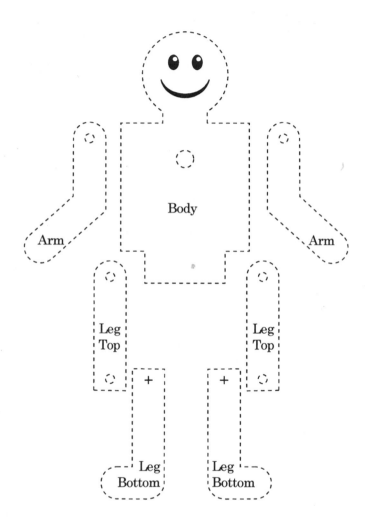

Figure 3–1. Appalachian Dancing Man. Photocopy this template to the desired size and cut along the dotted lines. Then use the body template to make the body from a piece of 1"-thick wood. The hole in the body is for insertion of a 20"-long wooden dowel. Use the arm and leg templates to make those pieces from a ¼"-thick piece of wood.

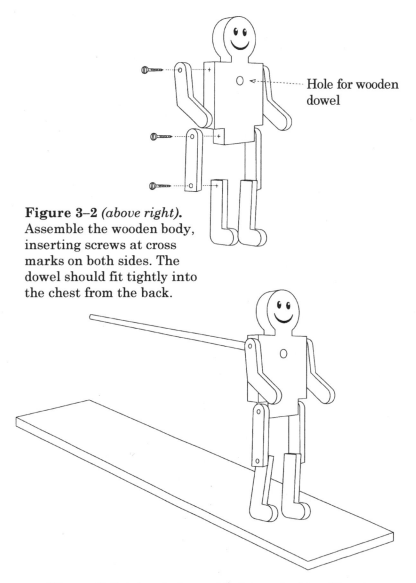

Figure 3–2 *(above right)*. Assemble the wooden body, inserting screws at cross marks on both sides. The dowel should fit tightly into the chest from the back.

Hole for wooden dowel

Figure 3–3 *(above)*. Assembled Appalachian Dancing Man on the dancing paddle. Cut the paddle 5" wide and at least 20" long from ¼"-thick wood.

Chapter 4

USING INSTRUMENTS

Participants need to explore each instrument thoroughly before they can be expected to relate to it and express themselves with it. If the instrument is unfamiliar, the performer will not know the sound dimensions, quality, or various techniques used to produce sounds. Also, and maybe most important, there can be competition among participants in approaching the instrument, possibly leading to misuse of the instrument. The activities in this chapter allow participants to get to know different instruments.

GETTING TO KNOW
THE INSTRUMENTS

Here are two exploratory activities that can be used for determining an instrument's qualities and that allow everyone to touch the instrument before it is used in any musical form:

(1)
There are loud *sounds*
And there are soft sounds.
Let me hear your *sounds!*
[Or: *Can you make the same sounds?*]

(2)
Big *sounds,*
Little sounds,
Big *sounds,*
Little sounds.
Let us hear your *sounds!*

Activities 1 and 2 can be very effective in controlling a group when there is a high level of noise after a very active session. The leader's doing the *big* sounds and little sounds on a tambour, reaching high and bending low, presents extremes and usually gets everyone's attention. Add the requirement of closing the eyes if necessary to get more control over the group. I encourage the participants to make loud or big sounds and little or soft sounds. Different instruments can then be presented to the group one at a time to allow them to experience each instrument's loud and soft sounds.

Here's another activity that is useful for individual exploration of an instrument in a quiet, controlled environment:

(3)
Listen, listen,
Listen to the sounds __[instrument's name]__ makes.

If the instrument is large, have the participants go to the center of the circle to the instrument. If a small instrument is used, pass it around the circle. If the participants can hand the instrument to the next person, encourage this social process. If you need to collect the instrument each time, put each participant through the motions of taking the instrument, turning to the next person, and handing it to that person. If you are there, you can protect the instrument from being dropped, assist with the release, encourage eye contact, and quickly reinforce the behavior. Releasing the instrument certainly is a developmental step in socialization. If you can work with two people, sometimes it is nice to have the person working behind the participants assist in passing the instrument while the one in front reinforces. Also, the person working behind can help relax the performer by rubbing his or her shoulders, upper arms, head, and the back of the neck if appropriate. This is useful particularly when approaching the tone bar instruments. Hender, a developmental specialist who works with music therapists, uses brush-downs in groups and has taught colleagues techniques for eliciting maximum relaxation and awareness of body parts.

THE CLAVES

When your group uses the claves, pass them around the circle with this:

(4)
Woodpecker, woodpecker
In the tree,
Give us a rhythm
That really is free.

Here's another clave activity that's fun to use with movement while the group is standing in a circle:

(5)
Listen, my children,
And you shall hear
Horses' hoofbeats drawing near!

With this activity, it works well to divide a group in half, pass two sets of sticks around, and have two rhythms with matched footwork from participants in each of the groups. The activity effectively develops two parts.

BELLS

Next are some simple bell activities that employ a large variety of bells, which are readily available at minimal cost.

(6)
I can clap.
I can sing.
Can you make
This little bell ring?

(7)
Ring-a-ling,
Ding-a-ling,
Hear my bell
Sing-a-ling.

(8)
Swingin', flingin',
Who will make the bells
Go ringin'?

I like to pass around a large tambour with a variety of bells in it for activities 6 through 9. The bells can also be placed in the center of the circle and participants join together in developing bell ostinati and composition form.

(9)
Dinnnnng, donnnnng,
Dinnnnng, donnnnng,
Bells have a special sound.
Dinnnnng, donnnnng,
Dinnnnng, donnnnng,
Bells have a special sound.

Random singing develops with this activity. It encourages harmonic exploration. The tune used is in the minor and is the same as "Yeah, Ho, Nobody Home." The melody sets a seriousness to the bell ringing and participants attend. I place the melody in a lower register. Instruments could be added if you have available the spare tone bars for developing a minor scale.

DRUMS AND PERCUSSION

I've told you of my concerns about drums/timpani already. Here are a few activities for getting to know the drum.

(10)
Everyone's a drummer,
A drummer, a drummer.
I have a special drummer...
Right inside of me.

Activity 10 can be done either by a drummer on drums or by drumming on the body.

(11)
Playing in the sun,
Having so much fun,
Playing on my drum,
Seeing who will come.

Activity 11 can encourage others to join in with the initial beat of the drum. Movement, body accompaniment, and other instruments all can be part of the fun.

(12)
Make the drum pitter;
Make the drum patter.
Fast . . . or slow,
It doesn't matter.

Conversation on drums requiring listening and then speaking and the dimensions that might enter into a conversation, such as whispering, yelling, and chatting, helps group members explore the properties of the drum while participating in both receptive and expressive communication, participating in a socialization process, expressing emotions through affect, and having fun.

Activity 13 sometimes excites the group with the possibility that there will be a real party, but that quickly passes. The pleasure in choosing all to be invited is fun and makes the host or hostess feel very important. When the conversation is through, then the host/hostess sits down and the guest assumes the role of host/hostess and invites someone to the party. I have participated in some interesting sessions with this activity. Sometimes participants need encouragement in listening, then speaking and proper use of mallets. Once, while I was running a session with very disturbed adolescents, a young man invited his counselor to the drum. The drum endured treatment that none thought it could endure—including me. Finally, the young man achieved closure, made eye contact, sighed deeply, and, rather pleased, returned to the circle. What the transaction was, we didn't know, but it did happen.

(13)
We're having a party.
Who will come
And sit with me
And play on my drum?

(14)
I went down to my garden patch
To see if my old hen had hatched.
She'd hatched out her chickens and
The peas were green;
She sat there a-pickin' on a tambourine.[1]

(15)
Stand up
And take a bow.
We'd like to hear
Your music . . . now!

For activity 16, instruments of the same type could be passed out and a combination of sounds could be used. One person at a time could play a song or a combination of sounds could continue, with the *ch-ch-ch-ch-ch-ch-ch-ch* continuing. The last idea would force closure if necessary. Movement is an obvious inclusion.

(16)
Ch-ch-ch-ch-ch-ch-ch-ch-ch-ch,
Ch-ch-ch-ch-ch-ch-ch-ch-ch-ch,
Charlie Chili Choo-Choo Chugger.
One by one,
Let's play a song for everyone.

INSTRUMENTS OF ALL KINDS

Once everyone is comfortable with the various instruments, they will enjoy the activities in this section.

(17)
Tambourines, bells,
Triangles, and a gong.
Now it's your turn to
Make up a song.

---

[1] From Withers, C. (1948). In *A rocket in my pocket: The rhymes and chants of young Americans* (p. 14). New York: H. Holt.

(18)
Music, music in the air—
Make some music
A friend can share.

(19)
Music man, music man,
Can you play
For the band?

(20)
Sounds, sounds
All around.
Choose an instrument and
Make your sounds [quick paced].

Pause between the stanzas of activity 21[2] for the individual to initiate sounds and then name a friend to play with him or her. Roxie added the name requirement to the activity because we found that without it, participants wouldn't bother to remember names even after we'd spent a lot of time exploring names.

(21)

There are man–y sounds we hear.
5 5 3 3 5 5 3

Play your sounds for us.
5 5 3 3 1

[Pause]

Choose a friend to play with you.
5 3 3 3 5 5 3

Choose a friend by name.
5 5 3 3 1

[2]Throughout this book, the small numerals below lyrics represent scale tones: 1 = do, 2 = re, 3 = mi, 4 = fa, 5 = sol, 6 = la, 7 = ti.

(22)
Secrets, secrets
Fill the room.
Find a secret and
Tell it with a tune.

The concept of developing pretty things in the mind and then playing these thoughts with accompaniment is a nice two-part development that can help establish phrasing. Judy, a nurse coordinator at Fairview, brought activity 23 to a University of California, Irvine class and the students found it an enjoyable resource. Establish an accompaniment for the tune in the key of G, playing G and down to E.

(23)

Play the above sequence during the tune and then repeat it using the same pattern as used with the tune. The "things that are pretty" then are played in a short period of time by the person whose turn it is to develop a melody. You may not want to control the piece so tightly, instead having extended explanation of pretty things and closure from the person presenting the story/melody. Just keep the G–E base going until the melody of what is pretty to the participant is completed.

With activity 24, have group members close their eyes and maybe sway a bit, and bring in a glockenspiel for the verse. Then have the wish verbalized, whispered, sung, played, or whatever. This is a very quiet activity. The glockenspiel can be turned so the leader can develop an ostinato and have the player randomize dreaming, starlike thoughts, encouraging glissandos.

(24)
Star light, star bright,
First star I see tonight,
What, oh what
Will I dream tonight?
[Or end with this version, which I prefer:
Wish I may, wish I might
Have the wish I wish tonight.]

Familiar verses like "Star Light" are useful because they are immediately bring back memories. Sometimes I've been surprised when introducing a familiar old rhyme to see an unexpected response or participation in the chanting with obvious stirring from rather limited individuals.

Here's another nice star activity that can slowly build, then come together:

(25)
They shine and tingle in the night
And in the dark, they move around
And all at once they
Tingle together as always.[3]

An activity that was developed by a group of participants in a workshop at Fairview can be used by placing instruments in the center of the circle, developing rhythms, or using just body rhythms.

---

[3]Lewis, R. (1969). In *Journeys: Prose by children of the English-speaking world* (p. 192). New York: Simon & Schuster.

(26)
Rhythms are fun—uhhhh!
Rhythms are free—wheeee!
Can you make a
Rhythm for me?

Activity 27, discussion-provoking and sometimes cathartic, deals with the sounds of night. When I used it with clients from Fairview, it was impressive to hear what sounds they heard in the night. Shortly after that, I visited their residences, and the sounds they had described in our activity came back to me. Their bodies were contorted in sleep, some in fetal position, some way under the sheets and blankets, some flat on the back and snoring; some clients even wanted to take their blankets under the mattress or bed and onto the floor. Some wandered restlessly; others just lay and listened to the sounds. The Address-O-Plates stamping, the buffer purring, keys jangling, doors opening, toilets flushing, and phones being dialed were all sounds of their night. The silence of their night was really quite noisy.

(27)
Sometimes at night
When everything is dark,
Sounds I think about
Get so loud
I can't even sleep.

The ostinati of night breathing, with strange accents coming into the composition, are curious.

For activity 28, group members move, following the leader with the instruments they have selected and brought to the parade line, taking their turn one by one.

(28, Part I)
Parades, parades,
Such wonderful times.
Play your music
And join the line!

For the second part of activity 28, the leader goes to someone sitting in the circle and that person chooses an instrument and takes on leadership of the parade.

(28, Part II)
_____[Name]_____ , _____[Name]_____ ,
It's your turn now.
What will you do?
What will you choose?
It's your turn
To lead the line.

This activity certainly could be a typical rhythm band activity. The separation of theme and response makes the activity structured and allows individual contribution and diversity—a description of the rondo form.

Activity 29 is a musical concept orchestrating the change from daytime to nighttime.

(29)
I know how daytime changes to nighttime.
Daytime melts.[4]

For activity 30, you can have participants draw pictures out of a hat and orchestrate them. The pictures can relate to affect but also can encourage an individual or a group to orchestrate a scene or story.

(30)
Picture this and picture that.
What did you pull from the hat?
[Pause and show the picture.]
Can you orchestrate that?"
[Or: *Can you make a sound like that?*]

The pictures could be of actual instruments on the floor; the matching of picture and object would follow with sounds. This activity was originally developed by an instrument teacher to teach the names of instruments.

There are numerous activities for using instruments throughout this book. The ones appearing in this chapter were chosen for inclusion here because they illustrate some of my philosophy of teaching and learning. Use instruments to bring an activity alive. Enjoy the

---

[4]Lewis, R. (1969). In *Journeys: Prose by children of the English-speaking world* (p. 182). New York: Simon & Schuster.

attending enthusiasm and joy the participants will share. When sound and movement are added to a story, well known or not, you have a different level of attending and greater diversity.

It's time to move on . . . to modeling and imitation.

Chapter 5

MODELING AND IMITATION

The whole creative process involved in the activities presented in this book provides opportunities for modeling. The rondo form, ostinato, call–response, and mime all include imitation with reinforcement yet also reinforce diversity. This is a rather strange combination, but it is a unique quality of Orff-Schulwerk that works well. The pattern of repetition and expansion and then repetition involved in Orff-Schulwerk has come under a variety of criticisms, none of which I consider insurmountable if one approaches each Orff-Schulwerk activity attentively.

This chapter presents some obvious imitation activities; there are many activities throughout this book that are useful when modeling is desirable.

(1)
Skittly, kittily,
Skittly, shi.
Do what I do
After me.

(2)
I can make a beat
That you can all keep.
I can make a beat
From my seat.

(3)
I'm a mirror;
Look at me.
Stand up tall
And follow me.

Here are some follow-the-leader activities:

(4)
Copycat is
The name of the game.
Anything you do,
We'll do the same.

(5)
Shadow, shadow
That I see—
Try to, try to
Follow me!

(6)
Riddle, riddle,
Riddle, ree.
Do what I do
After me!

(7)
Let's be copycats
And play a game.
Let's copy ____[Name]____
And do the same!

(8)
Shadow, shadow
That I see—
I am you and
You are me.
Shadow, shadow
That I see—
Try to, try to
Follow me.

It is very easy to encourage modeling and imitation to the point that a turn becomes community property. The wise manipulator soon finds, though, that he or she can easily control turns by being quick and assertive. Some imitation allows a contribution to grow, but it imitation can be distracting and get very boring. Try to insert activities that do not include modeling all the time, to encourage diversity of response. There certainly is plenty of modeling and imitation in the theme presentation.

At Fairview Developmental Center for the Learning Disabled, Dr. T. S. Ball and I conducted research to evaluate the degree to which generalized imitation develops in profoundly retarded individuals as a by-product of their participation in the Orff-Schulwerk sessions. In the discussion section of the article we wrote, we made the following observations:

> The data analysis reveals that generalized imitation was generated by Schulwerk but not by a varied schedule of group recreational activities. However, with so modest a level of statistical significance, the practical clinical value of the training vis-à-vis generalized imitation is limited. Within the experimental group a significant trend toward improvement was seen in no more than three or four participants.
>
> . . . It is also possible that a combination of formal imitation training and separate Schulwerk sessions might yield a facilitative effect in the acquisition of generalized imitation.
>
> Even though Schulwerk is probably much less efficient in promoting generalized imitation than is formal imitation training, it is important to note that at least for some profoundly retarded children, this propensity can be developed as a by-product of Schulwerk. It can be much more readily adapted to institutional, recreational and developmental programs than the laborious shaping procedures required in formal imitation training, elements which are sources of motivation for both patients and staff. The rehabilitative effects of Schulwerk are many and varied.[1]

In an article written for the *Music Therapy Journal,* Louise Hauck Ponath and I described modeling as one of the behavioral techniques:

> . . . Modeling is another behavioral technique which frequently occurs in Orff. Bandura (1969) emphasizes this as

---

[1]Ball, T. S., & Bitcon, C. H. (1974). Generalized imitation in Orff-Schulwerk. *Mental Retardation, 3*(7), 36–39.

one of the fundamental means by which new modes of behavior are acquired and existing patterns are modified. In the Orff setting, modeling occurs not only when the client imitates the therapist but also through vicarious processes (i.e., when the child observes the reinforcement of a particular behavior in another patient). Its occurrence, however, must be facilitated by the use of reinforcement, a necessary condition for observational learning (Skinner, 1953).

Bandura and Walters (1963) clearly define the effects of modeling (vicarious) influences resulting from exposure to modeling stimuli. The influences are threefold, each determined by a separate set of variables. The first is the acquisition of new response patterns that were previously absent from the person's behavior repertoire. For this to occur, the model must demonstrate novel responses which the observer has not learned to make, and which he must later reproduce in nearly identical form (Bandura, 1969, defines a novel response as any behavior that has a very low or zero probability of occurrence in the presence of appropriate stimuli). Novel responses in an Orff group would include a broad range of skills, varying from the select responses of playing an instrument such as the xylophone, a tambourine or a gong, down to what the casual observer would see as minimal social skills, such as taking turns or attending to a central figure—responses which certainly are not minimal or easily acquired skills with disabled clients.

The second effect is the strengthening or weakening of inhibitory responses in observers, as a result of the observation of modeled actions and their consequences to the performer. For example, when the observing client witnesses the reinforcement (applause, hugging by therapist, etc.) of the performer who has "used his imagination" and brought a clever, imaginative object into the circle, that rather unstructured response is likely to be strengthened in the observer. Likewise, the observer's response to inappropriate behavior is likely to weaken the behavior when the performer receives no positive reinforcement, but rather a form of time-out, when the therapist either removes him (avoiding eye contact, which may be reinforcing) from the group or noticeably skips his turn, and others in the group also ignore him.

The last effect of modeling is that of response facilitation, when the behaviors of others serve as discriminative stimuli . . . for the observer in facilitating the occurrence of previously learned responses in the same general class. This means that the behavior of those in the group as a whole will set the occasion and facilitate the occurrence of previously learned responses (no new responses are learned). Responses emitted in this "socially sanctioned" environment will rarely receive punishment and will therefore tend to increase.

In conclusion, the Orff-Schulwerk activity establishes an environment which can facilitate the application of behavior techniques. It must be emphasized however, that it only does this by providing the prescribed routines and setting for such applications. The activity itself cannot bring about effective results without the conscious effort of the "behavioral-minded" therapist who sets up individual client goals, takes notice of observable behavior and adapts the activity accordingly.[2]

Here are a few other activities I want to share with you:

(9, Part I)
Hey shadow, ho shadow,
Show us what you do.
Hey shadow, ho shadow,
Show us what you do.
[Shadow enters circle
while group chants.]

---

[2]Ponath, L. H., and Bitcon, C. H. (1972). A behavioral analysis of Orff-Schulwerk. *Journal of Music Therapy, 9*(2), 56–63.

(9, Part II)
Show us what you do;
Show us what you do.

(9, Part III)
[As action is initiated, everyone imitates
the center figure while chanting.]
This is what he[/she] does;
This is what he[/she] does.

I use a hat for activity 9. Because of the possibility of transmission of lice, use clean hats each time. The hat is passed from the person in the center to someone in the circle and is used to identify the shadow. Wheelchairs can be rolled out; movement can be extensive or minimal. If you can't easily model the activity in the center, then you should just "shine it on" and move along. When I use this activity, I stamp one foot and clap my hands with heavy rhythmic emphasis, adapting the pressure and speed of "this is what she does" to the particular response. Sometimes I stop the chanting until something is initiated and then reinforce it with "this is what she does" with excitement and encouragement in my voice. With some clients, it can be very difficult to tell when a pattern of movement is initiated, so you must use your own judgment. Sometimes bizarre mannerisms are imitated. This can be effective or can reinforce a behavior that others are trying to extinguish.

Call–response activities, such as in rhythmic patterns that require accurate recall, are useful for modeling, particularly when movement is integrated in the activity. An activity that Toni and Rose developed for a class at the University of California, Irvine has been excellent for developing call–response. It encourages everyone's favorite sound effects to come forth. With an adult class, it is always interesting to find out what special sounds participants are proud of. Again, many times you will not be able to make others' sounds. It's no big deal. Don't put yourself in the position of having to duplicate sounds that are specific words if the presenter has great investment in the exact reproduction of his or her sound. You can spend a lot of time trying to understand and may never succeed. Just move right along after each turn without discussion or interpretation.

(10)
Pumpkin, pumpkin,
Diddle, diddle, dumpkin.
Pumpkin, pumpkin,
Diddle, diddle, say!

Try activity 10 with everyone standing in a circle, swinging arms from side to side and snapping fingers. This activity requires clear framing—the person presenting sounds must provide closure so that the imitators can move ahead. It is so easy as a leader to cut off part of the "call" and lose so much of what you have been seeking in the co-authorship. Require closure of some form. Clearly demonstrate what you want to have happen during the activity so imitation is quickly established. Use a large range of sounds and motions yourself so that you will be modeled and then reinforce diversity immediately.

Below is an activity that Martha Wampler brought to us; it is drawn from Mother Goose. This is an activity where success can be delayed and thus perhaps more successful when finally earned and cheered on by group members.

(11, Part I)
Leader Lock: *Find the key,*
Find the key
That opens the lock.

The leader moves around the circle with two instruments that are similar in quality but have two different pitches.

(11, Part II)
Leader Lock: *I am a wooden lock.*
Response Key: *I am a wooden key.*
Leader Lock: *To open the lock, you must do*
The same as me.

The leader lock offers a rhythmic pattern. The key responds, whether intricately or simply, listening carefully with encouragement, and attempts duplication of the rhythm.

(11, Part III)
Leader Lock [Asking of group]:   *Did she open the lock?*
        Group: [Use either]   *She opened the lock.*
                                She opened the lock.
            [Or]   *Nooooooooo!*
                        Try again, try again!

Different combinations of rhythms are presented according to the individual's ability. Initially, it might be necessary to present the same pattern presented to each person. Count out loud if it is necessary and stop the stick that will strike once too often if it appears the participant is not going to succeed after a number of tries. The crowd cheers on, joy appears on the face of the less able participant, and the beat goes on.

Exploration of different textures and properties of instruments can be made with different presentations of locks and keys. A body lock and key can be used, modeling body sounds and movement. (The Mother Goose verse ends with "I am a monk lock" and the response "I am a monkey.") When changing the qualities of the instruments, you may be a musical lock if using tone bells, or a glass lock, metal lock, people lock, and so forth. The game can be extended to opening a door and peering in and then playing a tune. Some of the sharper participants quickly learn that if they make mistakes, they will get the attention and fun a little longer, so manipulation can cause some problems. Add a follow-up, such as playing a tune after opening the door or expanding on what is inside the door and quickly slamming it so it doesn't get out! And then move right along.

Whenever possible, test whether there is generalization in the modeling. Is learning occurring? The type of lock and key used can easily be varied and you can determine whether different patterns presented out of sequence are imitated. Are loud and soft or big and little really being learned? As a test, request a response that must be accurate. Are specific cues or prompts needed?

Chapter 6

SENSORIMOTOR
DEVELOPMENT

I have purposely organized this book so that movement (discussed in Chapter 7) immediately follows sensorimotor development (discussed in this chapter). They are inseparable, as are communication and movement and affect and voice. Many of the activities presented here as appropriate for sensorimotor development could also serve well in other categories. That's why you should read this book with an open-ended approach, examining, exploring, and expanding on the ideas in it. Mix and mold, as you would with any good recipe; change it to meet your likes and needs.

There are so many excellent books on movement that what I present here is just a small sampling of activities. Please see the bibliography for other books. Turn to such sensorimotor books as *Motoric Aids to Perceptual Training* by Clara M. Chaney and Newell C. Kephart and you will find pages of activities that can quickly become Orff-Schulwerk. I started to develop new material from Chaney and Kephart's book and decided that because it was so easy to do so, you can turn to such resources on your own. I'll get you started, but the task is still yours . . . if you plan to meet the challenge.

ACTIVITIES FOR
THE VERY YOUNG

So many children's games, such as Patty Cake, Peekaboo, Peas Porridge Hot, Rock-a-Bye Baby, and Seesaw Margery Daw, are excellent sensorimotor activities. Jump rope activities are a great resource for Schulwerk activities. Children can be pretty good at selecting activities appropriate to their needs. I guess it's a chicken-or-egg issue: do the children play because that is what they are able to do, or do they play in order to do what they are able to do?

I'm including just a few activities here that are usually used for very young children because they are also useful when you are going from bed to bed when working with very young or with very handicapped individuals.

(1)
Soooooooooooooooo big.
_____[Name]_____ *is soooooooooo big.*

You've probably used activity 1 with children or even had your own parents pull your arms above your head, stretching, reaching, saying "Soooo big." With this activity, small babies quickly learn to pull their arms up, grasping an adult's fingers for support.

Tickling is a natural stimulus if not overdone—tickling too much can be very cruel. Kathy, Fairview staff, and I developed this activity, a very social one used frequently with our teenagers.

(2)
I'm a tickle, tickle,
Tickle, tickle, tickle bee!
If I tickle you,
Will you smile for me?

The response to activity 2 is a result of noncompatible behaviors. It certainly would be strange to tickle and get a frown—but it does sometimes happen. For older participants, tickling each other and staff is fun. A tickling activity represents an acceptable time to touch and get acquainted physically with others in training. Different textures can be introduced for the tickling tool. When we were in training, Kathy used an artichoke thistle. Carpet samples, the kind that are clipped and pulled in to a shaggy brush about the size of an egg, are colorful and easy to carry. Getting to choose what color brush to use for tickling someone adds another dimension to this activity for the more advanced.

(3)
Peekaboo—
I see you!
[Toss a diaper, towel, or scarf over the face
so it can be pulled away.]

(4)
Who's that underneath that hat,
That hat?
Who's that underneath that hat?

For activity 4, I use a funny pink cotton floppy hat that covers the face and manages to cling to the head however loosely it is dropped. The participant's hands creep up and pull off the hat and everyone calls out the participant's name or says, "There he/she is!" Take care in presenting the hat so it doesn't startle. Also, remember the potential for a lice problem; you might want a collection of sloppy hats that are cotton and washable.

I carry around a nonbreakable mirror that is useful for a number of activities.

(5)
Look, look.
Look—come see.
Can you find
A face for me?

The mirror will be licked, dropped, and clutched and so will need frequent polishing. Help position it and then pass it on. Whether the person sees him-/herself can be immaterial. The social process of taking a turn and then relinquishing the tool to someone else is valuable; both are desirable. For an added dimension, stress the name and parts of the face. *Who's that? Where are your eyes? Is there a monkey in there?* Many playful exchanges emerge.

With activity 6, I use a scarf that floats through the air, dropping it on someone's head. Then that someone has to reach and pull it off. With little children, there is often silly clowning, wrapping the scarf around the head, throwing it, peeking out from under it, and so on. When it's appropriate, I use both parts of the activity.

(6, Part I)
Feather, feather
In the sky
Dropped on me
As it passed by.

(6, Part II)
Catch it,
Catch it—
Send it
On its way.

You're right: the activity is not teaching the concept of feather but is dealing with imagery. Pulling the cloth from the head and passing it on while attending and remaining in the circle is the behavioral goal. If you want to teach *feather*, do another activity. Chapter 16, Native Americans, is full of feathers.

Kathy, music therapist at Fairview, developed this next very simple activity using a washcloth and a shower cap as props.

(7)
Wash, wash,
Washing me!

Emphasize sounds and parts of the body. The participant is given a shower cap and a washcloth, which is then grasped and rubbed on the face in a circular motion. For hygiene's sake, have ready a supply of clean, damp washcloths and clean shower caps and a pan to hold the used cloths and caps, so that each participant gets a new washcloth and a new shower cap. Both cloths and caps can be disposable.

(8)
Jelly beans, bubble gum,
Licorice, too.
Show us how
You can chew.

For activity 8, you may want to pass out something chewy, like jelly beans, for each child. Have a box of tissues nearby in case someone decides he or she doesn't like the candy.

The next two activities focus on basic identification with body parts.

(9)
Mouths can open;
Mouths can close.
Show us how
Your mouth goes.

(10)
Sighs, sighs
And good-byes.
Where, oh where
Are your eyes?
[Then on to *my eyes*.]

Next is an activity brought into one of my first University of California, Irvine classes by the same person who brought in "The Witch Has an Itch" (activity 66 in this chapter).

(11)
Pumpernickel, pumpernickel,
Pumpkin pie—
Look at me
Straight in the eye.

In activity 11, each person relates to the leader with the eyes. Any approximation of the eye area is encouraged and any tiny glance is rewarded.

(12)
Peaches, plums,
And pumpkin pie—
Show me how
You wink your eye.

Eye contact is needed for activity 12; without eye contact, there is limited control. People who cannot handle eye contact may not be ready for a group process. Here is a basic command activity:

(13)
You are you [pointing]*;*
I am me.
Won't you please
Look at me?
[Then use *stand for me, come to me, sit for me;*
then on to *clap for me, laugh for me,* and so on.]

Next is a vibrator activity developed by a technician working with small, physically limited children:

(14)
Buzzzzzzzz, buzzzzzzzz, buzzzzzzzz.
Make a part of me tingle.
I feel a tingle in my ____[part of body]____ *.*

The teacher names the part of the body and applies the vibrator, then restates the part. Eventually, the participant will point to where he or she wants to be buzzed.

GETTING INTO MOTION

Here are some fun movement-inducing activities:

(15, Part I)
Leader: *Give me a giggle*
When I wiggle.

(15, Part II)
Participant: *I'll give a wiggle*
When you giggle.

(16)
Smile, smile,
Laugh, and wiggle.
Show me a face to
Make me giggle.

(17)
I have a friend—
She's a weird, weird witch.
You should see her
Big nose twitch.

With activity 17, get each nose twitching. Change *nose* to *ears* if you want to play a bit. Participants will reach for their noses and ears and make them move if they can't be sure they are moving them without aid. At the Shriners Crippled Children's Hospital, I used a musical activity that encouraged shaking and wiggling parts of the body. I would call out *ears* and the boys would work most intently on wiggling their ears. There were funny faces, wrinkled brows, and clinched teeth, and once in a while, ears did move. . . . I believe in fairies—Tinkerbell, please don't die.

I've used activities 18 through 21 with everyone developmentally disabled, from the aged to adolescents to young adults. I think the memories of smells, good and bad, work nicely with the mentally disabled.

(18)
I have a nose
That helps me to smell.
[Present odors; find nose.]

(19)
All smells go up the chimney of your nose,
Bringing messages.

(20)
Breathe in.
Up they go—
The good smells
And the bad.

(21)
What is your favorite,
Most favorite smell?
[Or: *taste?*]

Use a flashlight with activity 22. Have the participants hit sticks or the surface of a drum when the light goes on and off while one person is tracking the light.

(22)
Lights go off;
Lights go on.
Off!
On!

For activity 23, use lights, signs, whatever, but use an instrument for movement and to indicate *stop!* A tape or CD can be used for green light or red light, just as in musical chairs. Musical chairs itself would be a good stop-and-go activity to use, but it requires some social skills and balance. Many is the time musical chairs has landed me on the floor . . . with music I just adore!

(23)

Green light, go—
Fast or slow;
Red light, stop—
Right on the spot.

For activity 24, place a variety of textures in a bag for hands to reach in and pull out a particular texture. Gadget boxes and feel boxes are also useful. Rub the textured item on the body or encourage the participant to rub it and feel it.

(24)

Textures soft,
Textures smooth.
What are the textures
That you choose?

(25)

Reach deep into this mysterious bag.
Look with your hands, not your eyes—
Your hands.

Squeeze toys, with different sounds and textures, are very elementary.

(26)

I am squeaky, squeaky, squeaky.
What can you do with me?

The way you present a toy for activity 26 will make the activity closer to being age appropriate. Move on to more appropriate activity choices as the client moves on—or don't choose the activities!

The next activity focuses on parts of the body and is taken from activities on *Sesame Street,* a program of the Public Broadcasting Service (PBS). Watch the show if you can; it has plenty of great ideas.

(27)
I have two;
You have two.
We all have two.
What do you have two of?

PBS's *Zoom* is also supposed to have good resources. I see the show so seldom that I have only a passing acquaintance with it, so you are on your own.

FOLLOWING INSTRUCTIONS

Here are some activities that involve following instructions.

(28)
Clap your hands
In front of your face.
Clap your hands
Way out in space—now freeze!

(29)
You can clap your hands fast;
You can clap your hands slow.
Will you clap your hands
And show me how they go?

(30)
Eeny, meeny,
Miney moe—
Where, oh where
Are your toes?
[Or: *my toes?*]

(31)
Magic hands,
Magic hands—
Let us hear
Your magic hands.
[Make up a simple tune
for the hands to follow.]

(32)
We have fingers;
We have toes.
Can you move
All of those?

PHYSICAL COORDINATION

Grasping and timed release are involved in activity 33.

(33)
Beanbag, beanbag
In your hand;
Can you, can you
Toss it in the pan?

For activity 33, I use a tambour and encourage using alternate hands and tossing beanbags of different texture into the pan. The loose bags, with beans settling at the bottom, drag the hand down and help with timed release. There are occupational hazards to being music therapist—and activity 33 can present a few. An old hand with some grasp quickly drops the beanbag into the pan, whereas an old hand that is spry and angry will let it fly.

(34)
We're building a city.
We're building it tall.
How many stack
Before they fall?

With activity 34, I have been surprised to see how well the slow, difficult-to-manage hands of the adults in programs for the physically handicapped can carefully stack the light wood blocks, one on top of the other. I also use cones from yarn, given away by yarn mills. They look great painted and can also be given a variety of textures.

For activity 35, participants can lie on their stomachs on the floor in a circle and squirm like a worm. Activity 36 can result in some giggle-producing movements.

(35)
Oooey Gooey was a worm.
You should see
How that worm squirmed.

(36)
Wiggle waddle,
Wiggle waddle,
To and fro.
Wiggle waddle, wiggle waddle,
Watch me go!

Touching each other and being allowed to touch staff is always a treat—strange but true! As therapists, we do develop a "no touch" presentation to many. Activities 37 and 38 deal with touching one another.

(37)
Crawly, crawly caterpillar
Crawling up on me—
Crawly, crawly caterpillar
Where will you be?

For activity 37, crawl with your fingers on the next person and tell where you'll be. The activity is useful in overcoming tactile defensiveness and localization of tactile stimuli; it could be done with eyes closed. Have the person being touched put his or her fingers where the previous person stopped. Activity 37 was brought to a class by a student for a project

(38)
Touch new,
Touch new—
Touch you!

Activity 38 was originally done with *touch blue and your wish will come true*. I used it that way and was not comfortable. Then a group I was working with at Pacific State Hospital (now known as Laterman Development Center) decided that the activity was dumb the way I was doing it and made the change that helps in teaching this activity. Staff members and I decided that when we used this activity, we would establish parts of the body to be touched around the circle initially, then decide which part the "toucher" will use to touch the other person, and finally touch and identify some part. At Fairview, we had some interesting tapes with this activity. Toni, Gwyn, and Cathy, therapists at Fairview at the time, had a tape showing most of the severely physically limited young boys in the group lying on the floor. Their motivation is clearly documented, as is the group process, when each person struggles to get into the correct position to accomplish what he wants. The group waits, each member anticipating success. I love that tape.

Another tape that I did for a class at Chapman College in California is interesting in that it clearly documents the problem in learning to touch something using other than a finger or hand. On the tape, two young men working with the problem struggle to understand and finally laugh and push each other away, never succeeding. When someone has limited tactile stimulation, the maximum input should be encouraged. Why always touch with your finger? I've had a funny tongue touch my knee, lips touch my eye, and fingers (that had to pinch) touch my bottom, and it has been in an acceptable, explorative manner in Schulwerk.

During pretests and post-tests in Fairview's Rehabilitation Services Department when a research project was in process, parts of the body were to be identified on the participant's own body and on the tester's body. Again, participants were first hesitant and then delighted when allowed to touch the tester's body. It is difficult, I know, for those with limited social skills to discriminate when something, like touch, is acceptable and when it is not. That is all the more reason for clear framing of an activity and defined closure clarifying that a touch activity, like activity 38, is over.

In activity 39, an instrument at the end of the mat waits for the person rolling, with or without assistance, to get there and play a tune. Then the roller rolls back "home."

(39, Part I)
Rolling, rolling,
Rolling along;
Roll until you
Play us a song.

(39, Part II)
The music is over;
We heard you play.
Roll on back
Until another day.

A tambour, struck by the body as it turns, can orchestrate the rolling. Difficulties can be accompanied by an encouraging sound, as can successes. Two rollers at one time, coming from opposite directions, can be accompanied by tambours, each with his or her own rhythm, and then there can be a two-part composition at the end of the mats. The tambour is just an added reinforcement for each effort made in turning. The tambour alone on this activity would be nice, so the words *roll until you feel so strong,* instead of *play us a song,* would be used. Play around with this activity. Those sitting and watching a sensorimotor activity that requires one-on-one work can participate by chanting, marking success through use of instruments, and cheering success. That way, the environment becomes less sterile but is still goal oriented.

A number of the sensorimotor activities I have observed require a group to sit in chairs while each person takes a turn with the attention of the staff. I believe that anytime socialization, group support, and reinforcement can be achieved, the program is more effective and the cost of sensorimotor training is more dispersed and less difficult to justify. Socialization, verbalization, and attending all are typical needs and can be incorporated into very applied learning situations. Even trampoline activities, air-flow mattress activities, springboard activities, and waterbed activities can include the group in the process. Success is an accident trying to happen.

Linda, a developmental specialist in the Adolescent Social Development Program at Fairview, used Orff-Schulwerk, as did other developmental specialists in the program. Linda developed activity 40 for a class at Fairview. I like it because it is musical and repetitious and the melody and words can easily instruct participants about the task to be completed.

(40[1], Part I)
Put the ball in the bucket,
Dear ___[Name]___ , dear ___[Name]___ .
Put the ball in the bucket,
Dear ___[Name]___ , the ball.

(40, Part II)
Take the ball from the bucket,
Dear ___[Name]___ , dear ___[Name]___ .
Take the ball from the bucket,
Dear ___[Name]___ , the ball.

The inclusion of names is always meaningful. You can use items other than balls and baskets for activity 41.

(41)
A tisket, a tasket,
A ball and a basket.
Throw the ball into the basket.
[Pause until the action is completed.]
Why, the ball is in the basket!

Here is another adaptive activity:

(42)
Belly boards, belly boards—
Let's go for a ride.
Belly boards, belly boards—
Watch us slip and slide.

Therapists Dawn and Bev work with a group of teenagers; when they do activity 43, participants sit on T-stools. The ones most likely to fall initially were Dawn and Bev. Micki, a group leader in Fairview's adolescent program, works with T-stools with the deaf.

---

[1]Sing activity 40 to the tune of "There's a Hole in My Bucket."

(43)
Sitting on a T-stool,
Sitting straight and tall,
Let us hear your music.
Be careful not to fall!

It's not easy to do! Ladder and stair activities can also be used for sensorimotor development.

(44)
Let's get a ladder and climb to the moon.
You can take a look around
And come back soon.
[Or: *And play us a tune.*]

For activities 44 and 45, the base of the ladder is on the floor, with the top propped against the wall. The participant walks up, it going forward (a mirror at the end is nice), then backs down the ladder to return to the place that is still vacant in the circle/semicircle.

(45, Part I)
Up and down,
Up and down—
Climb to the top
And turn around.

(45, Part II)
What do you see?
[Or: *Look at _____ (Name) _____ .*]

(45, Part III)
Up and down,
Up and down—
Come to the bottom,
Then sit down!

A mirror with a few dress-up clothes, such as a veil, gloves, hat, flowers in a bouquet, and even makeup if there is time, adds to activity 46, which has a sequence of instructions.

(46, Part I)
Carry a flower
Up to the tower.

(46, Part II)
Throw the flower
From the tower.

(46, Part III)
Now down the trail
To take off your veil [if veil is used].
[Or: *Now down from the tower*
To find your flower.]

The sequence of events in activity 46 alone make it fun, but the dramatics and silliness of dressing up add to the event. The word *tower* may have no actual meaning here, but the concept of climbing up is easy to grasp, as is what is being accomplished. You can change the rhyme to use concepts more meaningful to your group.

An occupational therapist developed activity 47 for her clients' specific needs on parallel bars. She was interested in getting group socialization while working on very specific tasks.

(47)
One step, two steps, three steps, four.
Let us see you do some more.
One step, two steps, three steps, four.
[Cheering] *You have done . . . many more!*

Activity 48 is another way to get everyone moving. Use plastic feet cut out and placed on the floor.

(48)
Left, right, left,
Left, right, left.
Marching up,
Marching down,
Marching all around—
Where are you going?
Move from wall to wall!

Accompany the movement in activity 48 with march beats on a drum, adapted to the pace of the person taking the steps on the plastic feet. The feet can be colored plastic or even textured rug samples—I've seen all sorts of things used. The person who developed this activity used the rough plastic that is made into runners to protect carpet from heavy foot traffic. The activity allows free movement at the end by any means desired, such as rolling, crawling, running, and hopping.

With places in the circle well established by space, by carpet samples, or even by big X's or names taped on the floor, individuals are called away and asked to return, following auditory clues. Introduce an instrument for participants to strike, blow, or strum when they get to you and then have them return. Use different dynamics in your voice, different sounds in various areas of the circle, and eventually in the room. Have everyone close their eyes, move the instrument sounds around, and when they stop or while playing, have the participants point toward the sounds.

For activities 49 through 51, put instruments in a box and on a tambour. Place the tambour in front of each participant, at first with only two instruments and then with more. Play an instrument down in the box and have a participant match that sound. If there are problems with this activity, then select the same instruments, place them on two tambours, and use visual clues in combination with auditory clues. The activities are fun, functional, and an excellent way to explore instruments in a controlled situation.

(49)

There's something in a big box.
It sounds like this.
[Play the instrument.]
What do you think it is?
[Or: *What do you think is hiding in it?*]

(50)

Tiptoe, tippytoe,
Twinkletoe,
Twinkletoe,
Tiptoe, tippytoe—
Away you go!

(51)
Wiggle, twiggle—
You've got a beat.
Wiggle, twiggle—
Now move your feet!

Activity 52 can be useful for an introductory activity if you want shoes to come off quickly.

(52, Part I)
My shoes are off.
My socks are showing.

(52, Part II)
Leader: *My socks are off.*
Do you know how I'm going?
Participant: *Barefoot.*

(52, Part III)
How do you walk in your barefoot feet?
How do you walk in your barefoot feet?

The closing activity to get shoes back on—still to be followed by something quiet such as a good-bye song—could be this:

(52, Part IV)
Shoes, shoes
On our feet.
Shoes, shoes
On our feet . . . !
[Leave the last phrase open and sustained,
waiting for completion.]

(52, Part V)
Shoes, shoes
On our feet.
Tell us how to keep the beat.

After activities involving walking on toes, stamping—as in activities 53 through 55—seems a nice contrast.

(53)
Stamp one foot;
Keep the other foot still.
Stamp both feet
And move at will!

(54)
Bump, clop,
romp, stomp.
Show us the dragon hop!

(55)
Danny and his dragon
Did a dance one day.
They stomped and shuffled;
It didn't matter which way.

A University of California, Irvine student used activity 55 with a storytelling session.

This next game has the children sitting or squatting. The leader goes to a member of the group with sticks and taps them, which means the member is to jump up. If you want to get more complex, the number of times that the sticks are hit (an established number between, say, one and five) determines the number of jumps or movements the jack-in-the-box can have. When the turn is complete, then the jack-in-the-box trades places with the leader and goes to someone else in the circle.

(56)
Leader: *Jack-in-the-box*
Sitting so still
Will you jump up?
Participant: *Yes, I will* [Or: *No, I won't*;
falls to his/her rear from a squatting position or turns
his/her back—encourage a *yes*].
Leader: [Hits sticks, with group counting
number of strokes; establish a maximum of
one to five strokes.]
Participant: [Moves/jumps the number of times
sticks were struck while group counts.]
Leader: [Trades places with jack-in-the-box;
new leader finds a new jack-in-the-box.]

(57)
Jack be nimble,
Jack be quick.
Jack jump over
The candlestick.

The candlestick can be a Hula Hoop, rope, stick, and so on. An expansion: *Now let us see another trick!*

Hula Hoop activities are part of many curricula. You can adjust the complexity of activity 58 by incorporating maybe only one task before *Here's what I can do.*

(58)
Round and round,
Up and down,
In and out and through.
[Pause for completion.]
Hitchety, skitchety,
Hitchety, skooooo!
Here's what I can do!

Spring-a-lings, like the one in activity 59, are used in some programs, although not commonly. You can make a spring-a-ling with two 2' x 2' pieces of wood with a strong spring in between.

(59)
Spring-a-ling,
Ding-a-ling,
Hop! Pop!

A parachute is very impressive in group activities. You'll need a good-size group to hold one up and keep it moving. Working with balloons, thrown into the parachute and tossed back and forth, requires good upper arm strength. It is nice to eye dye the parachute so that it becomes something completely different. Blues and greens create a moonlike atmosphere. Running from one side to the other under the chute within a specific time period will put participants to the test. Movement under the parachute while it is on the floor is mysterious, but unfortunately, participants don't get to see the strange combination of forms while they're underneath. Videotape would be helpful.

Ball activities are plentiful. Here are a few:

(60, Part I)
A ball is round.
It can roll on the ground.
[Roll it.]

(60, Part II)
A ball is round.
It can bounce up and down.
[Bounce it.]

(60, Part III)
Show us how
A ball can sound.

Toss a ball to a group member for ball sounds. Toss two balls and have them "talk" back and forth with receptive and expressive communication.

(61)
Big ball, bounce around.
Tell us,
Tell us,
Who you've found.

For activity 61, the ball is tossed to a group member, who takes the ball and bounces it, calling out his or her name. The group repeats the chant and the person with the ball tosses it to someone else. I use large beach balls that will not hurt or startle anyone. Have a spare ball so that if a set of teeth meet the ball, the game will not end.

Make up a minor-key tune for activity 62 that is simple, sad, and then glad. Wipe tears away. Have a person in the middle squatting all alone. Have another member volunteer to go to Joan and jump with her, smiling and happy! Continue with activity 63, using a major-key happy tune.

(62)
Here I am,
Little jumping Joan.
When nobody's with me,
I am all alone.[2]

(63)
Here I am,
Little jumping Joan.
When somebody's with me,
I am not alone.

There are many varieties of activities for body parts. Painting the parts or putting stickers or magazine coupons on them work well for body part identification.

(64)
One thumb, one thumb
Beat on the drum.
One thumb, one thumb,
Rummy tum tum.

Change *thumb* in activity 64 to other parts of the body after you've gone through the chant once. I use a tambour, but a floor drum would be fine. In fact, a floor drum would perhaps be better because both hands could be free. Each person plays a patter with a thumb and then moves on to *one hand, one nose,* and so on. Encourage feeling the surface of the total drum. This is an excellent means of exploring the drum with control. Bobbie developed activity 64 in Stockton, California, while attending a session at the University of the Pacific. She hasn't stopped developing resources since.

For activity 65, accent the *itch* in *witch* and be dramatic, scratching at your body. When a particular body part is identified, everyone scratches at the same place. Do not be surprised with what may well occur. Let it land where it falls!

---

[2]A Mother Goose nursery rhyme.

(65)
The witch *has an* itch.
The witch *has an* itch.
Where, oh where
Is the witch's itch?

Beth, a music therapist at Napa, California, developed activity 66 in a training session at Fairview. She did it a bit differently; I changed it to meet my comfort level/needs. It's an excellent speech exercise, as is activity 67.

(66)
The big *bugs* bite.
The big *bugs* bite.
Where, oh where
Do the big *bugs* bite?

(67)
Busy body,
Body busy.
Busy body
Move!

For activities 68 and 69, set up a full-length mirror that does not distort. Encourage discussion if appropriate. Location of body parts, colors, and clothes can all be explored.

(68)
This is my body;
This is me.
Look in the mirror
And what do you see?

(69)
Shake-a-shake,
A-shake-a-shake-a-shake-shake-shake.
Show us what you can
Shake-a-shake-shake.

Activities 70 through 72 will definitely get everyone moving.

(70)
Move your arms
And move your feet
While ____[Name]____
Plays a beat.
[One person plays a beat
while the other moves to it.]

(71)
Oliver Twist,
Oliver Twist, Twist, Twist.
He can do this.
He can do this, this, this!
[A Hula Hoop can
be used with this activity.]

For activities 72 and 73, have one person initiate movement of body parts and another person, or the whole group, imitate. If it's sunny and there are shadows, use activity 74 and have each person develop a shadow; then the group can participate or just watch.

(72)
One jump! Two jumps!
Three jumps! Four!
Jump, jump
Across the floor.
[You may want to establish
four jumps or more if appropriate.]

(73)
Jumping, jumping,
Jumping high!
Can you stretch
For the sky?

(74)
Shadow, oh, shadow—
Come, shadow, and dance
This way and that way.
Come, shadow, and dance.

Have each galloping horse move out for activity 75. Accompaniment would be nice; claves, drum, piano, or body parts could be effective.

(75)
Galloping horses
All in a row—
Some go fast
And some go slow.

(76)
Slop, hop, clop,
Nimble as a top.
Proud pony prances.
When will he[/she] stop?

VARIATIONS

In this book, I have divided sensorimotor and movement activities even though I realize that they greatly overlap. I did so because I wanted to emphasize that some very similar activities can serve different purposes in different contexts. I am interested in developing organic dance form, so it is discussed in the next chapter.

Meanwhile, get resourceful and make the activities in this chapter both functional and enjoyable. If you are turned on and imaginative, the mundane things in life can become highlights. To spark your creativity, here are a few variations you can add to sensorimotor activities:

- Take a mannequin apart and then have participants put parts back on, identifying specific body parts.
- Build parts of the body on a flannel board.
- Tie down part of the body, like arms, and have just feet move while someone else just has arms to move because the feet are wrapped (with a real or imaginary tape).

There are *many* resources not explored in this chapter. Go out and find them!

Chapter 7

MOVEMENT:
ORGANIC DANCE FORM

Rhythm is the inner life of a movement, enabling it to grow and evolve out of itself like a living thing. In our study of dance as a creative art activity, we learn to create body movements according to natural laws of rhythm. By allowing our body movement to evolve naturally, one growing out of another, we achieve what we call organic dance form.

The opposite of organic dance form is a sequence of movements arbitrarily constructed to fit into a preconceived form. Organic dance form allows movements to develop in accordance with natural rhythmic laws. These laws are biologically founded and only partially subject to the will of the dancer. The more craftsmanship the dancer has in working with them, the more perfectly he can form the movement as an expression of himself, and the more satisfying will be the dance.

In organic dance form, the form of the dance is the result of its function. Its function is the expression of the rhythmic feeling of a particular individual or group.

No two dances are alike. Each one is unique, being an expression of the uniqueness of the individual dancer or group. Nature provides us with an unlimited variety of unique forms; no two trees, no two snow-flakes, no two human beings are alike. The form of a dance, if it is a living growth, is also unique, vital, true, and inevitable.[1]

I've already mentioned that I don't spend extensive time on movement in this book because there are many other excellent resources available. However, I do want to give you some useful movement activities; they often can be used for other purposes discussed in other chapters of this book. I am interested in combining contrasting movements and creating tension so relaxation will follow. In this

---

[1]Mettler, B. (1960). *Materials of dance as a creative art activity*. Mettler Studios, Box 4456, University Station, Tucson, AZ 85722.

chapter, I introduce ideas that expand on movement without directing movement, because I am interested in *movement through discovery.*

I think dance activities should be free structured, striving for expansion. Specific activities may well result in expansion, but eventually you must leave them. Teaching steps or dance techniques can be most problematic with less developed children because it tends to make them constrained, imitative, and overly concerned with the critical judgment of others. Activity songs with routine actions create the same problems: There is the tendency to compare one's dancing with how well someone else has danced. Routine steps can become boring and tense. I am *not* saying that learned dance steps are inappropriate; I *am* saying, however, that they can be misused. I have included definite actions in many activities, but there is still plenty of room for expansion.

WARMING UP

Here are a few warm-up activities:

(1)
Exercise
Is lots of fun.
Move your body
And show us one.
[Choose whether to have everyone imitate
or watch. If you're tired, the obvious occurs.]

(2)
Exercises, exercises—
Let's do our exercises.
Hands over head,
Fingers on toes,
Show us how
Your exercise goes.

Try activity 3 for stretching and moving with particular concepts in mind.

(3)

Great big people
Stamp around.
Little tiny people
Touch the ground.

Have the "great big" movement accompanied by drum or some other resounding instrument and use a contrasting instrument for "little tiny." Fast sounds tend to mean little sounds. Combine "giant" and "tiny" people and have them move diagonally across the room for a change from being in a circle.

For activity 4, have booming sounds accompanying the movement of individuals. Move one at a time diagonally across the room, remaining in a new line. Ask for closure . . . the punctuation.

(4, Part I)

Big sounds,
Big movement.
Big sounds,
Big movement.

(4, Part II)

Little sounds,
Little movement.
Little sounds,
Little movement.

I use little-sounding instruments sometimes to get the idea across, like finger cymbals in the ear. To get the size concepts into participants' movements, I call out descriptive words for *big* versus *little,* such as *giant, huge,* and *enormous* versus *teeny, tiny,* and *baby.* There is always plenty of modeling, and you never know, as the leader, how the movers will interpret the changes from *little* to *big.* Is that participant moving like a small elephant—or a large ant? What will you do with that? Test out the concepts.

(4, Part III)
[Start out with *either* big *or* little sounds
and switch them.
Does the movement switch?
Have each dancer move alone at first.
I use two drums, each with a different sound—
one, small and high pitched;
the other, big and low pitched.
You can add *Stop!* when there is no sound
if you have a group that attends well
while continuing to move.]

(4, Part IV)
Big sounds,
Little sounds—
Your *sounds!*

In part IV of activity 4, accompany the mover as he or she wishes to move. Until this part of the activity, the music has said what to do; now it is time for the dancer to tell the music what to do. Encourage grabbing partners and leaving the diagonal line across the room to join hands at times if a dancer indicates such movement . . . and away you go!

Alfredo from Colombia brought this activity into a class at California State University, Long Beach, where there is a very active music therapy program.

(5)
Imagine that you have
Something [heavy, funny, light, and so on]
On your back.
How would you walk?
How would you walk?
How would you walk?

EMPHASIS ON
PARTS OF THE BODY

Make up a tune to sing with activity 6.

(6)
My elbow and my knee—
They're both part of me.
What can I do with
My elbow and my knee?

Martha Wampler brought activity 7 into training at Fairview.

(7)
I look at my hands:
My hands see me;
I see my hands.
My hands see _____ !

I use activity 7 with other parts of the body. too. What do your hands see? The session can be either serious or playful. Imagine looking through a part of your body. It reminds me of this activity:

(8)
My two eyes
Are the windows
Of my face.

DANCING

You can have a lot of fun with dances based on feelings or sounds, like these:

- Crying dance
- Whispering dance
- Growling dance
- Laughing dance
- Roaring dance
- Silly dance
- Mad dance

Here's a specific feeling dance:

(9)
Moving, moving,
Moving my own way.
Watch how ___[Name]___
Moves ___[adverb]___ *today!*

A little bit of bongo madness is appropriate for activities 11 through 12 . . . although intensity will be determined by either the dancer or the musician. Who will set the pace? Who will dictate movement? This is always an issue either to be settled as the process evolves or to be decided before the activity starts. The skill level of the musician frequently will determine whether the dancer or the musician leads. Some volunteer musicians get locked into repetitious rhythms that soon become boring. If you can't change the musician, try to make a dramatic change of instrument if the same movement evolves. Such themes as kindling a fire; building the fire; and the dying, rekindling, sparking, mixing, and then lowering to a simmer of the flames (enacted by individual bodies) can be described loosely in prose or in a discussion of the qualities of fire. Suddenly drama, music, and movement will become very exciting. I have found some of my most spontaneous activities have developed in a movement exercise that pops out of a mind and gels. As exciting as these activities are, though, they can be most disappointing if you try them again soon, because such expectations have been placed on them that new expansion can be inhibited and culmination can be anticlimactic.

(10)
I hear the drum.
It calls to me.
I hear its voice.
It sets me free!

(11)
Abracadabra,
Alacazam!
See what a magical creature
I am!

(12)
Your feet can dance;
Your feet can walk.
Show me how your feet
Can talk.

With chants like activity 13, I frequently give the full chant in opening and then cut it to a shorter version because there are just too many words to remember. Just *Twisted or twirled, snagged or swirled/ How does a pretzel bend?* is more than adequate. Once in a while, just to get the group focused and stimulated to move a bit, go through the whole verse and have everyone try the suggested movement prior to the time for individual contributions.

(13)
Curled or straight,
They sit on my plate.
Pretzels are my friends.
[Pause to get groups into a position.]
Twisted or twirled,
Snagged or swirled,
How does a pretzel bend?
[Have group or individuals bend.]

Have one participant accompany while another other moves; then continue around the circle if working with neighbors, or exchange roles if working with partners.

(14)
Reach high,
Bend low.
Now, body,
Here we go!

(15)
Moooooooooove,
Moooooooooove,
Move to your
Neighbor's sound.
[Or: *Partner's sound.*]

(16)
Icka becca soda cracker—
What a silly sound.
Icka becca soda cracker—
Get up and move around.

For activity 17, you might pause after each motion so a little bit of dancing and a little bit of singing occurs with the group prior to each individual statement.

(17)
We all can dance;
[Pause for dancing.]
We all can sing
[Pause for singing.]
Now it's your turn, ___[Name]___ ,
So do your thing!

With activities 18 and 19, the instrument will determine the movement, perhaps changing or stopping. You can require either attending to the musician or just responding to music made by someone else. If there is a large space, or even in a circle, you can have different instruments and players assigned to spots. When the walker/dancer gets to the instrument, the player will change the pace until the walker/dancer moves to a new section. There will be an overlapping of players/instruments developing two parts at times. The musician then is directing the movement but does not play unless the mover indicates it by moving to him or her.

(18)
To market, to market
To buy a fat pig.
On the way there,
I did a jig.

(19)
Walks are fast;
Walks are slow.
Make your music tell me
The walk that will make me go.

Gongs can encourage attending. Use activities 20 and 21 with a gong.

(20)
Ding dong,
Listen to the gong.
Listen to the gong
And move!

(21)
Move, move,
Move to the gong.
Move to the gong,
Then freeze!

While the gong resounds in activity 21, move, but as its sound diminishes, diminish your movements until hardly a sound is heard, then freeze. Gongs are often taken by someone who uses them for nonmusical chores, so hold on to them!

Moving through some imaginary substance is an excellent way to get extended movement. An activity that I think Martha Wampler brought to us, which we have since learned in different forms, was with the gong. The gong sits in the middle of the group. Someone, probably the leader the first time, strikes the gong and calls out a substance—perhaps it's peanut butter. Everyone moves throughout the room freely, as if going through the substance, until the gong is quiet, at which point everyone stops. Then someone else goes to the gong, calls out a substance first (remember this order of events or you will never hear the substance), and then strikes the gong. Encourage everyone to move in response to the substance and gong so that all is quiet at the end and there are definite breaks between substances.

For activity 22, I use the Appalachian Dancing Man and have him dance on a wooden paddle with arms and feet flying. (See the end of Chapter 3 for instructions.) The person to whom the Appalachian man points should move and then trade places with the person working the dancing man. This activity could be done without a dancing man, however; you may find you have tap dancers in the group.

(22)

Tiptoe, tappy toe.
Tiptoe, tappy toe.
Tiptoe, tappy toe—
Awaaaaaaaaay you go!

Feet can make many sounds—happy sounds, clappy sounds, mad sounds, funny sounds—or just reproduced sound that everyone imitates. You can change activity 23 to focus on to other parts of the body so you get *Hands do, My head does,* and so forth. Focus on that part of the body and encourage the participants to do the same. This is a good activity for exploring the various movements each part of the body can make. Focusing on the eyes is less inhibiting; it is somewhat like working with the eyes closed where others will not look at you.

(23)

Feet do, feet do,
Feet do this!
Feet do, feet do,
Feet do this!
Feet make a [happy, mad, and so on] sound,
A _____ sound,
A _____ sound.
Feet make a _____ sound!

When you are developing movement activities, it is certainly necessary to have an uncluttered environment. Mirrors are nice but can be very distracting. I do not like them for initial movement development, but later, when correction might be desirable or when working with groups when video recorders are not available, mirrors can be useful.

Encourage participants to move in their own space, to avoid bumping, and to avoid touching others. If you start with imagery and free movement around the room without such instructions, boys and girls alike will have each other knocked to the floor within a minute.

Activity 24 involves mime; pulling in air from the space around oneself becomes an exercise for extending the body. Encourage presentation of a gift of space from the air. The gift could be very caring or could be a fun gift to be passed from person to person; maybe it will maintain its shape and maybe it won't.

(24)
Gather space from the air.
Gather space and hold it there.
Now make a gift
That all can share.

Here's another activity that deals with passing surprises along:

(25)
Who has a secret to share?
What size is it?
What shape is it?
Carefully—send it on its way!

Perhaps the secret is large and light. As it is passed around the circle, different or additional characteristics of the secret will emerge: big, little, heavy, light, soft, tender, ugly, slimy, and so on. Have that secret defined in the mind of the sender, then (if you wish) have the secret revealed at the end. Some of the participants will learn to just turn to a neighbor and touch hands. Fine! I remind participants to take care of the secret because "It belongs to [name]." This is a playful activity in which the item may be dropped and change shape each time it moves on. The way an object is passed on can be most revealing.

Putting an elastic band with bells on one arm or ankle can add a distinctive accent to rhythms developed in movement activities. The difference in sound between a foot hitting toe to heel and one hitting heel to toe evolves into a captivating two-part rhythmic invention. Two feet, one with a bell, combined with the heel-to-toe and the toe-to-heel rhythms, can be fun—and then suddenly, a body appears and moves as the melody. If this doesn't happen spontaneously, you may have to ask a participant to move or even do it yourself to draw others in.

(26)
Jungle jive,
Come alive.
Move . . . to . . .
The count . . .
Of five!
One, two, three, four, five!

In activity 26, the movement is free within a set period of time. The meter you develop will determine the type of movement. Perhaps it will be fast and jerky or maybe slow and intense. It may well change as each person or group has a turn.

A group movement activity is one where the leader determines a number that the group will move on, freezing for the rest of the time. For example, you could have the group always on the "one." Take the tambour and start a count to eight, then suddenly drop it to four and finally to two. Suddenly, everyone is active, moving without a second thought. The same idea can be used with jumping facing one way, then turning on "one" to face another way. This is also a way to get movement on an offbeat.

Activity 27 will certainly wake everyone up.

(27[2])
Let your feet go stamp, stamp, stamp!
Let your hands go clap, clap, clap!
Ask a friend to move with you,
Then sit down to show you're through.

For activity 28, the group moves in a circular motion to and fro, into the center and out while turning, and then the drum speaks and the movers respond. The drummer can be a specific leader or participants can trade off. There could be a combination of sounds, using tambours and timpani.

---

[2]Sung to the tune of "Tra-la-la Boom-de-aye."

(28)
Happiness runs in a circular motion.
It moves to and fro.
To the sound of the drum,
Happiness runs,
Happiness runs.

Rose and Sherrie developed activity 29. Adolescents enjoy it a great deal. I have the group line up in two lines facing each other, and I stand at the end with a tambour. The lines cross through each other as participants move. Different drum patterns get different responses. Rhythms can be established that others imitate, or counter-rhythms can be developed. The activity can really "groove."

(29)
Dance and move,
Dance and move.
We're gonna groove,
We're gonna groove.
Move to the rhythm of
   [A person's name or name of the drum]   .

OTHER KINDS OF MOTION

Now I'll describe two other activities I use. One is rear-projected shadow play. The most minute movement is magnified when rear-projected on a screen. I take any type of projector, remove the lens so the light is more dispersed, and place the projector behind the participants. Then I have the instrumentalists sit at the screen, facing it with instruments. The mover, whether in a wheelchair or standing, is stationed between the screen and the projector. The movement becomes very reinforcing. I assign instruments to accompany movement of different parts of the body.

The second activity involves using a black light. Use blacklight paint and cover sticks or instruments with it. Get clothing that is easily visible in the light, such as light-colored gardening gloves. Have the movements of different parts of the body accompanied by instruments (which you assign prior to turning off the regular lights) and you'll have a magical show under the black light. (You'll need a powerful black light.) This activity is great fun; everyone will experiment with glowing teeth and clothing. Beware of the heat of the lightbulb and the possibility of a getting headache from looking into the light too much.

The design that spins the spider
Allows him no rest
Until it's done.

Chapter 8

VOICE

For voice projects, there are many basic activities that can produce some very enjoyable singing developments. Remember to use those good old rounds and songs that have become the staples of evenings around campfires.

For activity 1, encourage finding the mouth by gently squeezing the mouth, icing it, or tickling it to help participants get the idea of "where the food slips in." This activity would be useful while working with feeding, unless you are training clients to keep their hands in their laps at the same time.

LEARNING TO BE COMFORTABLE
WITH THE MOUTH

(1)
Chin chopper, chin chopper,
Chin, chin, chin.
Show us the place
Where the food slips in.

Make activity 2 very dramatic by making a "yucky" face. Be warned, though: this activity may get you into trouble. Every once in a while, I find I'm teaching something that someone else is trying to change, and this activity is certainly a candidate for such a scenario. To avoid such problems, communicate closely with the inter-disciplinary team members who work with the same clients you do. Team members can reinforce what you are teaching and give you feedback; you can do the same for them.

(2)
There's something yucky
In your mouth—
Spit it out!
Spit it out!

With activities 3 and 4, make exaggerated mouth and cheek sounds. Blow with your tongue and lips. Be silly and functional at the same time, because always, you are working on modeling. Get a mirror in on the action whenever it seems helpful. When activities involve spitting and blowing, sometimes it is nice to have a mirror between you and the performer. To encourage spitting activities, you might use little colored candies, such as Red Hots, that stand out on a surface; other items you could use include rice (any color other than white) and watermelon seeds (although they are very flat and small). Sunflower seeds go down, rather than out, as can many items you might use, so beware! Marshmallows fly if they are not too chewed or wet, and they stick very well on surfaces. Then there are raisins, grapes, fresh peas, and olives—I've seen them all fly.

(3)
Motorboat, motorboat,
Puttttttt, putttttttt, puttttttt.
Let's hear your mouth go
Puttttttt, putttttttt, puttttttt.

(4)
Do what I do,
Silly, silly you.
Do what I do.
[Make sounds to be imitated.]

Does the end justify the means? Only you will know . . . or quickly find out! For inspiration, read *Soprano on Her Head: Reflections on Life and Other Right-Side-Up Performances,* a book by Eloise Ristad. It's a great resource. The author explains how she used various activities for controlling her breathing, singing in tune, and relaxing her body. I always wanted to attend one of her workshops, but unfortunately, I never had the chance. The author died in a freak drowning accident in a lake; she had been in the middle of writing another book.

If you're working in mud or doing body painting, you're already messy and it is easier to justify spitting activities, but if you're in a classroom or at a dinner table, the consequences of engaging in spitting activities would indeed be negative!

MOVING ON TO SOUNDS

With activity 5, encourage licking and pushing against the teeth with the tongue and then using the motion to make some type of sound.

(5)
Lick your lips;
Push your teeth.
Now make a sound
With these.

I have a number of props for activity 6. Frequently I use a tambour with feathers or cotton balls placed in the middle of the skin and have the participants blow them off. I can adjust the distance to be blown by moving away or drawing closer; then I count how many things fly. Ping-Pong balls, glitter, sequins, and tissue paper strips all fly—but remember, *you* get to retrieve them. I also use a long carpet tube, with sandpaper glued on one end and foam rubber on the other, for tactile input related to the quality of blowing or of the voice. The tube can be rolled on the floor with different tactile messages on each side. Balloons, candles on a birthday cake, pinwheels that have been tested to be sure they work, and weeds that scatter messages with their seeds are all interesting to use in activity 6. The level of intellect can vary tremendously among participants who need such a basic activity, so it's necessary to have a variety of props available. I have used this blowing activity extensively with the aged.

(6)
Blow, blow,
Blow a long blast.

Activities 7 through 9 can use some of the same props.

(7)
Round and round
The pinwheel will go.
Let's see how hard
You can blow!

For activity 7, some of the light plastic pinwheels, with a number of small pinwheels on them, are nice because *something* is bound to move.

(8)

I'm the north wind.
I bring winter's snow
And I make windmills go.

With activity 8, you can introduce an electric fan blowing from behind the head or into the face.

(9)

Shimmering, shimmering
Light so bright.
Blow out the candle and
Make it night.

With activity 9, you can use a flashlight, which you control. Roxie developed this activity:

(10)

Take the fire;
Light the candle;
Light the room.

This activity was used at the University of Southern California for a demonstration at an Orff institute where Martha Wampler and Gertrud Orff were teaching. A nun who was working with us loaned us a flashlight resembling a candle. The room was darkened, then was suddenly filled with light from the candle-flashlight. It was most impressive. The darkness was mysterious and the power of filling the room with light allowed expansive movement. I have since seen the candles advertised with choir robes and church supplies.

For activity 11, use a feather as a nice tool for sending messages to the sky. As the verse says, ". . . A feather is a letter from a bird and it says, 'Think of me.' "[1]

(11)

---

[1] From de Regniers, B. S., and Haas, I. (1950). If you find a little feather. In *Something special*. New York: Harcourt, Brace and World.

Blow it,
Blow it
Way up high.
Send a message to the sky.

Activity 12 can be used to help participants distinguish between gentle and strong breathing.

(12)
Jeremiah, blow the fire,
Puff, puff, puff.
First you blow it gently,
Then you blow it rough.[2]

Here's a puppet activity developed by a nurse at Fairview:

(13)
Hi. My name is Miss Bliss.
Blow me a kiss.
[Pause for a response.]
Here is Mr. Busic [name pronounced to rhyme with *music*].
He wants to hear your music.

In activity 14, each participant develops a sneeze—covering it, of course!

(14)
Air comes in tickly
Through your nose.
Then very quickly,
Out it goes:
Aaaahhhhhhh chhhhhhooooo!

With activity 15, get the humming going. Your bees will likely be playful—and may even pinch!

---

[2]A Mother Goose rhyme.

(15)
A big bumblebee
Sat on a wall;
He said he could hmmmmmmmm
And that was all.[3]

Have each "insect" in activity 16 produce a hum and then build it around the circle for all the insect sounds. Instruments could be added effectively to this activity.

(16)
The sun has set;
Night has come.
Different insects
Start to hummmmmmm.

For activity 17, pass the sounds around the circle after each participant initiates a shum, chum, or hum sound. The sounds will build like insects sharing secrets in one another's ears, covering their mouths as they gossip and call into each ear.

(17)
Shummmmmmm, chummmmmmm.
Let us hear
Your special
Hummmmmmm, chummmmmmm.

It's not just insects that can hum, you know:

(18)
Feeeeee, fiiiiii,
Fohhhhhh, fummmmmmm.
Listen to _____ [Name] _____
Hummmmmmm some.

---

[3]From Withers, C. (1948). *A rocket in my pocket: The rhymes and chants of young Americans* (p. 4). New York: H. Holt.

Activity 19 is fun because participants somewhat hide the sound and come up with some strange results. Each person takes a turn at making his or her own special sound.

(19)
Hand over your face—
Your own special sound.

A student in a class at the University of California, Irvine brought in activity 20 as part of a project. It may be inappropriate if members can't whistle, but if most can, you can help those who can't to pucker their lips. It's fun, so there really is no such thing as failure. You'll even spot participants attempting to whistle later, outside of Orff sessions.

(20)
Kitty, kitty, kistle;
Bitty, bitty, bistle.
Let us hear your
Very best whistle.

Activity 21 is good for developing circle ostinati.[4] (The concept of circle ostinati is explained further in Chapter 20.) In this activity, a combination of sounds and movement can create an active machine. Take one sound that comes from the motor activity and ask for movement to be added in the center of the circle. Then, one by one, add another ostinato of a motor sound, with movement. Finally, you'll have one large motor with a variety of workings—composition form. The person who initiated the first sound and movement should be responsible for closure, which might be a gradual wearing down, crashing, or exploding. If you have access to video equipment, take the time to set it up before this activity. Taping will be reinforcing to all. The group might want to try the activity again and make some corrections; if so, great! A new sound and leader can be introduced, or the same leader again can develop a similar activity.

---

[4]Author's note: An ostinato (plural: ostinati) is a repetitious pattern of sound. In this book, I extend the concept of *ostinato* to include a repetitious pattern of movement. Ostinato provides the basis for elemental music, using the pentatonic scales. Melodies enter and leave at will, whereas ostinati sustain the composition's initial thoughts.

(21)
Wheels whirl round;
Engines roar loud.
Click, clack, squeal, hummmmmm—
Make a motor sound.

Echo activities and call–response activities are excellent for developing inflection, sounds, and new words. I have included a few useful ones in Chapter 5. Many echo activities can easily be drawn from participants' actions. For example, you can develop a mountain with a climber, who when he or she reaches the top, calls to different group members; the other members respond.

GETTING BOLDER

Activity 22 has both functionality and concepts on which to focus, and it encourages voice projection. For once, participants are asked to shout. I don't know that I was ever given permission to shout as a child . . . but I do know why.

(22)
Over the drum,
Under the drum,
In the drum and out.
I get so excited
That I want to shout.

The carpet tube that I mentioned earlier can be used with activity 23.

(23)
Breathe deep;
Let it out.
I get so excited
That I want to shout.

Strangely enough, activity 24 tends to be a quieting activity. It is nice when done just before lying on the floor or whispering.

(24)
Monster, Monster
Shriek and howl
Be a monster
And scare us all.

Here's a puppet activity:

(25)
My name is Mr. McCloud;
Talk to me loud.
[Pause for a response.]
My name is Miss Moe;
Talk to me very, very slow.
[Or: *very, very low.*]

Receptive communication and expressive communication can be established effectively with instruments because they allow "listening" and expression without the need to draw on language skills. The large bass xylophone is what I most frequently use. I sit on one side of the instrument and a group member sits on the other side of it; we talk back and forth by using mallets to strike tone bars instead of by using our vocal cords. This requires "listening" and "speaking." I've included many more such activities in Chapter 11, but here is one:

(26)
Take my hand
And walk with me.
Be my friend
And talk with me.

Have one person choose another, walk to an instrument or to two instruments, and talk with each other, developing a two-part conversation on instruments.

With activity 27, I've used a phone as a prop. At Fairview, I was interested to find that some of the more sophisticated young men (who are no longer at Fairview) would carry on rather extensive phone discussions. The best phone I had was a wall phone mounted on a wood stand that sat on the floor and could be moved from person to person. I also borrowed a training unit from the local telephone company and actually developed two-way discussion with dialing and phone ringing. Phones have changed since then, though, so you'll either need to use more contemporary equipment or just not use "talking on the phone" for this activity.

(27)
What kind of sounds do you make
When you're   [mad, glad, sad, sleepy, hungry,
happy, reading, eating, talking on the phone, and so on]?

Activities 28 and 29 are very simplistic and can be modeled, or you can encourage individual responses. Activity 28 could grow on the spot, with participants adding reasons for sighing, for example.

(28)
People say hi!
Bees buzz by. Buzzzzzz!
We'd like to hear you
Give us a sigh,
____[Name]____ !

(29)
The owl says,
"Whoooooo,
Whoooooo,
Whoooooo are you?"

A theme of animals or of just personal names can be used for developing a response in activity 29. A television character giving a description of what he or she is doing or wearing and also add to the conversation.

THE KAZOO

The kazoo, used in many activities like number 30, is hard to understand at first. I went to a party for adults one time where kazoos were used, and my colleague Kay complained all night that her horn was broken. It never dawned on me that she didn't know that you don't blow a kazoo—you hum into it. You'll have to spend time teaching the kazoo's sound process, and you should have some type of disinfectant for afterward. Pull the kazoos out of a fun box or bag; try to have on hand different shapes of kazoos all for the fun of it. Kazoos are very cheap, and some are fancier than others. Nose harps and combs with cellophane work also, but these are harder to teach.

(30)
Kazoo, kazoo,
Crazy kazoo.
Sing us a song saying,
"Do dooo dooooooooo."

THE GONG

The hanging gong, used in activities 31 through 33, has mystical powers. I spent a weekend working with "gong therapy," and it was most exciting. I have respected the gong ever since. The gong speaks back, as do many other instruments that you can explore. The tambour gives feedback, but usually only to the speaker. The gong hangs, and when spoken to, it feeds back very strange overtones. People who under no other circumstances are eager to participate will, when the gong is brought out, get on their knees, with their rear ends in the air, and speak to the gong. I thought about calling this book *A Hard Day at Work Calling into the Gong.* . . . I also thought about *Splendor on Your Ass* but was voted down.

Children who seldom speak *will* speak or make sounds into a gong. When do consultations for the general public, I can easily get a reputation as a miracle worker because with a gong I often can get someone to talk who has never verbally expressed him- or herself before. Sometimes this is a result of my not knowing limitations, so special things happen because I expect them to happen—but also, it's just that gongs attract people. Gongs are expensive; it is difficult to substitute another instrument for them; and cheap ones are miserable. If you get a chance to buy one, test it first if you can. Gongs mysteriously disappear, so keep them under lock and key when you're not using them.

I had some students from a developmental center housed in a church bring in a big stainless steel dishpan (which probably cost as much as a gong but was more easily available to them); it sounded great. Another nice substitute for a gong is a big bass drum, the old kind with hide heads. For this, take off one side so participants can climb into the frame and get a conversation going.

(31)

Ring, gong, ring.
1   ↓5   ↑1

Sing, gong, sing.
1   ↓5   ↑1

Take a mess-age
1   2   3   2

To the king.
1   ↓5   ↑1

Each participant has a special message for the king in activity 31. Maybe the message entails telling a secret, being silly, being a bit of a tattletale, or uttering a unique sound. The king may answer back or he may not; it doesn't really seem to matter that much. I've sat on the sidelines or behind the group (with everyone knowing I was there) and assumed the role of the king. Each speaker talked away into the gong, responding to my prompts or answering questions I asked.

(32)

Listen to the gong;
Hear it ring.
It will ring
When you sing.
Who will sing?

Sing songs for activity 32; you'll hear them later outside of class or after the activities. Keep the musical elemental. Different participants will likely use different forms.

I had a fun session with my colleague Kay one time with a group of elderly women at Laterman Developmental Center. Calling into a big bass drum instead of a gong, they started talking about their trip to the fair. They were charming. They had their aprons on, so typical of grandmas, and were gossipy, fun, and willing to try new things. They were really a very special, social group.

Occasionally, it's necessary to let each person hit that gong or drum. When this is the case, make sure you are up to it, are in good shape, do not have a headache, and have no activities scheduled nearby in the building.

Bea, working in a program for blind clients, developed activity 33 for use with the gong.

(33)
How will you know
When the king is near?
How will you know
That the king is here?

For activity 33, have each person announce the king's presence by striking the gong while another person approaches the gong regally. The announcer then presents the king. You usually will hear a number of gong strikes just because it is so hard to stop after only one strike. Take care in the mallet you choose; make sure it will help make all that sound tolerable—that is, not too loud and brassy. Use a very fuzzy mallet.

You might lead up to activities that involve hitting the gong by using activity 34, which makes big instruments whisper.

(34)
Big instruments can talk soft.
Big instruments can talk low.
Let's hear them.
Shhhhhh!
[Make a face for silence and
put a finger to your mouth
to help indicate soft sounds.]

The gong activities in this chapter use such words as *sing, ring,* and *king;* these words should be extended and accented to mimic the sound of the gong.

WORDS TO
BRING ACTIVITIES TO LIFE

When developing project resources, use words that sound like what they are describing . . . use onomatopoeia.[5] Look at the following list of onomatopoeic words. I've left space in the list so that you can keep adding such words for your own projects. Using onomatopoeia is really fun, and these are good resource words.

Onomatopoeia

Buzzing	Wiggle	Pout	_____
Rattling	Giggle	Burp	_____
Sneezing	Cough	Squeeze	_____
Sizzling	Vomit	Blow	_____
Popping	Whisper	Swirl	_____
Tickling	Squirm	Sneer	_____
Honking	Swoop	Scratch	_____
Fluffy	Scream	Cringe	_____
Coarse	Hush	Scurry	_____
Smooth	Swish	Sag	_____
Prickly	Stick	Jostle	_____
Velvety	Harsh	Meander	_____
Greasy	Hiccup	Freeze	_____
Misty	Glitter	Explode	_____
Hot	Dazzle	Rub	_____
Bumpy	Rush	Cut	_____
Disgust	Hurrying	Itch	_____
Rebellious	Waiting	Slow	_____
Zing	Twitch	Low	_____
Splash	Ugly	Hissing	_____
Gobble	Lovely	Breathing	_____
Cuckoo	Yes	Mumbling	_____

[5]Onomatopoeia is the formation of words imitative of natural sounds, the formation of name words by imitating the sound associated with the thing designated, or the use of imitative and naturally suggestive words for rhetorical effect.

Meow	No	Squeaking	_____
Bark	Clicking	Spit	_____
Yuck	Spitting		_____
Creepy	Whistling		_____
Brat	Yawning		_____
Float	Groaning		_____
Sneezing	Panting		_____

SINGING AND SPEECH

Getting people to sing can be difficult, but every once in a while I'll assume there is a hesitancy to sing and be happily mistaken. We are losing our ability to sing, and that is sad. People seldom sit as a family and sing songs. There are obvious reasons why: hectic schedules, TV programs to watch, video games to play. . . . We music therapists must encourage singing, because we are the models.

I think most of us have experienced great disapproval from our children when we sing. When I sing in the car, I get elbows in my side and I see scowling eyebrows indicating playful but true disgust. My parents spent so much money on my voice, yet I use it so seldom and poorly. I am constantly teased about my $8,000 voice because that is how much I once estimated what my parents had spent on it. I love to sing. If you ever meet me—or if you know me—please let me sing!

When you sing loudly, whether beautifully or not so beautifully, everyone will stop to listen and others' small voices will be stilled. Singing is a powerful group process, but it requires sensitivity and respect for each person's worth.

If you are learning these activities or participating in workshops and you discover that you still can't sing, then don't sing. I've observed students using activities I've taught them and seen such painful modeling! If you can't do a particular presentation as is, then don't. If you do, everyone will be miserable. Just use good dramatics and speech inflections and change the material. The material in this book is meant only to be a starting point. Please shape them and improve on them—or use them in developing other ideas—but please don't model them so perfectly that you aren't yourself. Listen to yourself, know yourself, and be yourself. If you need some other dynamic that you can't easily provide, invite someone to work with you who can provide it.

Pitch your voice to the needs of the group. Singing requires listening. Use call–response and canon activities with words that are heavy on rhythm and vowel sounds. Encourage inflection in talking and then in singing.

If your activities start to sound similar, check your movement and rhythm selections and maybe add some singing, and there will be dramatic change. Work with someone else so you point out problem areas for each other.

Strive for simplicity so each participant can make a contribution worthy of his or her intent. If one person has a great complex voice, what does Jane or Johnny One Note do? There is a time for complex music, and we can all celebrate it, but there is also a time for co-authorship and a need for noncomplex contributions to which others can relate as part of the development of a successful, sophisticated composition with exploration and full participation.

Now, let's get to the voice activities.

A student at the University of the Pacific in California brought in activity 35 as a project. He is a choral teacher of junior high students.

(35)
Make your voice high;
Make your voice low.
Make your voice go
Where you want it to go.

Use instruments for the sounds in activity 36 and ask that they be matched. Kathy brought this activity into a Fairview training session. I don't recall if she used a sequence of notes, but a single note would be fine. The singer could be the person at the instrument who asks someone else to sing what he or she plays. The whole group could sing back the notes, too, with the emphasis being on one person's choosing a note and everyone's trying to sing it back. That setup is less threatening than having only one person at a time sing.

(36)
A parrot says
The sounds I say.
Who will sing
The sounds I play?

Jessica brought activity 37 into a class I taught at the University of Missouri in Kansas City. I changed it a bit, but I'm sure it still has the same intent:

(37)
Little Johnny [Or: Janie] One Note
Can sing just one sound.
We can sing many notes
As our turn comes around.

Try developing some ostinati on various "one notes."

I was getting an alto xylophone for an activity for the same class, and while playing with it on the way back to the circle where I was teaching, I played this:

With the group standing (but you can have people sit if necessary), I started with "add one note to build a tune." Sing it in 4 :4.

With the group standing (but you can have people sit if necessary), I started with "add one note to build a tune." Sing it in 4 :4.

After everyone has turned to the person next to him or her, the tune starts and moves on with "add two notes," then "add three notes," then "add a tune and then pass it on"; slowly, closure and rest come with tune development. Instruments can be added or used instead of voices.

When I used this activity, I had the answering phrase sung by each person. It was bouncy, and as we passed the xylophone around, I removed all the other keys (just for demonstration purposes—the students certainly could have played it with all the keys). It really moved along and was very nice for developing vocal range. I used a C pentatonic scale. A recorder could have been used in place of voice. Movement was waiting because of the spring of the introductory phrase/question.

A familiar tune will be understood immediately with this next activity, which Sue, a music therapist, presented as a project at the University of the Pacific in a summer course I taught:

(38, Part I)
I've got a song;
Let me sing it for you
While the meaning is true.

(38, Part II)
Make up a song
And sing it with mine.
Singing together,
We'll have a good time.
[One person plus someone of choice—
random singing.]

(38, Part III)
We've made up a song
And the feeling was fine.
Singing together,
We've had a good time.

Different tricks have been developed for working with speech inflection. It is difficult to push speech inflection because many times, the person with poor speech inflection is painfully shy and/or has a poor self-image. One idea was brought in by a teacher from a developmental center. She got her husband to hook up colored lights behind a speaker that was attached to a phonograph and microphone. She called it her firefly activity, and she and her husband were going to patent the idea; I don't know if they ever did. When the inflection of the voice changed, the lights would reinforce the change by adding color and brightness. It was great. Sherrie Taylor of my staff used a dimmer switch with Christmas tree lights attached; she manually turned the switch when she heard voice inflection change.

Grace Nash, an Orff specialist and teacher, uses her arms for high, low, and middle sounds. She has groups repeat rhymes, such as "Hickory Dickory Dock," and as her arms move, the voices change. She then develops the voices into two parts. It's fun and functional.

I found some toys that were composed of a cone with a doll inside, with sticks beneath. I make the doll go up and down to encourage *down* and *up* and *soft.*

(39)
I'll sing you a song,
Though not very long,
Yet I think it is pretty as any. . . .[6]

Activity 40 is one I use for a large-group composition. Cheryl, Dawn, and Bonnie worked along with me in developing this activity at Milledgeville, Georgia. We had a whole auditorium full of people. We divided the group into fourths and had each group develop random melodies and movement. The composition was done in canon/round form.

(40)
Come laugh and be merry
And join with me.
We'll sing a chorus
Of ha, ha, hee*!*

We did activity 41 with the same group and in the same way. We removed all sound, leaving only the movement of laughter, which is a nice experience in silence (as silent as a whole auditorium full of gregarious people can be).

---

[6]A Mother Goose rhyme.

(41)
Laughter is
A universal language.
Laughter is
A universal language.

I had developed activity 41 at another conference. It was first done with a smaller group so that movement was more observable and coordinated, as was the style of laughter. *Universal language* is fun to play with, but I have since found that is not universal.

Chapter 9

UNIQUENESS

We each are constantly striving to find out what makes us who we are. How do we differ from others? If we cannot compare similarities and differences, how can we establish just who we are? Children always give intriguing answers when asked what is special about them: a scar, a funny mole, a different belly button, a cowlick, crossed eyes. They search openly for their uniqueness and are satisfied rather easily. Many times, they see their deficits as assets because they are "special." When we as adults have trouble identifying what makes us unique, we close in and become less certain of our worth; we focus on our deficits and cannot see our assets.

In Orff-Schulwerk, we constantly seek diverse responses that confer personal worth, possession, and uniqueness on those who give them. Poet Carl Sandburg identified such possession[1]:

I saluted a nobody,
I saw him in a looking-glass.
He smiled—so did I.
He crumpled the skin on his forehead, frowning—
    so did I.
Everything I did he did.
I said, "Hello, I know you."
And I was a liar to say so.

Ah, this looking-glass man!
Liar, fool, dreamer, play-actor,
Soldier, dusty drinker of dust—
Ah! He will go with me
Down the dark stairway
When nobody else is looking,
When everybody else is gone.
He locks his elbow in mine,
I lose all—but not him.

---

[1]Sandburg, C. (1978). Chicago poet. In *Early moon* (p. 41). New York: Harcourt Brace Jovanovich.

I have often told a story about Shari, my daughter, and her child-hood search for uniqueness. When she was a girl, she came to me one day, concerned over the fact that she was going to lose a silver tooth that had replaced a damaged tooth when she was younger. She wondered what would be special about her after the tooth was gone. She said she was the only one in her class with a "gold" tooth. (That is what she called the silver tooth; her brother called it her fang.) I was amazed at her concern because I had always considered her to be unique and special. I don't know what she found to replace the tooth, but she soon seemed content and self-assured, so I assumed she had fulfilled her need to identify something unique that she alone possesses. As do many adults, she may well have many new traumas as she becomes more critical of her unique qualities. I can only hope that she has the opportunity to discover herself and know that she relates, as a unique contribution, to the total composition of a group.

I decided to single out a few activities for a chapter on uniqueness even though I was tempted to discuss uniqueness in the chapter on psychosocial dynamics (Chapter 11), where it would have been most appropriate. I did so because uniqueness is too important to combine with other subjects. The title of this book, *Alike and Different*, itself implies a search for uniqueness.

I worked with a teacher in the San Jose area and encouraged her to try the following activity:

(1)
Alike and different,
Alike and different—
We are both
Alike and different.

I encouraged her to have each student turn to the person next to him or her and verbalize differences and similarities. The teacher was most concerned as to how her first-graders would react, but she took on the activity despite her feeling that it was high risk. She was quite pleasantly surprised. The students were perceptive and honest. When it came time for one of the children to turn to a little boy who had a cleft palate and who had been mimicked on different occasions, the teacher held her breath—but she trusted the children enough to let the activity move on. The child turned to the boy with the cleft palate and compared their similarities. When it came to differences, the child said, "You have beautiful blue eyes with a lot of eyelashes, and I have brown eyes." The teacher had initiated the activity with a positive attitude and had reinforced positive and explorative statements, and the child was able to model the teacher's intent.

If the child hadn't come through, what could the teacher have done? She could have listed some of the boy's other unique qualities, such as his eyes, his smile, his dark and neat hair, and his proud walk, and perhaps stated, "[Name] does have a different mouth from the rest of us, and he is using it very well." If the teacher were too concerned to allow the students to evaluate the boy, she could place herself next to him and serve as a model, using positive observations and perhaps being critical in a playful way of something least expected. As a teacher, be aware of what is being said—of the content, not the words being spoken. Children need models, not critics. Be comfortable with the special traits of each of the students, regardless of age, and be assertive when necessary. Everyone will be watching for your reaction because the teacher is the leader. With this one small activity, you can solve a very large problem, as the following poem illustrates.

Teacher, give me back my "I"—!
You promised, teacher,
You promised if I was good you'd give it back.
You have so many "I's" in the top drawer of your desk.
You wouldn't miss mine.[2]

As compositions are developed through co-authorship, each contribution makes a clear statement of "I am." The following activities are obviously focused on pinpointing participants' unique qualities:

(2)
Look at you;
Look at me.
When we look,
What do we see?

---

[2]From Cullum, A. (1971). *The geranium on the window sill just died, but teacher you went right on* (p. 56). New York: Harlan Quist.

(3)
Some people are big;
Some people are small.
People can be
Any way at all.

(4)
I'm a person and so are you
Jump into the circle
And show us what you do.

(5)
People, people,
All kinds of people:
Big ones, little ones,
Middle ones, too.
Stand up and
Show us you!

(6)
I'm special,
He's special,
She's special, too.
Tell us something that's
Special about you!

(7)
Have you heard [clap, clap]
One word [clap, clap]
All . . . about me [clap, clap]?

(8)
Special people,
Special people.
What makes you
So unique?

With these activities, encourage descriptions of each participant's appearance, differences, and uniqueness and encourage personal disclosures. These activities can be emotionally powerful; if your group is in the mood for encounter-type activities, there may be a lot of didactic exchange. There might be tears or anger. Growth can be painful, but poor leadership can be, too. Provide space for recovery so that individuals can move ahead and build positive uniquenesses. You may need to encourage the participants themselves to provide recovery for someone who is floundering, but you may find that participants assume this responsibility before you have to intervene. Sometimes participants may interfere because they are too uncomfortable with the process. As the leader, be alert and sensitive and allow some release through instruments and movement. Do not be oversolicitous; be comfortable with your group, knowing their traits, and be comfortable with yourself.

Determining what makes each person unique is very difficult unless your group has done some good work on building trust in prior activities. Movement that describes a uniqueness can be easier than verbalization for participants initially, unless your group has done a lot of talk sessions.

Chapter 10

AFFECT

This face you got,
This here phizzog you carry around,
You never picked it out for yourself, at all, at all—
    did you?
This here phizzog—somebody handed it to you—
    am I right?
Somebody said, "Here's yours; now go see what
    you can do with it."
Somebody slipped it to you
    and it was like a package marked:
"No goods exchanged after being taken away"—
This face you got.[1]

As a music therapist, you model facial affect. You are there in front, the person with the "phizzog," the leader. Your affect is what you are thinking and saying. Contrasts you may try, but you won't fool those working with you. It is necessary for appropriate facial affect to be used with the emotion, the idea, and the mood that is being explored and developed. If you smile while confused, feel pleased but show no facial approval, or stiffly present material with which you hope to spark spontaneity, you won't get creative, exciting results. You cannot decide to be creative and then wait for creativity to happen.

If you are seeking diversity, if you are looking for the unexplored or blissfully free, you must open yourself to this experience and allow it to grow and show. When "boudoirizing"[2] your material, scrutinize your affect. Have you developed an interesting idea? Do you have specific motions in mind that in fact are

---

[1]Sandburg, C. (1978). Phizzog. In *Early moon* (p. 41). New York: Harcourt Brace Jovanovich.

[2]Author's note: By *boudoirizing,* I mean developing your own material and exploring it, in the privacy of your own boudoir, until you are comfortable, before using the image in a group session.

not part of you? If you are uncomfortable with what you have developed, then let it change and become a part of you. You must change your way of thinking if you plan to change your way of being. It is not necessary for you to be all light and jolly, but it certainly helps if you give clear cues as to what is being communicated. We all must build on a repertoire of feelings, and this repertoire must be a spontaneous part of us. Affect is universal, in each situation I can think of. You might think of examples where I am wrong. Good! But hear me out. Granted, avoiding eye contact and hanging the head may be a cultural affect not intended to communicate shyness, disdain, disrespect, dishonesty, and so on. But affect resulting from obvious stimuli is universal. As you work with your group, it is necessary to realize that each person is working on a separate idea and that the mood you set, the affect you present, will either encourage diversity or control responses because it implies an expected response. When you discuss moods in a jovial, playful manner, it is likely that the moods presented will be the same. Using the same affect throughout a session with a group is just as ineffective as using the same rhythms throughout.

The message of Carl Sandburg's poem "Sky Pieces," which is about the hats we wear, is an excellent guideline for music therapists:

> ... Hats are sky-pieces;
> Hats have a destiny;
> Wish your hat slowly;
> Your hat is you.[3]

TEACHING THE CONCEPT
OF AFFECT

Use activity 1 to help participants explore the concept of affect.

(1)
[Elicit descriptive words, such as *happy* and *sad*,
and require that the face present the opposite.
Some examples:]

- *Happiness with sad affect*
- *Anger with joyful affect*
- *Loose feeling with tight affect*

---

[3]Sandburg, C. (1978). Chicago poet. In *Early moon* (p. 92). New York: Harcourt Brace Jovanovich.

The activity becomes playful but builds on the repertoire of feelings and affect; participants will learn through contrasts. Use music to dramatize these contrasts: for example, play happy music with an angry face.

Activity 2 focuses on another contrast: *yes* can sound like *no* and visa-versa. Let arguments evolve in which one person says no and another says yes. In the discussion afterward, you'll often get conflicting opinions on who was saying yes, who was saying no, and who won the argument.

(2)

Play the sounds of no.
[Pause.]
Play the sounds of yes.
[Pause.]
Play the sound of maybe.

In activity 3, the use of contrasts within the body again builds on the repertoire of affect.

(3)

Get your stomach
Laughing
And make your face
Frown.

With activities 4 and 5, take turns passing by the group and seeing each face presented.

(4)

My face can say yes;
My face can say no.
What other expressions
Can your face show?

(5)

Faces can smile and
Faces can cry.
Show me your face
When I pass by.

For activity 6, I use my collection of cards with different emotions on them. Mine are commercial, but you could use actual photographs or magazine pictures, one or two subjects in each, showing emotions. These pictures can also be used for storytelling or for building a story activities.

(6)
Faces, faces—
They show us bow you feel.
Take a picture from the stack
And make it look
And sound real.

I pass the stack around and have everyone choose a picture and then turn it over so others don't know what the picture is. Then I ask participants to choose an instrument and to use their facial expression to represent the feeling selected. After each participant makes a presentation, he or she shares the card. Discussion may follow.

For activity 7, have some pictures taken of each participant demonstrating various facial affects and then place them in a hat to be drawn at random by participants. Videotape is useful beforehand for helping participants identify affect. Have someone walk for the videotaping and then have the whole group, including the walker, accompany the movement when you play the tape back.

(7)
Body talk [Clap, clap],
Body talk [Clap, clap].
Communicate
By the way that you walk!

I take slides of various facial affects and body affects when participants first join my class. I usually need five or six different shots of each person to get one usable shot. When I show the slides on a screen with activity 8, I also throw a light from another projector on the wall next to the screen and have the person whose face is on the screen move with the same affect, using the light as a rear projection as his or her shadow communicates the movement. This activity must be appropriate to the mood of the group, however, or it will just fall flat— it's happened to me.

(8)
*Pictures, pictures
In the hat.
Who do you know
Who looks like that?*

HAPPINESS AND SADNESS

Bells seem the most obvious choice for activity 9, but triangles, glockenspiels, and finger cymbals all have a "ting-a-ling" sound. Pass the sound around, using a tinkling instrument for the first part of the development, and then have each participant make a vocal sound that is passed from person to person around the circle. You may want to use a chant with a simple melody, such as 5–3–5–3–5.

(9)
*Ting-a-ling-a-ling,
Sing a happy sound.
Ting-a-ling-a-ling,
Pass it all around.*

Rose Reeder developed the next activity when we were working in the Education Department at the University of California, Santa Cruz.

(10, Part I)
*I have a laugh inside of me;
It goes like this!
I have a laugh inside of me;
It goes like this.*
[Make up a major-key tune.]

Work on the affect of laughter. Some will cover their faces; others will laugh and fall over; others will giggle. The individuals at Fairview who participate in this activity love the laughter but are always a bit uncomfortable because the other half of the activity is this:

(10, Part II)
I have a cry inside of me;
It goes like this.
I have a cry inside of me;
It goes like this.
[Make up a minor-key tune.]

There is great anxiety in crying. Participants frequently will state that "big girls [or boys] don't cry" or will become very involved in grabbing tissues for someone else who is crying, taking obvious pains to keep from crying themselves. Paradoxically, you may find that there is little difference between crying and laughing in facial affect and body motion; sometimes you'll have to ask participants which they are doing—laughing or crying. I think it's most inappropriate to deny the need and right to cry, because it is one of the most basic ways of communicating emotion.

At Fairview, an interested psychologist, who was male, visited a group composed of young girls. When it came his turn during the activity, he pretended to cry. The girls expressed disgust, saying that "boys don't cry," and he told them he did cry and that boys do cry, just like girls. This created additional concern.

With the same group of girls, a few very emotional situations occurred when the activity moved into psychodrama. With this activity, there is such anticipation and concern about crying that surprise responses occur. Reasons for crying might be dramatized, and deep feelings may be revealed that are valuable and most important to the group. As leader of such a session, you must be prepared to move into heavy discussion and to deal with possible uncontrolled crying and manipulation. Consider the ramifications of the activity for the particular individuals in the group when you are deciding whether to use it or to draw on other resources to elicit the desired affect and dramatics.

Activity 11 is another crying activity, but it is less emotional than activity 10, merely showing crying without drawing it from inside.

(11)
Peanut butter, peanut butter,
Bread and rye.
Show us how
You can cry.

MAKEUP AS AN ENHANCER

I encourage the use of makeup (and costumes, if desired) when feasible with affect-centered activities to extend the repertoire of affect. I make this recommendation because of personal experience. I once attended a mime class, and the instructors started the class in whiteface and were most entertaining. However, because I was concentrating on the activity instructions, I never quite got into the mime exercises as I had planned and I felt that many of the activities were not rewarding. We participants never did get to paint our faces. When my daughter and I were fooling around later, though, I painted my face and found that many of the activities we had practiced were enhanced—even completely different—because wearing makeup encouraged extensive facial exploration.

Activity 12 provides an excellent chance to use makeup.

(12)
When you're happy, you smile;
When you're sad, you frown.
What kind of face are you
Wearing around?

TOUCH

Our society often discourages touching one another. The developmentally disabled and others lacking social skills frequently have problems in determining when it is appropriate to touch. This next activity can include hugging, but you will want to develop additional resources for demonstrating affection and caring.

(13)
I like you,
Don't you see?
Please show me
If you like me.

ANGER AND REGRET

Activities 14 and 15 help participants discern and express anger.

(14)

Sometimes I'm happy;
Sometimes I'm sad.
This is how I act
When I'm very, very mad.

(15)

Others get mad
Just like you.
When mothers get mad,
What do they do?

Tanci developed activity 16 at Fairview so that very simple expressions of regret could be developed. What makes each individual feel sorry? The activity could be playful and silly or serious and in depth.

(16)

Sor-ry, so sor-ry,
Eeeeeeh, eeeeeeh, ooooooh.
Sor-ry, so sor-ry,
Ooooooh, eeeeeeh, sor-r-ry.

DIFFERENTIATING EMOTIONS

Activities 17 and 18 provide practice in expressing and discerning emotions. Make up a simple questioning melody. After each person has demonstrated how he or she feels using facial and postural affect and then played individual feelings on instruments, have groups with similar feelings combine their music and develop a specific "feeling" composition.

(17)
Moods, moods—
They come and go.
Walk around the room
And let . . . your mood show.

(18)
How do you feel?
Reach inside
And pull it out.
How do you feel?

Chapter 11

PSYCHOSOCIAL DYNAMICS

Leader Goose
by Carol H. Bitcon

Na-Na-Nanny Goat,
Carol is a baby.
She keeps on making rules;
Leadership's her slavery.

Five copies—four for the gang,
One for the manual.
She really knows her stuff,
Freedom she does handle.

Did you see her sitting—*plop!*—
While others were dancing?
Fondling toys once part of play,
Her need for advancing.

Her muscles twitched in
Disguised despair.
Boredom reveled,
Stuck to a chair.

She'd grabbed her toys
With ample pull
While others danced on;
Her arms were only halfway full!

Na-Na-Nanny Goat,
Carol is a baby.
Leadership, she won't deny,
Can be a slavery.

WHY DO WE LEAD?

Exploring areas of play as an adult can be a high-risk experience. As adults, we note that risk through observing models—children. We all have seen or at least heard of the bossy child demanding control, threatened by failure, and concerned with lack of skill—frequently developmental and anticipated prematurely. This child, when challenged for leadership, will likely pick up his toys and go home. Adults frequently play the same way, displaying this "picking up of toys and going home" in such behavior as removing oneself from a group, intellectualizing a process rather than participating, standing near an exit with arms folded and ready to run, and denying what is happening.

As an adult moves through the developmental stages of play, uneasiness appears in inappropriate laughter, asides used as distracters, and interruptions or questions. Frequently, adults will ask the question "Why are we doing this?" Must we always explain our behavior rationally, though?

As part of my own personal development, I discovered that I was comfortable as a leader and did not frequently participate in activities others led. This comfort was a result of controlling the environment, subject material, and responses to the degree that if something was uncomfortable for me, I could redirect the energies of the total group without challenge. What in fact was happening was that I realized freedom only when in control and found myself "picking up my toys" and missing out. These "toys" were capable of hindering my development and total participation.

With discomfort, I forced myself to attend a variety of activities that were high risk. Roles were assigned to me, others influenced and controlled my participation, shaping my performance to their comforts, and I progressed to a new level of play. I learned to make the most of the environment and to enjoy basic play relationships that provided new "aha!" experiences, with others relating to me as a peer rather than performing for me, the teacher/leader. I lost the need to "skip to the back of the book" to read the final page while the mystery was still in progress. I am convinced that one does not experience true freedom and openness with others until one relinquishes leadership. Certainly, one can participate as leader and still be a part of the process and allow great freedom, but this takes practice; this an effective leader.

I must constantly expose myself to new adventures, not without concern. I must force myself to get to an activity, and then force myself to leave, resisting closure. All has not been joy, but at least it has been a learning experience that can be incorporated into my teaching resources. I still am more comfortable when I'm the leader when meeting new playmates. I am, however, pleased at what I discovered one day: I removed myself from a high-risk experience and watched magic working without me as others danced, sang, and participated together in celebrated climax; although I had "picked up my toys and gone home," everyone else went right on dancing![1]

ACTIVITIES FOCUSING ON
PSYCHOSOCIAL DYNAMICS

In my work with adults and adolescents, I've found a group of activities that are sophisticated yet simple. These very basic activities can produce complex results. Families can easily come together and communicate with the use of Orff-Schulwerk, as can church groups, social groups, crisis intervention groups, and anyone interested in letting go, exploring, and discovering. Some of these activities may be inappropriate for your particular group; some may be very similar to ones you already use. If you work with awareness books, therapy resources, encounter groups, gestalt therapy, transactional analysis, body language, and so forth, you already have many resources available to you. I hope that you will explore music-making in the group process as an added dimension to communication.

One qualification I place on Orff-Schulwerk activity is that participants should not have to explain what they "meant." Individual contributions are accepted and combined with those made by others in co-authorship. Having to explain spontaneity, diversity, and pre-intellectual participation diminishes organic participation. Sometimes at a later time, responses or activities come up again as topics of discussion and explanations are given if it seems appropriate to give them. But I turn off so quickly when someone asks me, "What did you mean?" or "Why did you do that?" during a process. Being able to let

---

[1]Author's note: I originally wrote this first part of the chapter as an article to be published elsewhere, but I ended up not publishing it separately.

loose does not leave one without responsibility for one's behavior, but it does leave one free to explore and discover.

When I visit with or lead groups that are into rap sessions, there is usually a lot of inside information to which I don't have access. It's fine for groups to use this information during a session if it seems contextually appropriate, but using inside information extensively with "outsiders" can become a protective device that "insiders" use to avoid opening up further when they feel scared or threatened. Encourage acceptance without a lot of verbalization. Try to rely on models to demonstrate what is happening so you do not get into heavy didactic instructions, become too controlling, or waste time.

Once in Vienna, I worked with young schoolchildren who did not speak English, and I did not speak their language. We still managed to work together, however, without being able to verbalize extensively. When they arrived for our session, they ran up the beautiful circular stairs, smiling with excitement. I leaned over the banister and called hello, and they called hello back. Two teachers panted along after the children, worrying, I am sure, what they were in for. Once we were all in the classroom, I taught the children my name, pounding on my chest, and soon they were modeling me. We did activities together in a circle. As we went through the first rondo on names, the teachers helped, but the children quickly understood the concept of modeling. Pam Healy and Charlotte Bostwick, who traveled with me, were in the circle too, using shoulder taps to indicate turns and modeling the activity. When it came time to say good-bye, everyone was sad; I truly wished I had at least one more day to work and play with the children. They left knowing about rondo form, call–response, ostinati, and closure, and they had new friends from the United States besides. Later on, I learned what I had missed and looked forward to returning another time.

Getting Acquainted

A student from the University of California, Irvine brought activity 1 to class. You'll enjoy seeing what happens with this activity; one word is hard for a group that is used to expanding on topics and getting into discussions. This activity also appears in Chapter 9.

(1)
Have you heard
One word
All about me?

Like activity 1, activities 2 through 5 will help group members get to know one another.

(2)
I've only begun
To become _____ .

(3)
A penny's worth of mirth
Is worth a pound of sorrow.
What small thing today
Will make you happy tomorrow?

(4)
Friends are fair and
Friends are true.
What does your best friend
Mean to you?

(5)
I as me,
You as you,
We are all together.
I think that I will play a tune
So you will know me better.

For activity 5, have each participant select someone whom he or she wishes to know better. This can be a very introspective activity and also a very caring one. You may want to reduce the lines to just these:

I think that I will play a tune
So you will know me better!

For activity 6, choose someone—or ask for a volunteer—to "talk" with you using instruments. The bass xylophone is often the instrument of choice. Facing each other, converse through the music. Then have two people join in by dubbing for the conversation. When one person plays, the assigned person talks about anything he or she chooses. When the player stops, the dubber stops; the other player resumes the conversation with music and the other dubber talks, usually sticking with the same subject. The playing may extend the verbal exchange. You'll find that all four people will be going at one time when excitement rises. Any particular dubber speaks only when the player to whom he or she is assigned is playing. The music forces conversation, but it does not force quality or conversation content. With young teenagers, you may hear a lot of phrases like these: "it's, like, I . . . ," "then he [she] goes, like . . . ," "you know." This activity can be fascinating.

(6)

Who will ta – lk,
5   5   3   1

Who will ta – lk,
5   5   3   1

Who will talk with me?
5   5   5   5   5

Who will ta – lk,
5   5   3   1

Who will ta – lk,
5   5   3   1

Who will talk with me?

5   5   5   5   1

Who will talk?

5   5   1

Expressing Feelings

Activity 7 is fun because participants have to work to find a way of secretly sticking out their tongue. It promotes a kind of "So what?" attitude that can save participants' self-esteem when they're working on personal accomplishments and feel threatened.

(7)

When people tease, hurt,
And make fun,
Secretly
Stick out your tongue.

I mentioned earlier in this chapter that I once worked in Vienna. While I was there, I also had an adult group. The participants spoke French, British English, German, and assorted other languages. At the start of our work together, their questions were about why I felt they needed therapy. One of the first activities we did together explained that I was there to share, not to provide therapy; I used it to discuss problems.

Another of our early activities used artwork that consisted of basic outlines of two human figures, just like the black and white figures at the beginning of this book, to symbolize the two sides each person has—outside and inside. Along with the artwork, I passed out colored pencils and gave participants 5 minutes to write down a description of each side of themselves. I imposed the limit so participants wouldn't have time to revise their original thoughts. When the activity (number 8 below) was chanted in rondo form, each participant shared both sides of him- or herself, some using instruments, some singing, some speaking. One woman cried; I went to the bathroom with her while the therapists traveling with me continued with the session. The woman shared that her husband had recently died and that she had not been able to cry about it before this. When we went back to the group, the other participants were surprised to hear that the woman had suffered such grief. We all talked some and then moved on to other activities.

When the second group came in for its session, I wanted to help participants open up more easily, so I spent a lot of time talking about communication problems. That session went smoothly.

(8)
There are two sides of me,
Two sides of me—
One on the inside,
One on the outside—
Two sides of me.

Activity 9 doesn't require the use of artwork, but it, too, can help participants express what's inside.

(9)
I can whisper;
I can shout!
How do you
Let your feelings out?

Kay, then an instructor at the University of California, Long Beach (now at Chapman University in Orange, California) brought this activity to a class:

(10)
I'm feelin' good [clap, clap].
I'm feelin' bad [clap, clap].
I'm feelin' happy [clap, clap].
I'm feelin' sad [clap, clap].
Good [clap], *bad* [clap],
Happy [clap], *sad* [clap]—
How [clap] *are* [clap] *you* [clap, clap]?

Activities 11 and 12 continue with the theme of feelings.

(11)
Life is good,
Life is real.
Play the sound that
Makes you feel great!

(12)
Hey, hey,
How was your day?
Take a turn
And have your say.

Debbie brought activity 13 to a class at the University of California, Irvine and developed it to handle anxieties. She used it with young children when they appeared worried or upset.

(13)
Feel better fast [clap, clap],
Feel better fast [clap, clap]—
What makes you [clap]
Feel better fast?

Lucy brought this rondo to the same class:

(14)
Feelings, feelings,
Feelings are true.
Today I'll share
My feelings with you.

Activity 15 is good to use when members of your group have acted as if or said they felt unnoticed.

(15)
Have you ever felt like nobody?
Just a tiny speck of air
When everyone's around you,
And you are just not there?[2]

For activity 16, each person takes a turn giving a warm fuzzy (through music or movement or a statement) to the next person in the circle. You might instead allow participants to choose to whom they'll give a fuzzy. This idea is, as you may well know, from Alvyn M. Freed's *T.A. for Tots (and Other Prinzes)*, a book with many other such good ideas.

(16)
I just found me
A nice warm fuzzy
I think I'll share!

What problems, fears, and surprises lurk in the outside world when people leave the protective environment of a hospital, an institution, or a family or a relationship? Activities 17 and 18 can help group participants get these feelings out in the open.

(17)
I'm leaving a place
Where I've been so long.
I'm scared to leave it,
For things may go wrong.

(18)
If you're going somewhere,
Where, oh where, is somewhere?

With activity 19, talk about fears, share and compare them, and act them out. I am always surprised to find out how many people were afraid, as children, to stretch their legs way out under the sheets in the middle of the night because they thought things like crabs, crocodiles, or snakes would get them. Act out the walking, and maybe

---

[2]Lewis, R. (1966). Being nobody. In *Miracles* (p. 163). New York: Simon & Schuster.

have each person orchestrate the walk and narrate it. This can help participants become desensitized to scary things.

(19)
Walking in the dark,
Scared as can be—
When you look around,
What do you see?

Identity

Another Kay from the University of the Pacific in California developed these next two activities:

(20)
I am woman [clap, clap].
I am woman [snap, snap].
What kind of woman? [Clap, clap.]
What kind of woman? [Snap, snap.]

(21)
Goals, goals,
Who needs goals?
We need goals;
You need goals.
What [clap] *are* [clap] *your* [clap] *goals?* [clap]

Encourage pantomime, movement, or music to demonstrate the various responses to activities 22 through 24.

(22)
Doobie, doobie,
Doobie, dee—
Tell us who
You'd like to be.

(23)
What did you
Want to be
When you were
Young and free?

(24)
Hey!
What do you like most about living?
Say!
What do you like most about life?

Activities 25 and 26 can boost self-esteem.

(25)
Sometimes I'm cool
And sometimes I'm not.
I like myself best when _____ .

(26)
Some people are big;
Some people are small.
Tell us your best
Characteristic of all!

What we wish for others tells a lot about us:

(27)
If wishes and dreams came true,
This I would wish for you:

_____ .

What are your dreams? It's fun to expand on dreams by orchestrating or dramatizing them, particularly for the person whose dream it is. For activity 28, develop a dream/plan and bring together all components with orchestration. Take care, though: the dreamer is liable to be compulsive about how the dream went and will not readily accept modifications to it.

(28)
The power to dream,
The power to plan—
Is this not
Our supreme endowment?
What are your dreams?

We all have something we need to get rid of. The something mentioned in activity 29 might be traits, habits, ideas, or even just old feelings that have lasted too long. Genola developed this cleaning-day activity for use at Stockton State Hospital:

(29)
Cleaning day, cleaning day—
Let's find something to
Throw away.

I developed activity 30 for working with questions and answers using body instruments. One person goes to another in the circle and asks questions using body sounds and movement. The answer is given in the same fashion, and then the questioner and the answerer change places. Instruments also can be used. If you choose, the activity can be done so that a variety of answers are developed to answer a single question, which is repeated for each participant.

(30)
Questions need answers;
Answers need questions.
Questions and answers,
Answers and questions.

Here's a mirror activity. In turn, each person goes to a "people" mirror and states:

(31)
Mirror, mirror on the wall,
Please be kind to me.
Mirror, mirror on the wall,
Tell me what you see.

For activity 32, have someone develop a concept, then have others make opposite-type rhythms as a contrast. Move on to a discussion of how people are similar and different.

(32)
Opposites attract.
What do you think of that?
Opposites attract.
Give me some feedback.

What participants have to say in activity 33 may be communicated by a musical message, a movement, or language. You can add new interest to the last line by changing it to *That is why I'm going to sing . . .* and using special songs with messages.

(33)
I'm okay;
You're okay.
That is why I'm going
to say_____ .

Sharing News

Newsworthy items are fun for young and old. When someone experiences a special event and has the opportunity to share it, the intensity of the relationships in the group grow. If you're a snoopy teacher, you can put to good use the free information that flows with news-oriented activities. The following activities are great for use in exploring and expanding on new materials and experiences. There may be times some "news" items must be reported, but it's difficult to report them when responses are freely given in a private group environment. Disclose early on that if something appears to be of danger to a participant, it will be necessary for you to report it.

(34)
Extra, extra—
Read all about it!
What is your news?
What is your news?

(35)
[Make up a simple tune based on a 1–3 interval.]
Ding, dong, ding,
News we bring.
Ding, dong, ding,
Who's brought something?

(36)
In every house, on every street,
Around and up and down,
There's something special going on
In every house in town.[3]

(37)
Sit by me
As quiet as can be—
I have a secret to tell.

The secrets in activity 38 through 42 can be fun fantasies developed and expanded on just as in a gossip game.

(38)
My nose,
Your nose—
Nobody knows
What I know.

(39)
Rumor here,
Rumor there,
Rumor, rumor, everywhere.

---

[3]From Fisher, A. (1969). At Christmas time. In *In one door and out the other* (p. 62). New York: Thomas Y. Crowell.

(40)
A nose for news,
Sharp eyes,
Clear eyes,
Quick mind.
I've got a noseful of news.

(41)
Share and tell,
Tell and swell.

(42)
News makes us proud;
Tell it to the crowd.

If you are working with a rather explosive group, use activity 43 to throw rumors out and then laugh at them, discuss them, and maybe correct them. Making up rumors is fun. Match opposite people together and you'll hear participants voice ridiculous thoughts about each other. Group members will get quite silly as they paradoxically explore issues; the seemingly ridiculous sometimes leads us to truth.

(43)
Short or tall,
Big or small,
It spreads like fire
Among us all.

Use activity 44 to bring things back the other way, away from rumor and toward truth.

(44)
Eyes are for seeing.
They're the windows of your face.

Dealing with Rules and Working for Change

We've all chafed under rules we thought were unnecessary. Activity 45 lets everyone vent—and think of ways to change the rules!

(45)
Signs, rules
Everywhere!
Don't do this!
Don't do that!
[Pause for (1) do's and don'ts and
(2) an *I'd like to* from each person.]

Activity 46 will pop into your mind even after group sessions. Many times, we hurry to wait or wait to hurry. I use this activity by alternating from one person to another, hurrying and waiting. The contrast of going from a panting pace to slow, stunted movement is nice. Try it with young people; you'll get complaints about your priorities.

(46, Part I)
[Done very slowly]
Waiting, waiting,
Always we're waiting—
Waiting for this
And waiting for that.

(46, Part II)
[Done quickly, out of breath]
Hurrying, hurrying,
Always we're hurrying—
Hurrying here,
Hurrying there,
Hurrying everywhere!

When I attended a symposium at the University of Southern California, a fellow presented this next activity. It provides the opportunity to make a statement against the establishment and then to come up with a positive idea for correction. It is surprising how often that when there is the opportunity to make corrections, no one has corrective ideas. This activity can be enlivened by using big paintbrushes on butcher paper. Build a city—and build it right. One of my groups developed a city council and worked with the reform contingent in a call–response pattern:

(47, Part I)
The city is sick;
The city is dying.
Each time I see it,
I feel like crying.
What's gone wrong?

(47, Part II)
We'll build a new city;
We'll build it right.
We'll build a new city;
We'll build it right!

Here's a similar activity:

(48)
Here comes the judge.
Here comes the judge.
Tell us what you'd like to budge.

Activity 49 focuses on working for freedom for everyone.

(49)
The world was created for you and me.
We can help
So we are all free!

You may be surprised at the creative solutions offered in answer to activity 50.

(50)
Hey, diddle diddle,
Hem, haw, and fiddle;
How do we integrate? [4]

---

[4]From Merriam, E. (1969). *The inner city mother goose.* New York: Simon & Schuster.

Spirituality

There are numerous activities that have been developed for religious services. These can be adapted for your group.

(51)
Songs of silence,
Songs of sound,
God will hear us;
God is around.

The results of using instruments for nonverbal prayer are impressive. I used this activity with Dawn and Chaplain MacOlash at Fairview, and it was really very touching. Different participants came forth and offered their prayers with music. Some combined their prayers. The ritualistic patterns some of the participants used in their presentation were reverent and treasured by those offering them.

Another variation to activity 51 is this one:

(52)
Prayer of silence,
Prayer of sound,
God will hear it;
God is around.

(53)
Lift a joyful voice
Unto our God.

(54)
I wonder why God gave us life
Instead of passing us by?

Activity 55 is not necessarily religious in nature, but there are special hymns that the clients at Fairview liked to sing for the congregation, and this was one activity developed for that purpose.

(55)
Sing, oh sing
To us a song—
Make it short or
Make it long.

Call forward the animals in activity 56 two by two; bring in the rain, have the water rise, and send out the dove. Tell the story after the ark is full. Build the story from the decision to build the ark, if your participants can attend for that length of time. Choose specific instruments for the sounds of rain pounding the ship, the animals walking up the plank, and then the animals disembarking two by two.

(56)
Noah called the animals
Two by two.
Which animal
Are you?
[Each participant acts out an animal.]

These next two activities focus on the fact that we are part of the world, not apart from it.

(57)
World, world,
Spin round and round.
What can we do
To make it a better sound?

(58)
Life is exciting;
Life is divine.
Life is all around you.
What can you find?

I developed activity 59 for wheelchair clients. You can use musical walls or beanbags thrown at objects to make the wall fall as the music ends.

(59)
*Joshua fit the battle of Jericho
And the walls came tumbling down.*

Activity 60 can evoke a great deal of tenderness.

(60)
*God gave us music
To tell us of love.
Give us your music;
Tell us your love.*

Trust and Opening Up

With activity 61, discuss what trust areas are difficult, when participants have trusted, and when they have not.

(61)
*Trust, one must!
Trust, one must!
Risk it—one must!*

Leslie, a music therapy intern from Camarillo State Hospital in California, brought activity 62 into a class at Fairview. Make up a tune for it because this activity needs to be sung.

(62, Part I)
*There are many things we like about our friends;
There is one thing that I do not like about you.*
[Response:] *Help!*

(62, Part II)
*There are many things I like about myself;
There is one thing I'd like to change within me.*

Leslie had a nice melody for the activity; you can make one up. When she presented this project, it was high risk in that the group could have easily gotten out of control; participants had to be prepared for criticism and be willing to be open with others.

It takes trust to allow someone to whisper in your ear. Whispering immediately adds to the mystery and excitement of talking. Sometimes it's easier to whisper something personal or exciting than it is to speak it. As a leader, try whispering when you want to draw very close attention to what you are presenting.

(63)
Whispers
Tickle through your ear,
Telling things you like to hear. . . .
Whispers come so they can blow
Secrets others never know.[5]

Joan, from the University of California, Irvine, brought in this:

(64)
Sometimes I'm cool
And sometimes I'm hot.
Sometimes I'm with it;
Sometimes I'm not.
I like myself best when _____ .

As the group process develops, so does the sensitivity of the group's music. Just as the group's conversation moves more freely and with greater depth, so does its music. In a 5-day workshop that starts on a Monday, music starts falling together by about Wednesday, with sensitive listening, entrances, and silences all appearing as part of the co-authored composition. Orff-Schulwerk surely is a social process; some social groups demonstrate more intensity than do others. It is such a pleasure to be part of a group with which one grows and explores and discovers. I am fortunate that as a participant/instructor/manager, I do not have to grow alone. What will happen within a group? None of us knows until it happens.

---

[5]From Livingston, M. C. (1958). Whispers. In *Whispers, and other poems* (p. 11). New York: Harcourt, Brace.

Chapter 12

THE AGED

Nobody grows old by merely living a number of years; people only grow old by deserting their ideals. Nor is youth simply a matter of ripe cheeks and supple knees. Youth is a temper of the will, a quality of imagination, a vigor of the emotions, and a freshness of the deep springs of life. Years may wrinkle the skin, but to give up enthusiasm wrinkles the soul.

Whether [one is] seventeen or seventy, if there is in one's heart the love of wonder, the childlike appetite of what's next, and the courage to play the game as the rules are written, [one] is young.

[People] do not quit playing because they grow old; they grow old because they quit playing.[1]

MEMORIES AND DREAMS EXPRESSED— NOT IN SILENCE

A phrase from an old song has always been a bit haunting to me. "When I grow too old to dream, I will try to remember." When do dreams stop and memories take over? Are memories expanded and really products of current dreams? Do we ever reach an age when we only remember? Should we try to generate dreams with the aged, or just memories?

When I first was contacted to consult as a registered music therapist at a convalescent hospital in Santa Ana, I was challenged, but I was concerned. Why was I suddenly moving into clinical work with the aged after working predominantly with younger people with various types of disabilities? As I questioned my motivation, I realized I was testing myself in accepting old age in my friends, family, and . . . myself. Meeting each of the aged individuals energized my thoughts. Why were some of the aged still very vital, determined, and conversant whereas others were crabby, negative, agitated, and generally depressed? Certainly there were some physiological explanations, but

---

[1]Author unknown.

there were some great inconsistencies in accepting the negative conditions as things to be expected with old age. I wondered if these patients had thoughts they wanted to share? Did they realize they had contributions to make that they could not have made in their youth? Did they have dreams?

As I worked with patients at the convalescent hospital, I realized their worth; this realization was facilitated by the Orff-Schulwerk work. Initially, I worked with various groupings of wheelchair and semiambulatory individuals, testing the experience, wondering if the service I provided was appropriate and effective. I found that many of the sessions were reinforcing another effective clinical program called Reality Orientation.[2] Through repetition and expansion, I was encouraging participation, subject-related responses, eye contact, and development of self-image, and perhaps most important of all, providing a social situation in which each person had an opportunity to communicate as an individual, learn one another's names, and discover others' unique traits. The communication of unique qualities became the priority of the sessions; the goal was to assist everyone in valuing the various cultures and backgrounds they represented, each of them with their secret bits of knowledge that we "youngsters" might never learn on our own. Many of the elderly in convalescent hospitals have had feelings we have not; they have, with unmatched determination, experienced hardships we'll never endure. All these things remain hidden from us, where we cannot learn from them, unless we use skill and sensitivity to provide the elderly with opportunities for expression and expansion through stimulating modalities.

As part of the expansion of the Orff-Schulwerk program at the hospital, two of the nursing staff were selected to participate in a 1-week workshop at Fairview, with staff members from different facilities, to be trained in meeting patients' special clinical needs. Soon the convalescent hospital had two effectively trained staff members ready to provide Orff-Schulwerk as part of a variety of treatment modalities for the aged. The hospital administrator had planned ahead so that carefully selected instruments were ready when the staff members returned from the workshop. Everyone would soon get a real treat.

-----

[2]Reality orientation is designed to assist patients in accepting life as it really is, now, on this date, in this situation.

The next visit I made to the convalescent hospital provided tremendous reinforcement to me. Guess what I heard as I walked in. You're right—Orff-Schulwerk was in progress! The circle of chairs and wheelchairs grew large as patients, family members, and staff members were all drawn in, unable to resist. Those not in the room could hardly ignore the fact that Orff-Schulwerk had arrived. There was hardly any stigma of old age. This was a hospital for the ill and dying? Life was everywhere, in everyone. The participants—both clients and staff—were involved and joyful.

Interestingly enough, there were clients in that group whom I had never seen on previous visits, and staff who had appeared disinterested when I had worked with the group before were now very actively observing. Before those two staff members went to the workshop, the staff had seen and heard what I was doing, but I was just a consultant. I was not one of them who intimately knew the needs of the patients and the staffing problems and who shared success and failures with them. Now, two of their own people were now people they could model. After that workshop, my value had expanded in many ways, but at the same time, it had diminished. Bringing in a consultant is certainly not always the answer to meeting clients' needs; it tends to foster dependence. However, sending those staff members for training and using me as a resource for clinical ideas and for expanding on that training was effective planning.

As I monitored the clinical objectives, I observed the establishment of rapport and some unexpected responses. Truly, something wonderful was rapidly expanding through the work of energetic and motivated staff members. Some of the comments clients typically made at first were "I never was handy at the piano"; "I can't do that"; "My sister sure was good at music"; "I've had a stroke, you know"; "Go away"; "Stop that noise—I can't stand it"; "Are you girls in your second childhood?"; and "I can't hold things very well." But despite denying their abilities and expressing concern about failure, clients would struggle to make a sound, to have others join in, and finally to close their contributions, and then be ready to move on to the other members of the group. Some clients would only smile with twinkling eyes and maintain a pleasant silence, but they were actively participating while encased in a limited body. Some clients would make harsh, insensitive, or undisciplined comments, but staff members ignored these, whereas they rewarded success and positive statements with a touch, a smile, or praise. The clients, in turn, began to frequently verbalize to staff members or touch them in order to reward them. Some family members began to come to the Orff-Schulwerk sessions to watch and would observe the active mental life of the elderly that they had long since failed to notice. A client can hardly be a nonperson when participating in Orff-Schulwerk, but in other settings, people sometimes assume that the conversation of the elderly is just the rambling typical of senility. Some elderly clients involved in Orff-Schulwerk sessions can be very much in contact, then suddenly slip into a pattern of behavior removed from the moment, and then just as easily return to make an active contribution.

One woman, complaining of the noise and referring to times long past, worried about when her parents would come to get her for a picnic. (The woman was in her nineties.) As the drums were being played loudly and continuously by an active participant, I suggested that the drums were talking, sending messages like Native Americans use to send. As the drums got louder, I said, "See—the Native Americans are getting closer." She, with twinkling eyes and a grin, said, "I hope to hell they get here soon!" We giggled together, and soon she was beating her drums, sending messages, periodically fading into another pattern of behavior and again returning to the group. How fortunate that the opportunity to participate was there and that she was motivated to participate. After that, clinicians felt that over time, the woman increasingly participated with the group, slipping into other behavior patterns less often. We realized success.

How many convalescent hospitals have you entered where you heard giggling, laughter, conversation, and the beat of music? A session I later participated in at the convalescent hospital produced one of those great "aha!" experiences that Orff-Schulwerk allows to creep up on you like Carl Sandburg's "fog on little cat's feet." Because it was a beautiful sunny day, perhaps the first in the new year, we decided to have an outdoor session. As each client came out, many feeling it too cold, too bright, or too windy, the staff hastened to provide comfort, bringing each individual his or her sweater, stole, or blanket as requested. Staff moved some clients out of the sun because they thought it too bright and moved others into the sun because they though the shade too cool. A small puppy visited each of the clients, who asked to touch and love him. He chased leaves and ignored the anxieties of people experiencing something different. A large poinsettia shrub was in full bloom on the patio wall, reminiscent of Christmas even though it felt like spring. We all had made it through to another new season.

A few jets flying overhead became an immediate point of interest, and conversation was active. As the Orff-Schulwerk session began, many clients made playful and social comments. One man, feeling too distressed to stay, asked to be removed and was. One of the other clients stated that "he just isn't quite himself today," reinforcing the efforts of the staff. Another woman could not accept the invitation of joining us because she was just too busy. (She and I had had an exchange on another day when she reminded me that I was paid whether I worked or not and she was paid by the hour and by how much she produced, a style of living that she could not shake even when in a wheelchair with simulated pressure and real anxiety.)

One of the activities planned for the session had been developed by a staff member at the Laterman Development Center; we wondered if the clients would enjoy it. The activity was initiated by looking around, talking a bit about the weather, and then moving on to chanting:

> *Happies are big;*
> *Happies are small.*
> *What makes you*
> *Happiest of all?*

Some responses were such things as "my grandchildren," "my son," "my children's success," and "when my family visits me." Generally, though, happy thoughts were initially based on past experiences and then focused on the present situation: "being out of doors on a beautiful day," "praying and singing in church," "being with this group out here today," and "being with you," the latter of which became, for many clients, something like "I had not really thought about it before, but I am happy right now!"

It is most important, when working with the elderly, to present activities that are age appropriate. Our attitudes can be inappropriate even if the planned activities are not. If our aged clients cannot tell us what is going on inside themselves, we can only project our observations, compare them with past experiences, and participate in our clients' growth. These people are so easily forgotten because they represent a future part of our lives that many times we wish to forget, but they, with their memories and dreams, are a resource for us. We cannot access this resource if we do not seek out the aged.

SPECIAL CONSIDERATIONS

Working with aged clients who have for one reason or another lost judgment, contentment, and orientation to life can prove a challenge but is worthwhile. Certainly, the aged need not be disabled to experience Orff-Schulwerk. What a great improvement over the kitchen band, where accompanying other music or beating repetitious sounds on an instrument with little dynamics is a lengthy activity. The aged had a wealth of experiences and memories that should not go to waste.

Therapists and students frequently contact me and question the use of Orff-Schulwerk with the aged. They fear that Orff-Schulwerk will come across as too childlike. It will be if it is presented in a childish manner, if the esteem of the participants is threatened and the participants are uncomfortable in relating with the leader. I must admit that I had great concern when first introducing Orff-Schulwerk to the aged. The group expected me to sing or play the piano and was most displeased that I was not entertaining. In addition, the disabled aged are notorious for being blunt and crabby. The group immediately made many derisive comments; after having worked with developmentally disabled clients who appreciated my every effort, I was quite shocked to suddenly be confronted with coarse language directed at me, the benevolent therapist! But then the group became curious about the new instruments and sounds, so they wanted me to succeed and thus they condescended to stay and help me out.

As sessions with such groups proceed, it is amazing to find how little these people, who live together 24 hours a day, know about each other and how little they think of their own abilities. How ready they are to tell you why they can't do something, to say they don't hear well, or to act confused. Quickly, you must determine whether someone can hear or whether someone can really move a hand or an arm. Does someone really need to go to the bathroom or is it all a way to get out of a situation that could be too hard, too silly, too dangerous, too painful—just another failure? Follow all their cues: anger, confusion, embarrassment, pain, frailty, depression, the need to talk, twinkling eyes, giggles, encouragement, and interest. I have found myself firmly grasping an arm or hand with the paper-thin skin of old age that was so frail that I thought I might destroy it. I have found myself clumsy with using instruments on tables because the height of the table was so important to the individual participating. I have learned to ignore the quick no and "I can't" and to reinforce any approximations of success. I have learned to continually relate to each individual by getting down right in his or her face, talking clearly, giving expansive facial feedback, touching a shoulder, brushing a hair off the forehead, doing anything to stimulate body parts and interest while relating that I am not immediately leaving and that success is forthcoming.

There are issues for which you must work out your own answers. Deciding which name to use is confusing. The elderly are from a different generation; many older women are used to being addressed with a *Mrs.* before their surname. Others who have lived in nursing home for a long time are used to being called by their first name and may be taken aback by being addressed by two names. Defining what behaviors to ignore is difficult because the inconsistency of attending is disarming. The most active participant in the group will suddenly surprise you with open hallucinations, disorientation, and/or emotional display. Likewise, the individual who seems to need the most primary approach may suddenly describe a cowbell and tell you how it was used many years ago, entertaining the group with memories.

Nursing home clients are very familiar with the sounds and signs of death, like the absence of a friend in church or in a music session. It certainly is unusual to enter such a facility and hear music, laughter, and chanting. The whole climate among staff members seems to change for the better as they pass through or by rooms where there is an Orff-Schulwerk session going on or as they take clients back to their rooms after a session. *Play* certainly is not a ready part of the vocabulary used in a convalescent hospital. There are bingo games and craft classes, but strong rules regarding success or failure with these are quickly drawn by active participants who don't like the sounds, the slowness, the smells, or the skill levels of other clients less capable of participating. Bringing an activity into such facilities and providing a group process with individual objectives and adaptations is unusual.

Family members can readily be drawn into an Orff-Schulwerk session, participating with the group or just observing and enjoying. Grandchildren are a great source of pride for nursing home residents. Sometimes an activity can include discussion of grandchildren, introducing any in attendance and, if the children are willing, letting them each touch or shake hands with the aged. A puppy, a baby duck, or a kitten is likewise an exciting subject for the aged and is and enjoyed by all. I have frequently taken my daughter Shari to activities with the aged. They wanted to touch her, squeeze her arms, and run their hands through her hair. She brought back so many memories to the participants that we were guaranteed a more animated group. Likewise, Shari got to have such experiences as meeting a 99-year-old who could tell her what Vienna used to be like. She experienced age in a joyful situation and realized another part of life not readily available to her but in her future, and learned to be around physical disability, fragility, sickness, and death.

One of the most unpleasant experiences I've had with the aged involved an elderly stroke victim who was functioning minimally (but twinkled with the celebration of the group) and his wife. The man had been a prominent judge until 6 months before his stroke. During an Orff-Schulwerk session, the wife observed her husband grasping a stick and beating a drum; he was laughing, raising a hand, lowering it, and being rewarded with a sound. The wife became most disturbed that her husband was playing with the other physically and/or mentally limited people. He had been capable of many things, and his being childlike now was most disturbing to his wife. I immediately realized what a mistake I'd made in having the woman in attendance: it was too painful for her. The man's success in the session was not a success to his wife in comparison with his successes before his stroke. He needed the activity, but she felt that the convalescent hospital should be training him to walk and talk again and that he should be off by himself recovering, not in the Orff-Schulwerk group. In no way do I want to belittle the man's wife; I merely want to tell you how awful both of us felt. What a tragedy. That wife's idea of a successful experience for her husband would likely would never be realized, but in other cases, spouses of nursing home residents have been ready for observing or participating in a group experience and have provided hints about how best to help their loved ones or have clarified their loved ones' verbal responses during group sessions.

This chapter contains some of the activities I've found useful with the aged.

(1)

[Group:]

Happiness is [clap, clap],

Happiness is [clap, clap]

Different things

To different people.

[Individual response here, then group:]

That's what happiness is!

Sessions should move at a pace adapted to each person's current abilities. Have participants repeat any responses you can't understand; don't try to be an interpreter if you can't understand what is being said. It can be very discouraging and stressful for everyone if someone is interpreted as saying something other than what he or she was trying to express. Have a response ready if it is needed, or just relax and accept; that will likely be understood.

(2[3])
Mmm-mmm good,
Mmm-mmm good.
Tell us what you think is
Mmm-mmm good!

Activity 2 elicits interesting food preferences, as does activity 3. By the end of such activities, discussion of foods can lead to socialization and spontaneity. If someone calls out a response out of turn, great!

(3)
Let's pack a picnic basket;
It's a beautiful spring.
What kinds of food
Would you like to bring?

There is no reason you can't make the effort to plan a special lunch with a theme relating to the sessions on foods. It always surprises me how patient-care staff, family members, and kitchen staff are very eager to help and will go beyond my expectations to pull off the event. Share the success!

A discussion of picnics and the sounds of spring are additional resources right in your pocket after activity 3. Move on to the sounds, sights, and new life of spring and try to get the group outside. It will be quite an adventure. You'll spend a good amount of time wrapping or unwrapping the sensitive bones of participants concerned about or frightened by venturing out where walls and people don't protect them, but though some participants may tire, you'll see new excitement by the end of the session.

---

[3]Sing this to the tune of the Campbell Soup song.

Exercises are popular with the aged. I use a big beach ball that will not break eyeglasses but quickly bounces into participants' laps or off their wheelchairs before they can refuse to take a turn. The ball is excellent for testing arm and leg control, reach, and general range of motion, but it is best at testing hidden disposition. Does a smile come forth? Does the ball disturb or fluster? Can you relate to the individuals? Only the beach ball knows! There is a large variety of balls that can be used to push or kick for other exercises; these are heavier than a beach ball.

(4)

Big ball,
Bounce around.
Tell us, tell us
Whom you've found.

For activity 5, bring in either a branch or twig with scented blossoms or a scented flower such as a rose or gardenia. Each person smells it, then comments about it (or ignores it). As you go around the group with the scent, recite:

(5)

Smells go
Up the chimney
Of your nose,
Bringing messages.

Vanilla, cinnamon, nutmeg, incense, and spray sachet all work well and can be useful when unpleasant odors make the environment less enjoyable. I always carry a spray can of citrus aroma for emergencies.

Bedside tables that are usually found in rooms with bedridden clients are useful for holding instruments because the table height can be adjusted and because they can be rolled around to each wheelchair or bed. If people are working behind the wheelchairs with you, they can pull the front of the wheelchair up and the bedside table will slip right under the front wheels of the chair. Watch for rigid feet and easily scraped ankles. You can place a larger striking instrument, such as an alto metallophone, on one side and then place a glockenspiel on the side of the table where you are standing to allow for two-part developments in which the glockenspiel quickly follows into either a melody or an ostinato.

With someone working behind the wheelchair, elbows can be prompted to raise, both sides of the body can be stimulated to move, and the grasping of instrument sticks can be facilitated. Be careful, though: it's easy to let the person working with you from behind the wheelchair fall into the pattern of helping too much or requiring just a minimal response. Work closely with such a partner so sensitivity between instructors and with the client will develop and enable maximum participation.

Have a variety of stick sizes available and adapt sticks with Aire-cast or cotton and tape if needed. Get acquainted with an occupational therapist or a physical therapist; they have tubing and other supplies that could help in adapting instruments, and they are usually happy to be helpful. You are not without bartering resources; you can help occupational and physical therapists in turn.

Using a metallophone and glockenspiel on a table works well for activity 6.

(6)

Friends, friends
All around.
Show your friendship
With your sounds.

For activity 7, place a variety of bells in a tambourine on a table, or in a drum or whatever. Bells come in many shapes and sounds and are fun to pick up when traveling. Many times, family members will look for bells for you, and you'll soon have a collection.

(7)

Swinging,
Flinging—
Who will make
The bells go ringing?

For activity 8, use claves or wood cylinders with mallet or sticks on a table or another piece of wood. Long strings or bells on leather straps can accompany the horses drawing nearer. A lot of improvisations can be developed for this activity. Cowbells have brought interesting comments from groups. Sometimes I walk around carrying a few different sizes of cowbells—or roll them around on a table—and ask if someone knows what they are and what that person can tell everyone about them. Some can only hold the bell with assistance, but they are still participating, aren't they? That's fine! Don't assume, though, that everyone can (or cannot) hold the bells. Let participants try; if something needs to be adjusted, clients often provide the best help.

(8)
Listen, my people,
And you shall hear
Horses' hoofsteps
Drawing near.

For activity 9, I sometimes use a tambour as I walk around asking for different parts of the body to beat on the drum. Sometimes I *carefully* grasp a hand and drop it on a drum to get the idea across or to give some reinforcement for attempts made to strike the surface of the tambour.

(9)
Everyone's a drummer,
A drummer, a drummer.
Everyone's a drummer.
Let's hear the drummer in you.

Be careful of someone swinging very hard and missing or letting a hand drum fly. Combining a group of drums is something to work toward. It usually takes a bit of time, but when it happens, you'll be thrilled. Bells used to strike the drum pick up vibrations the way gongs or cymbals do.

Reality orientation is always a concern of staff working with the aged. I have introduced exercise activities to such a program that relate directly to parts of the body, the identity of sounds and touch and smells, facial affect, sequence of events, weather, dates, holidays, current news events, and community trip activities.

(10)
[Introduction:]
What's today?
Everybody think [Pause] . . .
Now call it out!
[Chant:]
Play a tune today;
Soon it will be tomorrow!
[Closure:]
What's today?
Everybody think [Pause] . . .
Now call it out!
What's tomorrow?
Everybody think [Pause] . . .
Now call it out!

The use of familiar sounds and textures is appropriate when working with the aged. You can use activities that involve putting something in a coffee can or box, shaking the container, and having participants guess what is in it.

(11)
I have a box.
It sounds like this.
[Pause for sound.]
What do you think
Is hiding in it?

(12)
Jingle bell, jingle bell,
Jingle bell rock.
Tell us, tell us
What's in this sock.

For activity 12, get a long sock; place such items as a clothespin, a brush, a ball, and other "junk drawer" items in it and tie a big bow at the end. Participants will want to know what's in the sock, so at the end of the activity, open the sock and let them handle each item. Other activities involving the use of the imagination can be found throughout this book. Change the items used inside the sock when it appears that the group has memorized the sock's contents. With participants who need more time and exploration, start the activity with just one item in the sock. Develop your own activity to serve the same purpose. When an activity is yours, it is more valuable.

Here are some activities whose purpose is obvious:

(13)
Old MacDonald had a farm.
What's that noise
Coming from his barn?

(14)
Coffeepot, coffeepot,
Blip, blip, blip.
Where would you go
If you went on a trip?

(15)
When you're happy, you smile;
When you're sad, you frown.
What kind of face are you
Wearing around?

Many of the elderly have experienced facial changes because of disease or trauma and they must relearn to present the appropriate facial affect. Because of this, an aged person might look crotchety but have really sparkling eyes, daring you to play. A mirror can be useful in working with affect; have participants look in it and report what they've seen. Grooming activities, which appear in other sections of this book, are useful for this purpose.

A day after a trip to the hair salon or after a visit from the family, which means new clothes, perfume or cologne, and so forth, bring news of such trips and events to the group. Also bring in any new family news, current events, and show-and-tell ideas by using activities like this one:

(16)
Extra, extra—
Read all about it!
What is your news?
What is your news?

Activity 16 also appears in Chapter 11, which contains other news activities.

Weather is always an excellent discussion starter. It is always too cold or too hot! Activity 17, which was brought by Dawn Noll Lemonds to her first course in Orff-Schulwerk, at Fairview, can be used for announcing the weather or for a sensitive music-making activity.

(17)
Mr. Weather, Mr. Weather,
How are you today?
Is it hot? Is it cold?
What do you have to say?

This activity is obviously excellent for a variety of groups and can be used many ways. When working with reality orientation, we are dealing with the here and now, and the weather is definitely here and now. I usually describe what I've been doing outside just before coming into the session and I tell the group what the weather is like and what I've seen, such as mud, water puddles, blooming flowers, or a rainbow. Sometimes I bring in a flower or perhaps a handheld fan to introduce the weather report.

Of course, food activities are great for every group. But for the elderly, who often have cooked meals for many years and now no longer have such a responsibility, it might be difficult to remember much about food for a while. Such activities, one hopes, will provide open-ended closure, and the participants will carry away any exploration done with the group and bring new ideas back for another session. It is always interesting to review what someone has had for breakfast, lunch, or dinner. Press the issue and try to get the group to remember details. Also, explore what the participants miss in their meals, then consult with the dietitian or the administrator when you have some new recommendations. Reviewing recipes can be stimulating, and preparing cookies, soup, beans, a cake, pudding, and so on can be reinforcing if done immediately after review. Making bread is fun if the group leader has the skill. Group members will enjoy watching the dough rise during the day if other staff members are willing to work with you in such a project. Baking bread provides experience with remembering (ingredients and directions), exercising (preparing the dough), exploring textures, socializing, emoting (the excitement of making something), observing, and finally using the senses (a scrumptious odor and then the taste). And of course, what goes on bread? Why not make the butter, or serve a variety of fruit compotes to be tasted, or make up an activity about jams or what goes on bread? Following directions in a sequence of events is complex for many, so be sure to break the activity down into appropriate steps for approximations of success. Instruments can be selected to represent different ingredients, tastes, temperatures, and smells. You could use a bread-making machine.

Here are some other food activities; remember to use them with other types of groups.

(18)

Nothing says loving
Like something from the oven.[4]
What do you think says it best?

(19)

Bears eat honey;
Cows eat corn.
What do you eat
When you get up in the morn?

Sound, rhythms, songs, and movement can be added to this group of activities according to the needs and abilities of the participants. Try it your way—it might be better!

(20)

I scream,
You scream,
We all scream
For ice cream!

With activity 20, discuss flavors. Again, what a good idea to make the food being discussed!

---

[4]You should remember this from old Pillsbury TV commercials.

(21)
What is your favorite,
Most favorite taste? [Or: smell?]

(22)
In winter, summer,
Spring, and fall
What is your most favorite
Taste of all?
[Or: *smell of all, sight of all,* and so on.]

Activity 23 will not be appropriate for all participants because of the loss of senses, so use your clinical judgment.

(23)
Tickly, tickly,
Tickly tie.
What goes into
A great big pie?

Exercise activities have already been mentioned, but activities 24 through 28 are a few more useful ones.

(24)
Exercises, exercises,
Let's do our exercises.
Hands over head,
Fingers on toes—
Show us how
Your exercise goes!

For activity 24, participants can either each show their own exercise or all model the individual exercise contributed. This activity can get tiring quickly if you are working with an active group—you'll find yourself panting, yelling too loud when chanting, and just hoping it will end soon. If you plan frequent exercise activities, you will quickly be rewarded by greater ease in getting up from the floor or around the drum or down to the gong. Walk around and use tickling, brushing, or pushing to prompt participants to use parts of their body.

(25)
Exercise is lots of fun!
Move your body—
Show us one!

(26)
We can clap our hands up high;
We can clap our hands down low.
Now show us
How your hands will go.

With activity 26, lower your voice for low and raise it for high, emphasizing the upward movement. Once your voice is up, snap your fingers with emphasis to get participants to lift their arms and hands and make eye contact.

Beanbags are excellent for patients with arthritis or those who have had a stroke. If you use bags of different textures, loosely packed, these patients' fingers can grasp and toss the beanbag. The weight of the beans at the bottom will often encourage release (timed release). Work on timed release with both hands, using a tambour, a box, or drum—anything that can work as a pan for catching a beanbag. Move the pan to catch the beanbag when necessary. Watch out for beanbags that fly at you when you least expect them. Activity 27 is very popular; clients will work very hard to succeed. Men will often participate quite actively with beanbag games. If you have advanced participants, bring in something like a clown-face board and have them toss the bags through the mouth. Provide a reward for success, such as applause or having the achiever raise his or her arms over the head to get attention the way a sports champion would. Encourage praise and support from peers in the group.

(27)
Beanbag, beanbag
In your hand;
Can you, can you
Toss it in the pan?

The jig in activity 28 can be minimal movement done sitting or standing or from a bed.

(28)
To market, to market
To buy a fat pig.
On the way there,
I did a jig.

   Remember, activities can get very tiring for the aged even when they are having fun. Plan ways to have time out after the activity, or you could have serious problems. Relaxation between activities might be helpful for you and/or the participants. Use activities 29 through 31 to slow things down a little.

(29)
Open and close,
Open and close.
What can you open
And what can you close?

   Discussion of who the wise old man in activity 30 is or was can be interesting and may end up in lengthy discussion. Orchestrating a story with movement or dance can make this activity more exciting and is good when a play or performance is expected of you. Be prepared so you don't have to compromise process versus production in doing something required. You have to work hard so you won't be expected to perform.

(30)
When I was one and twenty,
I heard a wise old man say

_____ .

(31)
Shaking, shaking,
Everybody's shaking.
Where, oh where
Are you shaking?

Activities 32 through 34 are good for working on coordination.

(32)
You can clap your hands fast;
You can clap your hands slow.
Now clap your hands
And show us how they go.

(33)
Make the drum pitter,
Make the drum patter.
Fast or slow,
It doesn't matter.

(34)
A parade! A parade!
A-rum-a-tee-tum.
I know a parade
By the sound of the drum.

Other instruments can join in activity 34 for a parade sound, or you can have participants clap and march if they are able. Be sure to close the response when going back to the chant so that new rhythms and paces will be initiated.

You can encourage memory exploration with activities 35 and 36:

(35)
Mirror, mirror on the wall,
Please be kind to me.
Mirror, mirror on the wall,
Tell me what you see.
[Or: *Show me what you see.*]

(36)
When I was a child, _____ .
My favorite outfit was _____ .
My parents used to _____ .
The maddest I've ever been was when _____ .
I took a trip one time that _____ .
I used to work in the _____ .

For activity 36, develop an environment in which you can ring a bell to indicate when a turn is up. Establish this rule before you start. You may succeed in getting open-ended closure, with conversations continuing after you leave. Each person has his or her own memories to share.

This chapter duplicates some activities that appear elsewhere in this book. I felt it necessary to use them again here so that no one would assume that any particular activity is inappropriate for the aged just because it doesn't appear in a chapter devoted to working with the elderly. In fact, though, there are many other ideas elsewhere in this book that can be adapted for the aged. Chapters 4, 6, 7, 10, 17, 20, 21, and 23 all have resources appropriate for the aged. But most important of all, the aged themselves have resources that you can use in working with them. Draw on these resources and share. Bring in props that the elderly might remember from their past or might never have experienced, such as puppets, shadow play, bubbles, kazoos, crafts combined with music, storytelling, singing favorite tunes, and exploring new instruments and toys. Don't be discouraged by any "I never could and never would" attitudes. Just move slowly and consistently ahead and be thick skinned, because you're going to get it hard! But you also will experience some of your tenderest moments with the aged. Remember—neither you nor those you love will escape old age.

ဆာ∝ဒ   ဆာ∝ဒ   ဆာ∝ဒ

To touch an old person's hand
Is to touch the scales on a dry fish,
To be a giant touching frozen river's veins.[5]

Whose responsibility is it to melt the rivers?

ဆာ∝ဒ   ဆာ∝ဒ   ဆာ∝ဒ

---

[5]Lewis, R. (1969). In *Prose by children of the English-speaking world* (p. 200). New York: Simon & Schuster. This poem was written by David Urrows, age 10.

I shall be older than this
    one day
I shall think myself young
    when I remember.
Nothing can stop
    the slow change of masks my face must wear,
    one following one.
These gloves my hands have put on,
    the pleated skin, patterned by
    the pale tracing of my days . . .
These are not my hands!
    And yet, these gloves do not come off!
I shall wear them tomorrow,
    till, glove after glove,
    and mask after mask,
    I am buried beneath
    The baggage of Old Women.
Oh, then,
    shall I drop them off,
Unbutton the sagging misshapen apparel of age,
    and run, young and naked, into Eternity![6]

---

[6]Anglund, J. W. (1967). In *A cup of sun*. New York: Harcourt, Brace & World.

Chapter 13

THE BLIND AND
THE VISUALLY IMPAIRED

I had rather extensive experience with the blind as part of my clinical internship. In recent years, however, I have not worked much with the blind or the visually impaired. I do periodically have a blind student or work with a blind group for demonstration purposes. Working with the blind and visually impaired takes a lot of energy. You don't just sit and give instructions. Bea Olson at Fairview and Roberta Stevenson at Laterman Development Center are two therapists whom I have observed using Orff-Schulwerk very effectively with the blind. I also have worked on projects involving both blind and deaf clients and had illuminating experiences exploring new techniques with staff members.

Even if you are adequately prepared for the special needs of blind and visually impaired clients, things can still go awry. I have a personal videotaped illustration of this. The tape was made when I and my colleagues Bobbie and Roxie were working with four blind, disturbed, and developmentally disabled individuals who were a handful. During the session, I was hit, Roxie had to cope with a screaming young man, and one client, who had limited traveling vision, walked into a mirror mounted on a wooden dividing door. On the tape, he suddenly appeared to be very controlled because, one might speculate, the Orff-Schulwerk was working. In fact, however, the boy was very quiet—a rare state for him—because he was stunned; we were afraid he had sustained a concussion. Fortunately, though, he had not.

For leaders not familiar with behaviors common to the blind or visually impaired, many movements typical of these clients can appear to be made intentionally in response to Orff-Schulwerk activities. With practice, however, you will pick up on these behaviors. People who move with ease to varying rhythms because they are sure of their physical surroundings are aware of their breathing. Blind people, however, often breathe quite shallowly, so many of their movements are hesitant, jerky, and overly controlled. Breathing exercises would be useful; you can find some in Chapter 8.

Understanding others often depends on the ability to interpret not just their verbal language but also their body language. Because the blind are denied this resource, you, as teacher and therapist, must not rely only on typical verbal instructions. You must also use bodily touch and good voice inflection. The most obvious problem I have to remind myself of is that the reinforcement that typically occurs in a session is not totally available in work with the blind. The attending peers, the smiles of approval, and the recognition of one other that others take for granted must, for the blind, be translated verbally or by touch. It is necessary to say who is taking a turn, to make clear who is sitting next to each person, to assist in passing an instrument on (in some cases when clients are very young or have limited abilities), and to use performers' names. For example, say, "Juan is playing the glockenspiel" or "Listen to Latisha's sounds," instead of putting your finger over your lips dramatically and pointing to the performer. Many times, the blind leave the circle and go to the instrument, as do the deaf, when it is not their turn. I allow this, if at all possible, so the instrument can be explored and closeness to the performer can be realized. This can become manipulative and distracting, however, so allow this practice carefully.

There are so few resources available that are specialized for the blind and the visually impaired that sharing resources and tips for success with other therapists helps. Here are some techniques I have found useful for work with the blind and the visually impaired:

- Use of small group sizes with young or very disturbed clients. In such situations, four clients with four staff members would not be unusual. If you are short on staff members, you can use volunteers, students, parents, or higher-functioning clients.
- Have participants' knees touching in the circle to help establish more control.
- Use carpet squares as effective, constant markers of participants' positions in the circle.
- Snap your fingers on the floor and call the next participant's name after a turn has been taken.
- Be aware that in a group composed of some sighted clients and some blind clients, the sighted clients will find that the high level of activity and sound provides enough clues for themselves and so will frequently fail to give clues that the blind clients need.

This is a controlled activity for standing and holding hands:

(1, Part I)
Into the circle
And out again,
Into the circle
And out again!
[Move in and then out,
making specific sounds for *into* and *out*.]

(1, Part II)
Listen to me
Stamp my feet,
Clap my hands [, *Snap my fingers*, and so on].
[The group imitates; then go back to Part I.]

The floor surface can be used to give clues to blind participants. Use different textures for different areas so participants can confidently move freely and aggressively.

For activity 2, have participants move around the room, then freeze.

(2[1])
Leader: *Where is ____ [Name] ____ ?*
Where is ____ [Name] ____ ?
Person called: *Here I am!*
Here I am!
Leader [to group]: *Can you go and find him[/her]?*
Can you go and find him[/her]?
Touch his[/her] ear [, *nose, leg*, and so on].
Touch his[/her] ear [, *nose, leg*, and so on].

All participants go together, calling out the person's name and where he or she was found. Closure should develop spontaneously during this part.

One fun activity that works well with blind and visually impaired clients is taking a listening walk: participants are guided around the room, hearing different instruments played at each stopping point, and then they go back to their starting positions and

---

[1] To the tune of "Are You Sleeping, Brother John?"

try to reproduce some of the sounds heard on the instruments. The book *Listening Walk,* by Paul Showers, has good examples of such a walk.

The following activity was presented in a workshop at Fairview:

(3)
Rhythm, rhythm,
Show us your rhythm.
Rhythm, rhythm,
Show us your rhythm.

A garden hose was used with the activity. It was passed around the circle and a rhythm was established on it by those grasping it; everyone held onto the hose to feel the rhythm. An instrument can accompany the movement from outside the circle. If participants stand, the hose is lifted high; if they sit, it is placed on the floor. This activity would also be useful with the hearing impaired.

In related activities, use a large tire, such as one from an airplane or a tractor, in a circle. While someone moves within the center of the tire, have everyone else sit outside the tire and play it like a drum with their hands. The tire players could wear elastic bands studded with bells around their wrists. They could also use sticks to play the tire; sand tubes can be substituted for tires. Be aware that sticks not passed carefully are lost, that instruments are bumped against legs, and that all in all, there is a lot of floundering and intensive listening. Participants will quickly learn that the sticks should always be placed in the same spot.

For activity 4, find all different kinds of textured familiar items and place them in a bag, then have participants explore and possibly identify them.

(4)
Reach deep
Into this mysterious bag.
Look with your hands.
[Not: *with your eyes.*]

Bea developed activity 5. She passes an instrument around the circle while each person plays what his or her hands "see." The activity can even be quite impressive when used with sighted participants who sit with their eyes closed.

(5)
My hands see for me.
My hands see for me.
What they play
Is what I see.

As you go through this book, you'll find activities in other chapters that are also appropriate for the blind and the visually impaired.

Remember, when working with the blind:

- **Find appropriate ways to guide participants' movements:** Don't keep yelling or saying, "Over here, over here." Decide on an instrument or a body sound that can be played rhythmically and louder as the person approaches, making the directions part of the composition. I have observed very nonadaptive and thoughtless handling of such situations, which results in confusion and tension.
- **Keep clutter off the floors and out of pathways:** You will become most unpopular when you suddenly decide to place a gong in front of someone without informing him or her. When you do this, the first thing the person will do is knock it over, which will make a horrible sound, cause the participant to worry whether he or she broke the gong, and disrupt the participant's quality of participation.
- **Earn participants' trust as their leader:** Don't turn your head as you yell, sing, or giggle while you walk a blind person into something. Be aware of how much space is needed to guide someone around a corner or past an object. You must earn trust.
- **Develop texture aids on sticks, surfaces, specific areas in the group circle, and on floors.**
- **Use verbal and tactile reinforcement:** Neither facial affect nor eye contact can be used as reinforcement, so use your voice and touch.
- **Encourage socialization:** Giving information as to who is performing, who is moving, who is sitting next to whom, what two people are moving together, and so on. Use names and descriptive terms while reinforcing.

- **Encourage personal disclosure.**
- **Take steps to help participants feel confident in moving around during activities:** Encourage grasping hands or holding one other around the waist or shoulders when the group is moving during an activity. Also, develop the safety of the environment so aggressive individual movement can occur freely. Body boundaries can be developed by using soft blowing when the person appears to be getting very near. (Remember, you want to encourage deep breathing.) Awkward foot movement is a self-protective habit developed to avoid constantly bumping one's toes or having one's heels stepped on.
- **Don't yell:** The blind can hear—unless they are also deaf or hard of hearing. Just give precise directions. Being precise does not mean being loud.
- **Don't be concerned about offending anyone by using terms referring to things that require the use of sight:** The blind, just like the sighted, use words like *see* and *look* and use color words and descriptions.
- **Be resourceful and alert to how you can assist with success in exploration, development, expansion, and discovery.**
- **Don't be overly helpful in guiding participants; just be alert.**
- **Put things back where you found them.**

෫Ꮙ   ෫Ꮙ   ෫Ᏻ

It is a black jar or a dark tunnel with
No opening to the world outside.
The fog drifts around me.
I try to break it.
But it lasts forever and ever.

There are no lights,
It knows no shadows.
There is only the deep, rich black.
Tear a hole in it to reach day.
There is no day, but everlasting night so dark.
Does day ever break?

The soul beneath sees a different dazzle.
The mind reaches far and forever, not like
The breath that dies and never comes again.[2]

---

[2]Lewis, R. (1969). Blindness. In *Journeys: Prose by children of the English-speaking world* (p. 207). New York: Simon & Schuster. This poem was written by Lori Schectman, age 10.

Chapter 14

THE DEAF AND
THE HEARING IMPAIRED

I could have found it very easy to not do a separate chapter about the deaf and the hearing impaired simply because many of the activities discussed in other chapters are appropriate for the deaf also. However, as I've said in other chapters, if I don't specifically emphasize certain activities as appropriate for a particular use, you may infer that they are appropriate only for other uses; also there are special considerations in working with the deaf and the hearing impaired.

SPECIAL CONSIDERATIONS

In most cases, my experience with the hearing impaired has been in an integrated program. I have worked as a consultant with the hearing impaired and their teachers have used many of the activities appearing in other chapters. I do, however, place extensive emphasis on affect when working with the hearing impaired: talking back and forth on instruments and requiring facial affect appropriate to conversation is very necessary.

I use the back of the piano and other vibrating surfaces to give feedback. Many times, a participant will move forward toward the instrument and place his or her body in what appears to be a strange position near the instrument to obtain the best reception. Other times, I've had hearing impaired individuals climb under the frame of a drum or move around with me, watching my face intently. This has really not created problems, but in a group in which there was serious behavior problems, there could be some modeling of this behavior and group control could become a problem.

Another consideration to bear in mind is whether a particular activity will cause feedback from the hearing aids of some participants. Holding the head back or rolling over can cause hearing aids to hum and squeal. To deal with this problem, I've had a teacher work with me to handle malfunctioning hearing aids and to sign and speak the same material I was teaching so we could maximize the benefit of the activities being presented.

It's helpful to develop your own signs for quick communication. I have used two signs to indicate "line up" and "form a circle." I hold two claves or mallets up above my head to symbolize forming two straight lines, and one stick above my head to mean forming one straight line. I hold a tambour high in the air and move my hand around in it as a sign for forming a circle.

Encourage good eye contact and insist that you are given the courtesy of completing what you are saying. It is one thing to be deaf but another thing to conveniently not understand so that you can continue beating an instrument or otherwise doing as you please. Learn a few basic signs, if sign language is being used. Slow down your speech and enunciate. I find it best to both use signs and speak, because I cover all bases that way. I took a sign language course but then unfortunately did not use what I had learned. I have retained just a few of the basic signs, but I find them coming back, like a long-unused foreign language, when I use them for a period of time with the hearing impaired. The few signs I do remember are very helpful and can be easily learned by others. Your face and body will be your biggest communicator. "The body is a blabbermouth," as Trudi Schoop wrote in *Won't You Join the Dance? A Dancer's Essay into the Treatment of Psychosis.*

INSTRUMENTS, RHYTHMS, AND SPECIAL SOUNDS

The following instruments seem most appropriate for work with the deaf and hearing impaired. Encourage the hearing impaired to put their hands or other parts of their body on the instruments as they are being played. Feel free to add to this list.

- **Large timpani:** These are particularly useful, especially those that can be tuned as they are being played, providing extra variety in sound and presenting a new way to play an instrument.
- **Hanging gong:** This needs to be left hanging without anyone touching or holding it.

- **Bass metallophone:** This is very good for sound conduction and has a broad striking surface, making it easier for participants to create sound.
- **Bass xylophone:** This is less intense than the metallophone and it also has a broad striking surface.
- **String instruments:** The surfaces of autoharps, guitars, harps, and string bass instruments provide active feedback to the participants touching them.

The gong is most attractive as an instrument because of its large range of vibrations. One time while working with an active group of young men, I struck the gong when it was first being presented to the group. The fellows were in a line waiting to move across the room. One participant was grimacing strangely. I asked one of the nursing staff if he thought the fellow might be ill, because his face was distorted and he pulled his legs toward his chest as if in pain. But we realized that he was responding to the sound of the gong. The instrument went on to become quite attractive to him. He would greet it when he entered the room and would bid it farewell at the end of each session. We knew he was there!

The kazoo is fun to use if you can get adequate sounds from the participants. The vibrations felt on the lips during kazoo play are very intense, as are the vibrations from playing combs with cellophane over them.

Another instrument I like has the form of a flat guitar, with a circle of sandpaper in the center to represent the hole of a regular guitar. Use a stick or another piece of sandpaper attached to a piece of wood to scratchily strum the instrument.

A special instrument that worked well for me was a pipe bent into a triangle that I used when I was in training as a music therapist. The father of one of the clients was a plumber, and he made the triangle for me. It would vibrate so that the children's arms would rock back and forth when they held it.

I found one of my best instruments quite by mistake—a pole that is used to wrap up a window shade. I was teaching at Patton State Hospital when I went looking for a broomstick to use in an activity in which a pole is pounded on the floor. I found a shade pole, its shade missing, leaning against a wall in the closet. When I struck it on the floor, I could not believe the feedback. After extensive use, the spring inside the pole loosened, but I was told I could get it tightened. The shade was a heavy-duty institutional shade that I'm sure is available through companies that makes window shades. Try it—you'll like it! You can paint the poles bright colors or have the participants paint them for you.

Another serendipitous discovery was a chair rack. Rose, a program assistant at Fairview, accidentally discovered that large racks (which are on wheels) designed to hold chairs give great feedback when strummed. I tried it, and it reminded me of that pipe triangle I mentioned above.

Explore all sorts of resources for sounds. I found a footstool that gives great feedback when I lie on my back and place it on my stomach. When working with very young blind and deaf children, I discovered that when one or two children were in a large social ball, sounds resounded and were very intense. Also, I used drumsticks on the outside of the ball to beat rhythms into their "rolling womb."

I frequently work on a tile floor and then use a wooden stage that is about 10 inches above the tile floor. The stage allows all sorts of instruments and other sounds, such as those made by stamping feet, bouncing balls, and sticks on the floor, to resound.

ACTIVITIES

In work with the hearing impaired, I've used the shadow activities mentioned in other chapters in this book; frequently, friendship is the theme demonstrated on the screen. I've also used the facial affect activities, discussed in other chapters, with photographs, slides, and pictures.

Tactile stimuli are necessary for enriching any activities with the hearing impaired. The tactile activities in Chapter 6 are appropriate, as are many of the blowing, spitting, and whistling activities in Chapter 8.

The following activity, which doesn't appear in any other chapter of this book, is useful for promoting attending:

(1)
Put your ear [clap, clap, clap]
*To the ground
And listen to
The sounds.*
[Or: *Listen to* _____ [Name's] _____ *sound.*]

The activity is fun because everyone gets his or her rear in the air and ears to the floor.

If you can get the group to listen to the specific instruments and have a signal for when a sound starts and stops, you can work on having the participants attend to specific vibrations and signal when they stop and start or eventually signal when vibrations are higher or lower.

Develop simple rhythms on the floor and then have the participants duplicate them on their bodies, using strong accents when playing the instruments selected.

Some of the body-part compositions explored elsewhere in this book that use the body as an instrument are constructive. They could be extended to passing rhythms around the circle: first make the rhythmic sounds on one's own body and then pass the sound on by beating it on the next person's body; then that person passes it around, and so on.

Marching activities, where there is order in what is being presented, are good resources, particularly if movement accompanies dominant beats.

Chapter 15

HOLIDAYS

HALLOWEEN

The strangest sight
I've ever seen
Was a fat old witch
In a flying machine.

The witch flew high,
The witch flew low,
The witch flew fast,
The witch flew slow,
The witch flew up,
The witch flew down,
She circled all
Around the town.
Then, turning left
And turning right,
She disappeared
Into the night.

That fat old witch
In a flying machine
Is the strangest sight
I've ever seen.
Of course it happened
On Halloween.[1]

---

[1]Jacobs, L. (1964). Fat old witch. In *Just around the corner* (p. 32). San Francisco: Holt, Rinehart, & Winston.

Use stories and pictures for an initial activity. You will at first hear limited ideas and maybe repetitious answers, but suddenly when you present new ideas, the next session will expand and eyes will grow bigger, faces will grow scarier, and the sounds will develop a chamber of horrors that lets you grab, touch, tickle, tease, run from, run after, jump up, and jump down. You'll all go in search of costumes, paint, makeup, treats, tricks, and mirrors to reflect horrible faces. Now, don't be scared—at least not too much—but do be surprised!

People of all ages enjoy Halloween, with the chance it offers to dress up and remember what was and is fun. Socialization becomes the theme for participants of all ages, disabled or not.

Giant jack-o'-lanterns
Smile from every pane,
And happy little goblins
March boldly down the lane.

Eerie sounds now echo
From shadows and it's said
The witches ride their broomsticks
Swiftly overhead.

Black cats stalk quietly
About on padded paw.
'Tis a night to be remembered
With very special awe.[2]

The sounds of Halloween are so great because they demonstrate onomatopoeia[3]: *eerie, scary, swiftly, quietly, silently, grin* (your mouth does go up with that word, if you let it), *awe*! Dramatize the words, playing with their real sounds. You, too, can be bewitching.

Get out the projector, turn out the lights, and let the mysterious shadows expand movement, with sound that accompanies the voices and instruments. Perhaps use two jack-o'-lanterns, one smiling, one

---

[2]Larson, L. P. Night of mystery.

[3]Onomatopoeia is the formation of words imitative of natural sounds, the formation of name words by imitating the sound associated with the thing designated, or the use of imitative and naturally suggestive words for rhetorical effect.

most sad, glowing at each side of the reflected light. Maybe some cheesecloth, lightweight scarves, a mop, hat, and a few props will add to the movement on the lighted screen. You'll be surprised how tense the group will get. Have ready a good activity for deep breathing, relaxing, talking it over in the light without all the scary effects, and build on each minute.

Here is an introduction activity, developed by Toni and Rose for a class at the University of California, Irvine:

(1)
Tell the great pumpkin
Your name, your name.
Tell the great pumpkin
Your name.

The pumpkin can be imaginary or you can make one. If you are lucky enough to have a large drum, tambour, or gong, put a face on it, and for very elementary participants, let them hear their name resound from the pumpkin. You could stretch things a bit and have a leader or participant behind a lighted pumpkin made from a sheet or cardboard. Encourage conversation between the pumpkin and the participants—then move right on to the chant when closure is established.

Two flashlights glowing in the dark from under the chin would be a fun way to emphasize facial expression. Approach the participants with the flashlight glowing under your own chin, asking each person's name when you place the other flashlight under his or her face. If you have just one flashlight, pass it back and forth. Perhaps the addition of a mirror would make this even more rewarding. Participants would take turns going to the mirror, the flashlight under their chin, and telling their name to the scary-faced pumpkin—themselves—that they see there. This activity can be either very quick and simple or expansive. The light under the chin, emphasizing the face, might be good for prompting discussion of how the pumpkin feels—sad, sick, happy, scared, and so forth.

Here's another enjoyably scary activity:

(2)
Halloween, Halloween—
Such a fright!
Ghosts and goblins in the night!
The witching hour is very near—
Make a sound you might hear.

Activity 2 is an example of a rather long theme development that need not all be repeated, particularly when you have minimal verbal participation. Introduce the total theme, and then cut it back to just, for example:

The witching hour is very near.
Make a sound you might hear.

Once in a while, return to the full theme to review some of the imagery.

The response to activity 3 could include acting out what the costume is and then walking to an established door and knocking. Have someone open the door, and the visiting participant can yell, "Trick or treat!" There could even be a reinforcing piece of candy handed out if you want to add to the festivity, but the activity is reinforcing enough if you provide the right environment, so the treat will just be a bonus.

(3)
Put on your costume;
Stamp your feet;
Get ready to say,
"Trick or treat!"

For activity 4, makeup, a flashlight, mirrors, and clowning all contribute to the facial affect of the jack-o'-lantern. This also could be an art activity with paper plates or just butcher paper and paint-brushes. A flannel board might be useful for putting together parts of the face from various cutouts. Predesigned faces would be good for those of a lower developmental level; the completed face would just be selected and stuck onto the flannel board. It would also be neat to eat cookies that the group decorates.

(4)
Jack-o'-lantern,
Jack-o'-lantern,
Shining bright,
Show us your face
On Halloween night.

Some activities that might seem to be only for very young participants can also be appropriate for older participants depending on how you present the material. You've probably noticed in recent years that Halloween has become a big event for adults—it's not just for children anymore. These activities are elemental, but as fun as Halloween is, adults enjoy them as much as children do—maybe more. Take care with costumes and makeup so that no one is dressed in a way to draw ridicule; participants need to hold on to their dignity.

(5)
Wicked, wicked witches,
Stealing through the night,
Show us how you move
On Halloween night.

(6)
Goblins and ghosties,
Beasties and bats—
Show us a face
That looks like that!
[Model the face being made by
the participant taking a turn.]

(7)
If I were a witch,
I'd ride on a broom
And scatter the ghosts
With a zoom, zoom, zoom!
[The group can accompany the *zoom*.]

(8)
We are the witches—
The witches of the night—
To haunt you, to scare you,
To cause you great fright!
What kind of witch are you?

For activity 9, have all participants hold onto a parachute, moving it up and down, swooshing, soaring, grabbing, and scaring with it, while each person takes a turn calling out what scares him or her. Better yet, have each one taking a turn at calling out run under the swishing parachute. For closure, everyone gets under the parachute and makes eerie movements and weird sounds. Then, a gong or bell sounds, all is quiet, and a few are selected to roll up the parachute while others listen to their breathing and assimilate their experience. This activity can be used many ways at different times; give thought to how it can best be used by the group you are working with.

(9)

Ghosts and goblins,
Witches and ghouls—
What scares you?
Ooooooh!

Build a story, with each person adding to the theme, or have short, quick stories that are well defined in length, or they will go on forever. In fact, that would be good advice with many groups!

(10)

Ghosts and goblins—
Boo! Boo! Boo!

(11)

I know a scary story.
How about you?

(12)

Apples and candies
And good things to eat—
What will be your
Trick or treat?

(13)

Skeleton, skeleton
In the night;
Skeleton, skeleton—
What a fright!
[Pause.]
Quick, before I run home,
Show us how you rattle your bones.

(14)

House to house,
Round and round,
Let us hear
Your scary sound.

(15)
Knock on the door.
Trick or treat!
What did you get
In your bag to eat?

(16)
Swing, swing, swing,
Let's all go out for Halloween.
What'll you be?
What'll you be?

This Halloween section is a long one, but the activities are functional and could be used for a variety of ages and needs. They reinforce modeling and imitation, inflection, and many of the other concerns addressed in other chapters in this book.

THANKSGIVING

A student at a class at the University of California, Irvine brought in this Thanksgiving activity:

(17)
Oh my goodness,
The turkey got away!
What will we eat
On Thanksgiving Day?

The class participants extended it so that whatever was mentioned as the substitute for the item that got away then became the next item to escape:

[Dramatically throwing arms up,
while sitting in a circle:]
Group: *Oh my goodness,*
The turkey got away!
What will we eat
On Thanksgiving Day?
Individual response: *Hamburgers and Coke.*
Group: *Oh my goodness,*
The hamburgers and Coke got away!
What will we eat on Thanksgiving Day?
[Continue with alternating individual responses
and the group response.]

A more difficult way to play with this is to repeat every food item the participants have offered around the circle, which requires attending and retention in sequence. For example, you could say this:

Oh my goodness,
The hamburger and Coke,
Pizza,
Candy bar,
Macaroni and cheese,
And ham got away!
What will we eat on Thanksgiving Day?

I use contra bass, striking G–C–G, as the chant continues with this refrain:

Thanksgiving Day is a day for giving thanks.
Thanksgiving Day is a day for giving thanks.
Thanksgiving Day is a day for giving thanks.[4]

---

[4]You can adapt this activity for Christmas or even springtime:
Spring is the time for celebrating.
Spring is the time for celebrating.
Spring is the time for celebrating.
Spring [held, then start another chant with:]
We welcome spring.

The first part of the chant is heavier and slower, and the second one is lighter. Sing the activity using a melody you can easily remember.

There is a pause, and then the chant can move on to the next performer. It is really adds to the activity to find wording that can continue without a stop.

With activity 18, signing between the Indians and Pilgrims, with the two groups sitting facing each other, is nice. Also, try rear-projected light with the two groups standing or sitting in front of the projector and casting their sign language or body language onto the wall. Line up Virginia reel style with the two sides facing each other, about 10 feet apart.

(18)
The Pilgrims and the Indians,
They did care.
They sat down together
And offered a prayer.

For activity 19, the first in line on each side walks forward; the two people go down the line together, talking and walking like turkeys until they get to the other end. Then the chant begins again with the next two people. If you improvise, the activity will grow in quality and creativity. Take time to plan how you will reinforce, because the participants will be watching and will repeat the same response so they can please you. Teacher- and therapist-pleasing behavior limits responses.

(19)
Here come the turkeys—
Look at them walk!
Here come the turkeys—
Listen to them talk!

The lines are formed for Activity 20 in the same position as for the last activity. Each participant is asked to get some instrument that he or she can play and carry and that is special to him or her. You may need to assist—at least be ready to do so—because many participants will have problems setting an instrument down gently.

(20, Part I)
[The first person in one line says,
while pointing to the other line:]
Those are the Indians over there!

(20, Part II)
[The other side points back
and says, all together:]
Those are the Pilgrims over there!

(20, Part III)
[Both sides together:]
At Thanksgiving time, they learn to share.

The first two people from the head of the lines walk to the center and exchange their chosen instrument. Then, together, they move down between the lines, accompanying their movement with their new instrument. You will find that participants are reticent to forfeit their carefully selected special instruments; adults have as much difficulty with this as younger participants do. This activity provides an excellent opportunity to explore sharing.

Activity 21 can provoke discussions of food textures, colors, and tastes and of the memories associated with them.

(21)
Thanksgiving Day—
What a treat!
What do you think
You'll have to eat?

CHRISTMAS

I believe activity 22 came from one a special Christmas issue of *Creative Practices*, but I do not know who created it. We used it immediately at Fairview. The secrets can be spoken or musical. Clues can be given, or participants can remember surprises from the past. Roxie and Bobbie used this activity with wheelchair clients at Fairview. They carried instruments to the chairs for the nonverbal participants to use for sharing secrets. Make up a melody with rhythm and it all becomes yours. Keep the secrets flowing and help participants remember their contributions so they take ownership of their response.

(22)
Our house is full of secrets
'Cause Christmastime is here.
Our house is full of secrets
'Cause Christmastime is here.

Let the bells and hoof sounds be heard for the next few activities. Santa activities can be age inappropriate if not handled well. They can be playful, but they need not be childish if the participants are not children.

(23)
Here comes Santa!
Listen to the sleigh.
What will he bring on
Christmas Day?

(24)
Look, look under the tree—
A Christmas gift for you and me!
What can it be?
Oh, guess quickly!

(25)
I'm Dasher;
You're Dancer.
Let's make the sounds
Of hooves on the roofs
All over the town.

(26[5])
Come sit, come sit
On Santa's knee.
Tell him what
Your wish will be.

(27)
Christmas tree,
All green and bright,
What will happen
On this night?

(28)
Merry are the bells,
Merrily they ring.
What Christmas sounds
Do they bring?

A gaily wrapped box full of sounds (small instruments) could be passed around for activity 28 so that special sounds can be selected. Sounds of the body should also be encouraged.

(29)
Jingling bells,
Falling snow;
The laughter of Santa
Through the silence swells.

With activity 29, get good hearty laughter, patting of the belly, stroking of the beard, and perhaps some Santa-type statements.

---

[5]Have someone act as Santa sitting in a chair. This is a fun co-ed activity.

(30)
Candy and nuts,
Holly and pine—
What do you think about
At Christmastime?

With activity 31, bring in the bells, foot noises, and laughter for dramatic effects. Let different instruments develop the sounds of Christmas. Perhaps someone will want to be Santa getting out of his sleigh and climbing down the chimney. Use some mystery when chanting or move to humming and some musical sound to restate the Christmas theme.

(31)
Ho, ho, ho
Comes from the sleigh.
Bells ring softly,
Feet prance loudly;
What do they bring?

For activity 32, put elastic bands with bells on them around the participants so they jingle.

(32)
Jingle bell, jingle bell,
Jingle bell rock.
Listen to your feet
As they walk.

You can modify the activity by putting some fun-feeling treasures into a long sock and then pass it around as you say:

(33)
Jingle bell, jingle bell,
Jingle bell rock.
Tell us, tell us—
What's in this sock?

Activity 34 always reminds me of a special gift, which is described below. I take all but the first notes of the scale off the instruments and have the following song start after Santa, who has been selected to be in the center of the circle, gives a Santa laugh:

(34)
San – ta, San – ta,
1   1   1   1

In the air.
1   2   3

San – ta, San – ta,
1   1   1   1

What have you there?
1   2   2   3

Santa then takes a special gift from his pack and gives it to a special person. That person then goes to the center of the circle and initiates the activity with a Santa laugh. If the participants are relatively shy and not very verbal, it may take a while for the ha-ha-ha or ho-ho-ho to occur. Peers can encourage and wait, but nothing happens until Santa laughs. Everyone will be so intent on playing, tongues hanging out and sticks straining to go, that the pressure usually results in a laugh of some king and a shake of the bells.

One time when I was participating in this activity, a deaf boy who was shy and dear grasped his stomach and made a Santa laugh, to the surprise of all. But when it came time to offer a gift, he brought to me a very special gift, which he opened, all in mime, and produced two earrings and a necklace, which he ceremoniously placed around my neck as he grinned from ear to ear. I had one of the "aha!" experiences of Orff-Schulwerk, one of those experiences that sneak up. If you don't have all systems on alert, these experiences will pass you by unnoticed and you likely will not get a second chance at them.

For activity 35, work on the dimensions of soft and loud, with soft growing to loud through the use of a variety of bells. Perhaps start by having participants use the bells while away from the circle, playing first softly and then more loudly as they approach. That will dramatize the verse and also help teach the dimensions of sounds.

(35)
Bells far away,
Bells far away;
Bells drawing nearer,
Bells sounding clearer.

In activity 36, accent *Ho, ho, ho* by bending over and *Hee, hee, hee* by rising.

(36)
Ho, ho, ho,
Hee, hee, hee!
What did Santa
Put under the tree?

Have ornaments ready to be put on a bare tree for activity 37, or have a craft session on the spot and make the decorations then. It's fun for each person to select a special ornament from a box and watch as the tree is dressed. Perhaps before the activity, get the lights ready. You can use a cutout tree instead of a three-dimensional real or artificial one; color it with paint and bright felt-tip pens.

(37)
The tree is bare;
It needs to be dressed.
With great glowing garments,
We think it will be best.

For activity 38, have Santa burdened with a heavy bag that participants can dig in to find what's in the bottom of the pack.

(38)
What's that thing
On Santa's back?
What's at the bottom
Of his pack?

This next activity is a takeoff on a popular anonymous Mother Goose verse.

(39)
Christmas is a-comin';
The geese are getting fat.
Please put something
In the old man's hat!

Pass a real hat—or a pretend hat—around. Either actions or parcels of different sizes can be put in the hat. For participants at lower developmental levels, just placing a hand in the hat is most acceptable and an indicator that some modeling is occurring.

HANUKKAH

(40)
Hanukkah, Hanukkah,
Eight days of Hanukkah.
Light the candle with a drum.
[Group counts eight drumbeats
for the lighting of the eight candles.]

For activity 40, extend the sounds into group work. Movement can be incorporated as the group desires.

NEW YEAR'S DAY

A bell that was big
And gruff and bold
Bade good-bye
To the year grown old.

A bell that was small
And tinkled clear
Called greetings out
To the youngest year.

Then all the bells
Joined the merry din
And the bright new year
Was welcomed in.[6]

(41)
I resolve [clap, clap],
I resolve [clap, clap],
I resolve to change!
[Pause for a discussion of the changes
to occur in each person's life.]

(42)
Happy New Year!
Happy New Year!
What do I fear?
What do I cheer?

---

[6]Jacobs, L. B. In *Just around the corner*.

(43)
Ring out the old;
Cheer in the new.
In ___[year]___ ,
What do you plan to do?

ROSH HASHANAH

Encourage dramatic movement to the sounds of the shofar in activity 44.

(44)
Sound the shofar loud and clear—
Too-too! Too-too!
[Cup the hands and then move one out
to pantomime a shofar.]
Think of the past; move to the future.
Sound the shofar loud and clear.
Rosh Hashanah is now here.

EASTER

Heighten movement in activity 45 by having the Easter Bunny carry a Easter basket and visit others.

(45)
Hoppin', hoppin',
See how he's hoppin'.
The Easter Bunny is coming to town.
Hoppin', hoppin',
Everybody's watchin'
As he hops around.

You might want to use more than just imaginary chocolate in activity 46.

(46)
Easter ducks and chicks
Eggs with chocolate thick
Easter brings
Some pleasant things.

Activity 47 is a natural for a craft project. Paper plates make great bonnets!

(47)
Make an Easter bonnet—
We're going to have a parade.
Put on your Easter bonnet
And join our Easter parade.

You'll be surprised at the many ways the Easter Bunny can move in activity 48!

(48)
Hippity hop,
Hoppity hip,
Make like a bunny
And do your trick!

The shoes in activity 49 take the place of a bunny's basket. The bunny can have some wrapped-up candy treats to drop in each shoe as it is passed to him or her in the circle. In some cases, you will have trouble with participants helping themselves as the filled shoes come by, so you might want to have the shoes taken directly to the bunny instead of passing them.

(49)
Hippity hoppity
Bippity boooo—
What did the Easter Bunny
Put in your shoe?

The simple motions of licking an egg, whether it rolls around or is held in the hand can be used in the action for activity 50. (The shell is removed before the egg is popped in the mouth.)

(50)
Painting Easter eggs
Is a neat, neat trick.
I like the eggs
That you lick, lick, lick.

VALENTINE'S DAY

For activity 51, talk back and forth, using instruments for voices. Encourage singing messages.

(51)
A valentine message
I will play for you.
[Choose a special person.]
If you want to join me,
Our message will be for two.

The participants must find out some way to get the valentine in activity 52 to be his or hers. Doing tricks, making faces, and playing tunes are all ways valentines can be offered.

(52)
Valentine's Day
Is a special time.
Please, Valentine,
Won't you be mine?

For activity 53, decorate prebaked cookies in class and then share them with someone. Participants show them one at a time to the class and then carry them to a person in the circle. The leader should ensure that everyone gets a cookie. Carole presented activity 53 at a delicious Fairview session. Keep the cookies wrapped in a small plastic bag for use with the activity.

(53)
Decorating valentines
Is always lots of fun,
Especially if you get
To eat a special one.

The special item in activity 54 can be make-believe and never described, or it can be described explicitly. The item might be a valentine made at a craft table and delivered to someone special.

(54)
I've made something special;
It's behind my back.
If you play a tune for me,
I'll put it in your lap!

Then, of course, you have to do this activity:

(55)
Valentine, oh Valentine,
Won't you be my
Love divine?

Be aware, though, that activity 55 carries a high risk and may fail.

I'm certain by now that you can develop the Valentine's Day activity you desire to meet the needs of the group. Valentine activities can be fun!

BIRTHDAYS

(56[7])

This is a special day—
Someone's birthday!
Whose can it be?
Whose can it be?
[Pause for group to decide, point,
and call out a name.]
How many years?
Tell us with a drum.
We'll count along with you
Until you're done!

MISCELLANY

(57)
Fiddle tune,
Fiddle play,
Fiddle for
St. Patrick's Day.

---

[7]A Native American–style beat is nice played in fifths on tone bar
instruments and timpani.

A cake of cardboard or paper—or a real one—is great to decorate for activity 58, which could work for George, too!

(58)
Abraham's birthday cake—
What a special day!
We'll decorate the cake
Our own special way.

A special book full of fun, laughter, resources, and ideas for activities is *The Saga of Baby Divine*, written by Bette Midler. Here's a sample from it:

I am Anxiety, friend to Despair!
I appear when your Courage departs.
I find wherever your Confidence fails you
And Fear makes a Home in your Heart![8]

Many other sections of Midler's book should encourage you to develop resources for discussion, mime, drama, voice, and art. The art is helpful for different emotions. Try bright-colored art featuring hair and body parts along with landscapes. If you have art you would like to share with Midler, send it to her through the publisher (Crown Publishers, Inc., 201 East 50th Street, New York, NY 10022). Midler has worked with special people and might really enjoy your generosity. Remember to protect the privacy of clients unless they choose to share. You will likely have guidelines for providing that where you work.

---

[8]Midler, B. (1983). In *The saga of baby divine* (p. 36). New York: Crown Publishers.

Chapter 16

NATIVE AMERICANS[1]

Ka–trum,
Ka–trum,
Ka–trum.
When buffalo run,
They darken the sun.
They cover the sky
When they pass by.
Tall grasses lie flat
And wild birds cry
And dry earth trembles
When they pass by.
But
Indian hunters
Stay quiet as the grass,
Quiet as the shadows
Where buffalo pass
Until the zing of an arrow (ziiiinnnnnng),
The shish of a spear (shhiiiiissssssssh)
Tell you they must be
Somewhere
Near.[2]

Native American activities present many symbols of movement, body language, history, politics, bravery, nature, art, music, battle, outrage, sadness, questions, foods, and present-day societal issues. For this chapter, I have selected a number of activities that can be used in a variety of ways, with a variety of participants. The obvious activities involve dancing to drums; war paint; signs of past; making headdresses, necklaces, and jewelry; building a village (as mentioned in Chapter 22); and exploring what Native Americans felt hundreds of years ago and how they feel today. How did Native Americans play?

[1]*Indian* is used in some activities in this chapter; it is understood to mean *Native American*.
[2]Baylor, B. (1971). Ka-trum. In *Plink, plink, plink*. Boston: Houghton Mifflin.

How did they communicate? Has it changed? Ask Native Americans to share their dances and their history with your group and encourage them and group participants to work together.

Some of the activities in this chapter are playful for those who are not yet involved in the dynamics of history and society. The drumbeat and the natural movement require no speech, yet they are so engrossing that few do not respond. Control the drum at first, then as the rhythm becomes a part of the participants, relinquish control. Dynamics of soft and loud and quick and slow are easily learned with a controlled drumbeat. Bells enter compositions with ease. Participants can slip on elastic bands with bells onto an arm, a foot, or a leg so they can use specific parts of the body to respond to the basic beat.

Shadow play and painting specific parts of the body all contribute to learning, sparking imaginations as everyone explores his or her own repertoire of movements, forms, and feelings to reach a celebratory climax . . . in open-ended closure. Wait until next time, and the time after!

Instrumental or verbal response can be used for activity 1. A combination of all the sounds in the "forest deep" is a nice closure. Have silent moccasins exploring the sounds around the circle, moving loud, soft, fast, and slow.

(1)
Walk on the forest trail;
Silent moccasins creep.
What are the sounds you hear
In the forest deep?

(2)
The Indians are creeping—
Shhhhhh!
The Indians are creeping—
Shhhhhh!
They do not make a sound
As their feet touch the ground.

(3)
Indians, braves—
Dance and leap!
War dance, rain dance—
Stamp your feet!

For activity 4, use a heavy drumbeat during the chant, then stop! What will be the new beat? Georgia, a group leader from Fairview, brought this activity into a training session to use with teenage boys. She gave the playful, lively, light activity dignity by bringing in a beautiful headdress and having the boys accompany each other, presenting the headdress to the drummer or to the dancer who was ready to perform. The whooping and the movement around the circle with all kinds of beautiful bells on the wrists make for an active, high-spirited atmosphere that will need sudden control.

(4)
Big Chief Short Pants
Going off to war dance.
Big Chief Short Pants
Going off to war dance.
Who will dance?
Who will dance?

From activity 4, move on to a low-key activity, like activity 5 or 6. (I emphasize the need for this from experience!)

(5)
Indian feet
Make many sounds.
Listen to the drum
And then move those feet around.

(6)
Symbols and signs
[Demonstrate a few]
Rule the land.
Eyes . . . listen
To their hands!
[Two participants communicate
with their hands.]

Activity 6 is nice for hearing impaired and deaf. Words can be used with the signs, or the movement of body can be unexplained, depending on what you are trying to accomplish and what the participant develops with the resources. Throwing the signs onto a screen or wall with rear-projected light is effective. Use storytelling, asking for signs and symbols to accompany the story while the story is building, or have a story narrated with established sounds.

Activity 7 is not specific only to a focus on Native Americans; it can work well with other themes, too. The growing movement of the flame, shooting out, crackling, and sizzling, can easily be a group composition or a solo, with or without instruments. The dancers are victims of the flame, their movement controlled by the air moving the flame, the wood kindling the fire, or water from the skies that quickly ends the flame. You might start this activity by watching flames on a torch—but make sure you are not under a smoke detector or a sprinkler system. Beware of fire marshals!

(7)
The flame is kindled;
The sparks fly.
The dancers move in response
Until the flame dies.

Your group can also observe an outdoor barbecue, with flames shooting, blown, watered, and rekindled, and then move away to the activity; later, all can return to cook something special (an economical idea). For safety, do *not* squirt lighter fluid on the fire.

During the activity, scarves or crunched cellophane in the hand can add to the dramatics, resulting in the expansion of movement. A spotlight, just on the fire, is dramatic when all other lights are turned out. Again, rear projection can be used, with red cellophane over the light, and then maybe yellow and then blue. (I've used my pallets of colored Plexiglas.) Also the film activity mentioned in Chapter 21 would be dramatic if just colors of fires were intermixed on the lead film so everyone could move to the flames. . . . I can't wait to try that!

You could lead into activity 8 with a discussion of nature, and then pull out sample Native American names from a story. The names given in response to the activity might be in Indian "languages" the participants derive, or they could be English names with connotations of nature and bravery. Perhaps ask for the name in sign and then in spoken word. The spoken word could be excluded with nonverbal participants.

(8)
Indian children
Are given special names.
If you were an Indian child,
What name would be your fame?

Activity 9 will inspire the artists in your group.

(9)
Swwwwwwishhh—
Brushes of color
Whisper and shout.
Your work tells us tales
Of your past.
Swwwwwwwishhh—
Brushes of color!

Easels, butcher paper, and walls with only a wash of imaginary colors (which last only for seconds) can be included in this activity. You will think of many other ways to "swish" tales of the past. A narration of the past can be developed, each participant adding to the story line or each with a tale of his or her own. Orchestration or signs of the body can narrate the brushes' tales. The developmental age and sophistication of the participants will determine how this activity is used. This activity is appropriate for many other themes than just the Native American theme.

If you are working with visually impaired participants, add coarse pulp, papier mâché, flour, or other substances to the colors, so the messages can be felt. If you have visually impaired integrated with sighted participants, there are no problems in feeling the tales of history because it sounds like great fun. You could go all out and bring in rocks to paint them and make them into a cave.

With activity 10, develop individual sounds and motions, using solo, solo-tutti, two-part, three-part, and total ensemble, all with sensitive sounds, listening to each chore, and moving to accent that chore sound. Melodies can enter in the form of movement or voice as the composition develops.

(10)
The women in the pueblo
Do their daily chores.
Listen to the sounds they make:
A symphony—a symphony of chores!

Body painting could be included as part of activity 11, or participants can just mix colors, as the tensions build with anxiety over the next day's battle. The slow bubbling of brilliant colors evokes symbols of bravery, heritage, and perhaps fear. Even bright scarves can be used as flames and as bubbling paints to add to the imagery.

(11)
Day colors turn to night.
Drums tell of past and future;
Next day's colors—
Warriors fight.
[Pause.]
The dancers move;
The paint pots bubble.

Movement and orchestration build up and fade away into closure in activity 12. Let the participants work it out, and establish closure so that the battle does not last too long.

(12)
Dust . . . hooves,
Snorts . . . push—
Buffalo are running.
Hunters are coming,
Elbows cocked.
Arrows shot—
Hunters and buffalo . . .
Some have won.

Activity 13 can be done using the statuesque stance of a chief, pondering and sad. Responses can be instrumental with voice or voice only—perhaps statements of why the chief's people had to fight or die, then developing music to accent the statement. A review of problems Native Americans have experienced will help give some structure to the project and provide the basis for more extensive expansion. Assign further reading, if appropriate, or watch a special movie on Native American history, then culminate with this activity.

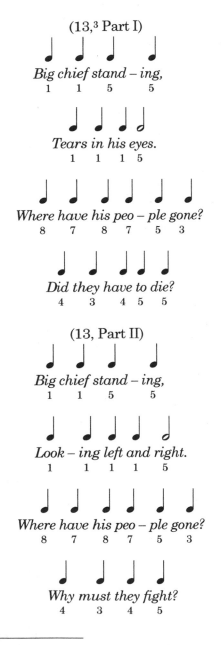

(13,[3] Part I)

Big chief stand – ing,
1   1   5   5

Tears in his eyes.
1   1   1   5

Where have his peo – ple gone?
8   7   8   7   5   3

Did they have to die?
4   3   4   5   5

(13, Part II)

Big chief stand – ing,
1   1   5   5

Look – ing left and right.
1   1   1   1   5

Where have his peo – ple gone?
8   7   8   7   5   3

Why must they fight?
4   3   4   5

---

[3]Minor key; slow, heavy accent, sad.

Arrow to the Sun[4], by Gerald McDermott, is a beautifully illustrated Pueblo Indian story with vivid imagery. I spent a day in Santa Barbara with the Creative Practices Council, Inc., reviewing the story, drawing symbols (later attached to shipping boxes), developing movement and music, and finally having it culminate in a collection of contributions relying on the narrator and dancer to spin each part of the story into a comprehensive unit. I felt excited during the performance, but better when it was all swelling forth, bringing together the energies of all participating in a joyous celebration of *Arrow to the Sun*. I cannot encourage you enough to browse through the book with your group, discussing shapes and forms, before doing any artwork or story development in your Native American project. I'm sure there are other resources; if you know of any, share them with a friend. Ideas are meant to be shared, and usually as they are discussed, they produce new ideas.

It's interesting that while putting together this chapter, I have written a number of spontaneous resources, with ease and reward. The Native American theme really has such an abundance of images that it sparks creativity!

So . . .

---

[4]McDermott, G. (1977). *Arrow to the sun: A Pueblo Indian tale.* Harmondsworth, UK: Kestral Books.

Get your
Moccasins creeping,
Ankle bells ringing,
Fire spitting,
Drums beating,
Brushes swishing,
For we have a tale to tell.

Release,
Moccasins
creeping,
Bells ringing,
Fire spitting,
Drums beating,
Brushes swishing.
What will happen?
None of us knows.[5]

Pam Healy

---

[5]By Carol Hampton Bitcon.

Chapter 17

NATURE

Nature is a rather broad area, so I have included activities focusing on a wide variety of themes, such as weather, wildlife, and seasons. Some are only impressionistic; others determine the process of the activities.

(1[1])
Winter's
Thunder
Is the world's
Wonder.

Get the thunder sounds going for activity 1, then develop another group with this:

(2)
Rain, rain,
Go away;
Come again
Some other day.

Orchestrate activity 2 to accompany winter's wonder—or use it when directed by the weather forecast.

(3)
Pitter patter—
What's the matter?
Pitter patter—
What's the matter?

Combine activity 3 with the rain in activity 2 and you have a good two-part development to work on, introduced by the thunder of activity 1. Then, enter the wind!

---

[1]A Mother Goose nursery rhyme.

(4)
The wind, the wind
Is passing through,
The wind, the wind
Is passing through.

Here are some more wind activities:

(5)
Rough and huffy,
The winds are puffy.
Blow, winds,
Blow.

(6²)
Blow, blow,
Blow a long blast!

You can easily come up with a multitude of seasonal activities after looking through books on seasons and weather. Have your students discuss weather and its sounds and then develop a complete composition on weather, starting with a weather report. The composition can be narrated or can just happen.

(7)
Mr. Weather³, Mr. Weather,
How are you today?
Is it hot?
Is it cold?
What do you have to say?

Dawn developed "Mr. Weather" in her first Orff-Schulwerk class and we've used it since. Participants can give only a weather report or can give a weather sequence or tell a story that includes the weather as the story moves along.

---

²This activity also appears in Chapter 8.
³You can use *Ms. Weather* instead of *Mr. Weather* if appropriate to the person playing the role.

Activity 8 can get everyone jumping.

(8)

When it rains,
Galoshes make splishes and sploshes.
What sounds do you make
When it rains?

In activity 9, participants are challenged to get the sun to go "our way." They can do this maybe by moving, by playing a drum or instrument, or by moving to the hot sun and then becoming colder when away from the sun. Put some mystery into developing the presence of the sun.

(9)

Hot, cold,
New, old—
All because of the sun,
All because of the sun.
Speak to it, speak to it;
Bring it our way.

In activity 10, orchestrate the A part of the rondo, with the wind developing and leaves rustling messages. Then seek variations on what was said by the wind. Stress the wind sound in the word *wind* (onomatopoeia[4]).

(10)

The wind, the wind
Is passing through,
Rustling leaves,
Whispering to the trees.

Most of the name activities are grouped together in Chapter 2, but I chose to put the wind sounds in this chapter, so that's why

---

[4]Onomatopoeia is the formation of words imitative of natural sounds, the formation of name words by imitating the sound associated with the thing designated, or the use of imitative and naturally suggestive words for rhetorical effect.

activity 11 appears below. You may want to use it in conjunction with the activities in Chapter 2.

(11)
I'm the west wind.
I bring summer rain,
And when I blow soft,
I whisper my name.

Next are some leaf activities that are great for fall.

For activity 12, use brightly colored leaves found on a walk or leaves made in the classroom out of tissue, so they float. Drop them down one by one, orchestrated with the music, or scoop them up and throw them so all the colors merge, a few leaves lingering behind.

(12)
Down, down—
Orange, yellow, and brown
Leaves are falling
All around.

(13[5])
The leaves laugh
Low in the wind,
Laugh low
With the wind at play.

With activity 14, I've used a circle, with participants' arms and bodies serving as the trees. The leaves—participants with instruments—go into the circle and play the secrets of the leaves. At the University of the Pacific, we brought in many magnolia tree leaves that we dropped to the singing of swaying trees and the accompaniment of the leaves.

(14[6])
Swaying trees,
Swaying trees,
Dropping secrets
With their leaves.

---

[5]Stevens, S. (1971). In *Awareness*. Moab, UT: Real People Press.
[6]Make up a swaying tune in a minor key.

Activity 15 is Carl Sandburg's famous poem. For advanced groups, it is very impressive to have the instruments develop the fog, the entrance of the cat on silent haunches, and then the cat's exit. A discussion of the nature of fog, how it can close in and then suddenly have open spots, of what happened one time in the fog when . . . helps lead up to an activity such as this.

(15)
The fog comes on little cat feet.
It sits looking over harbor and city
On silent haunches
And then moves on.[7]

Here are two other fog activities:

(16)
Stand still,
The fog wraps you up and
No one can find you.
Walk,
The fog opens up to let you through
And closes behind you.[8]

In activity 16, use scarves, or plain colored gauze, to wrap around a participant until the music moves away and a dancer unwinds the gauze so the captive is free to walk on. The next person must approach the fog/gauze/music; each participant will bring a unique style to the sequence. It's also effective to do the activity with only music and moving arms that eventually separate and let the participant through.

Easy in English, by Mauree Applegate, has a resource on fog (activity 17 here) that is great for creative production of movement, music, and dramatics while using colorful description that I know fifth-grade boys would love. I say fifth-grade boys because although they seem to be the most difficult to plan for (second to adolescents), they make the most enthusiastic participants when you get the right resources. Sound effects, motors, monsters, robots, and gore and guts

---

[7]Sandburg, C. (1958). Fog. In *Early moon* (p. 74). New York: Harcourt, Brace & World.
[8]By Lillian Moore.

are all intriguing to this age group. Help the group envision a wet string mop or a handful of gooey strings (or some other yucky thing that I'm sure participants could think up) being dragged across the group, swirling and touching, with those touched resisting. With this age group, I think there might also be a bit of choking each other out—but *you* figure out how to deal with that!

(17)

Fog is like a wet, cold, and slithering ghost
that creeps over the land with clammy fingers,
grasping everything that he can reach,
changing it into a ghostly shape.
Its wet, cold hands seem to cling to you
to make you feel lonesome and alone.
All living or moving things on the earth
seem to stand still when the misty fog moves in,
seeming to hold with
its cold, wet, slimy fingers.[9]

You'll see everything from birds to hurricanes with activity 18.

(18)

Sun, water, and
Morning mist dew.
What in nature
Is most like you?

This weather development might need narration:

(19)

I want to make some weather.
Does anybody know
How to make thunder, lightning,
Sunshine, rain, or snow?

---

[9]Applegate, M. (1960). Fog. In *Easy in English: An imaginative approach to the teaching of the language arts* (pp. 380–381). Evanston, IL: Row, Peterson.

Haiku[10] is excellent for developing nature activities. One poem that appears in just about every haiku book and can be nicely orchestrated with the movement of water, when the frog jumps, is this:

(20)

The old pond
A frog jumps in,
The sound of water.

If you have a group of participants who are able, have them write their own haiku. Then orchestrate it and dramatize it. Perhaps start with assignments of dramatizing haikus that have already been published and then move on to an assignment for participants to write and develop their own haiku. Individuals may want to write their own and have the group develop it, or they may want to direct the production as a completion of their own work.

Here's another haiku that can be made lovely with music accompanying the movement of a butterfly while the group is lying down:

(21)

That butterfly's wing
Barely grazed my cheek,
And yet
I felt his surprise!

For activity 22, sometimes I divide a group of children into five groups and have them represent the four seasons (groups 1 through 4) and Mother Nature (group 5), who changes and combines seasons and weather conditions. Spring, summer, winter, and fall could each take a corner of the room, where each seasonal group decides on instruments, words, and movements. I usually assign a number—perhaps three—of words (impressions) that can be used. Perhaps spring would choose *sunshine, warmth,* and *flowers,* whereas winter might choose *thunder, lightning,* and *rain.* Each group then puts movement to the words and chooses instruments to represent the words. The Mother Nature group then carries instruments, such as sticks and bells, and when they approach a season group, the sticks

---

[10]I'm sorry not to be able to give credit to the authors of most of the haiku used in this book, but the authors many times are not credited in publications in which I found them.

draw the group nearer and bells send them away, giving clues to the seasonal groups that their season is either about to end or about to begin. The Mother Nature group can split and draw two seasons together. If you want to go further, get some big packing boxes, or portable frames of some type, and have each season draw a backdrop for them; the Mother Nature participants could develop some streamers to tie to their bodies.

(22)
What are summer nights made of?
Oh—
What are summer [Or winter or spring or fall] nights made of?

Here's an exciting volcano activity that was used as a project by a University of Pacific student. The imagery is vivid, and it suggests violent, earthshaking movement that boys might really enjoy, with flashing lights, waving scarves, and orchestration of *bubble and boil and quake.*

(23)
The mountain is angry!
We feel it shake.
The lava will bubble
And boil and quake!

Be dramatic. Work out a closure so the activity is not rapidly put to death by falling apart or just ending abruptly.

Activity 24 suggests contrasting moods, affect, and movement that can be accompanied by instruments.

(24)
In the winter
When people arc cold,
They look cross
And walk very fast.
In the summer
When people are warm,
They look kind
And go slowly past.[11]

---

[11]Segal, E. (1952). Be my friend. In *Be my friend and other poems for girls and boys.* New York: Citadel Press.

With activity 25, there should be some good croaking, jumping, and music-making, Use a wand and a wild wizard hat to enhance the atmosphere. Hats sometimes make a performer more comfortable because they give cues for an activity and help one divert attention from oneself.

(25)
The wizard waved his wand;
Frogs jumped out of a pond.
They danced and sang and played—
What beautiful music they made!

The next two activities are difficult if you hate snakes. I have trouble getting into the movement of a snake, but I have seen other teachers move with grace and cleverness when depicting something as ugly as a snake. I wrote activity 26 because the thought of a basket of humans covering a snake that responds when music beckons is exciting. The *sssss* sounds and the mystery of the snake coming out of the basket, tongue flashing, add to the color of the activity. I really don't think I've had much success with this activity, perhaps because I've used it only with adults. Watching a snake would suggest great movement. If someone plays a recorder, flute, or even a kazoo, that adds the intrigue of the Far East. Closure is obvious as the snake coils back down into the basket.

I hate snakes. I think I'd like to kill this one!

(26)
The snake
Coils up in his basket.
The music beckons;
The snake responds.

(27)
Rattles that shake
Move, move, move
To a rattle–snake.

Out on the lawn, under a tree on a hot summer day, activity 28 is wonderful. Handle it with sensitivity and you'll get many different responses. Beware, though: this activity can get a bit heavy. I once got this response: "None of your business!"

(28)
I heard the grass weep
Beneath my feet.
I said to the grass,
"Why do you weep?"

Here's a quiet activity relating to breezes:

(29[12])
Breeze
Gentle as a feather
Cat quiet, snow soft
Gentle, gentle as a feather
Softer than snow, quiet as a cat
Comes
The evening breeze.

This activity is quieting to me even as I type:

(30)
Raining, raining, all night long —
Sometimes loud, sometimes soft.
Sometimes you can't hear it at all.

Emphasize the concepts of *soft, loud,* and *silent.* The group can slap thighs (*patchen*) and pass the tambour for each person to use for a finger-tapping composition of rain, using loud sounds, soft sounds, and silence.

The purpose of activity 31 is to identify parts of the body while the rain is pattering overhead. If you want to be realistic, use a dropper or squirt toy to make "rain."

(31)
The rain, the rain
Is coming down.
What part of your body
Has it found?

---

[12]Lewis, R. (1966). Breeze. In *Miracles* (p. 198). New York: Simon & Schuster.

Trying to catch as much water as you can will cause growing excitement. Roxie brought this activity into one of our very early sessions at Fairview. Once you have water, what do you do with it? You'll get some intriguing answers.

(32)
Rain falling over our heads,
Filling the world with water.
Catch it up, catch it up.
What do you do with your water?

Here are a few spring activities:

(33)
The wind is in a bad mood,
Raging, crying, howling, and moaning.
When will the mood change?

(34)
March winds,
April showers
Bring forth May flowers.

(35)
The cold wind blows
All around—bloooooow!
Let's hear your
Cold wind blow.

(36)
The wind blows,
The wolves howl
While the moon moves
Along the sky.

The imagery in the last verse is terrific descriptive material for a quiet, slow buildup and then a fade while the powerful, mystical moon moves over the composition. A light could be a nice moon, but the good old tambour is a great moon that slowly rises and then disappears.

This next activity was developed by a class participant to encourage high and low sounds on the instruments. The movement and type of flower could certainly enter into the activity.

(37)
I have a musical garden.
It has high plants
And it has low plants.
May we hear
How your musical garden grows?

Snow is seldom experienced where I live. If it does snow, it's a special time for exploring. I worked with Cheryl in demonstrating Orff-Schulwerk with a group of learning-disabled children who were truly charming. Even though it wasn't snowing, snow was brought into one of our activities, which was this one:

(38)
Chooooo cha chooooo cha chooooo,
The train stops for you.
Where does it take you?
Where does it take you?

The children made dramatic train sounds by turning a cabasa/Afuche in their palms. One small great brat of a boy (I love brats) had been very hyperactive and had contributed little to the group. I asked him to come up because a snowman had entered his train trip. We immediately left the train stranded on the track and started building the snowman on this little boy. Each child came to him and touched a part of his body as the snowman was built. Then as he stood tall in the group, a complete snowman, the sun came out and slowly he melted away. The activity was great for identifying parts of the body, for control, movement, and imagery. We all had fun.

My sister Janet brought activity 39 into a session with teachers and clinicians who had experienced snow, and there was gentle movement and music. But more preparation would have been necessary with participants who had not experienced miserable, cold, wet snowflakes that look great from a lodge or cabin window or the beautiful light powdering of snow on a protected body.

(39)
Snowflakes
Sifting through the trees—
Who can shake
And twist like these?

This haiku's beautiful imagery can inspire group compositions:

(40)
A leaf on the stream
Suddenly whirls round and round
And then vanishes.

Mother Goose rhymes also have some nice imagery, particularly for creative writing. Here's one example:

(41)
Spring is showery, flowery, bowery;
Summer: happy, croppy, poppy;
Autumn: wheezy, sneezy, freezy;
Winter: slippy, drippy, nippy.

Nature controls many of our forms of entertainment. Kite flying is of special attraction to me when I think of the apparent freedom of the kite soaring, its tail whipping, but the wind and string really are what control the kite. The wind withdraws and the kite crashes, the trees grab and tear, and the kite struggles to escape. Developing a kite and tail and the wind results in a movement activity that reacts to various forces, such as the wind blowing harder or softer and the kite constantly testing its freedom.

(42)
Kite flying high,
Thoughts of freedom,
Tail rebelling,
Wind controlling.

(43)
Wish that I
Could be a kite
Up in the sky
And ride upon the breeze
And go
Whichever way I
Chanced to blow.

When your group is outdoors near a natural area with various trees, plants, birds, and so on, a symphony of nature is in order:

(44)
We are going to have
A symphony of nature.
We are going to have
A symphony of nature.

This activity requires a very quiet environment in which birds are singing and water is running, but not too loud. If you are near a freeway, an airport, a dance club, or a school with outdoor recess activities, I don't suggest trying it. I start the activity with everyone in a circle, listening quietly. Then I start discussing sounds of nature, combinations of sounds, controlled sounds, noncontrolled sounds, loud sounds, soft sounds, and silent sounds. Then I ask that each member go out in search of a sound of nature and bring it back; I usually impose a time limit of about 10 minutes. When all have returned, we move on with this:

(45)
Nature's full of sights
And sounds.
Let us see
What you have found.

For activity 46, each person plays the nature sound selected. Periodically, I ask someone with a strong ostinato to select other nature instruments and join in on two- and three-part developments. Eventually, a conductor or a lead instrument develops a symphony of nature. The sounds are quiet and intense, and the musicians are sensitive. Melodies from birds come forth, and sounds from bugs frequently can be heard if you are at a campsite or in the woods. It is obvious that the environment must be very quiet enough so that a stick striking a pine cone, one rock hitting another, or water cascading from one container to another can be heard solo or solo-tutti.

There will be a few who bring ugly cans, flip tops, and trash as a statement of nature. You may want to accept these resources; I have chosen to go with whatever was selected.

(46)
We are going to play
A symphony of nature.
We are going to play our
Instruments of nature.

When participants bring in such human-made items, you may want to go on to focus on pollution of the environment. Have everyone bring in ideas for taking care of the environment. Then, for activity 47, get a Latin beat going:

(47)
What's the solution
To the pollution?
What's the solution
To the pollution?

I should mention that bringing in items from nature can be very messy. Participants will want to make the sounds of crushing leaves, running water, crashing rocks, falling dirt, snapping branches, and heaven only knows what else. I anticipate the day a live creature is brought in—it will be fun . . . but awful! Activities with a nature focus should probably be outside if at all possible. You can create a more comprehensive program when you follow your nature activities with an art project. For example, make collages or cast participants' nature items in plaster of Paris.

Here are two more outdoor activities:

(48)
Sit in the sunshine
And lift your face.
Close your eyes
And sun-dream.

(49)
Bright flashes stroke the sky.
It is the sun—
Mother Nature is painting.
Look out the window;
See the sky.
What do you feel
When a cloud goes by?

Chapter 18

SILENCE

Hark, hark, the dogs do BARK,
The neighbors YELL,
The babies CRY.
The buses GRIND,
The bongos BONG,
The telephones RING,
The jet planes FLY,
The car horns HONK,
The taxis SCREECH,
The radio's ON,
The Teevee's HIGH,
The ROCK-AND-ROLL pours from the record stores,
The subway ROARS,
The old women MUTTER in the gutter,
The rats SQUEAK,
The flies BUZZ.
Only the roaches quietly crawl.[1]

Sound has meaning only in relation to silence, just as light has meaning only in relation to darkness. Silence is accent. It is dramatic. It is the privacy of those participating in it. Silence has many messages, many anxieties but is in fact is a vital part of the total composition.

An immediate exploration of silence is aided by having one's eyes closed, listening to one's breathing as one lies down in a private spot, where silence can be risked.

I've pulled together a variety of resources on silence for this chapter, many of which I will share with silent explanation!

---

[1]Merriam, E. (1969). Hark, hark, the dogs do bark. In *The inner city mother goose*. New York: Simon & Schuster.

(1)
Understand the big sounds
Underneath the big silences.
Listen for the little secret sounds,
Listen for the little secret sounds.
Secret sounds.[2]

(2)
Let your hands go clap, clap, clap.
Let your fingers go snap, snap, snap.
Let your lips go very round
But . . . do not make a sound.
Fold your hands and close each eye;
Take a breath and softly sigh—
Ahhhhhh!

(3)
Listen!
There are sounds
All around—
Soft sounds.

(4)
The noise of the city is all around.
Can you hear it?
Stop—don't look but listen.
What is the sound?

For activity 5, use soft music, whispering, or a whispered statement with music if desired. Let it just happen.

(5)
Whisper, whisper,
Talk real low.
Whisper, whisper
What you know.

---

[2]From de Regniers, B. S., and Haas, I. (1958). Little sounds. In *Something special*. New York: Harcourt, Brace & World.

(6)
Listen to the quiet.
What do you hear?
Listen to the quiet.
What do you hear?

(7)
Quiet is a splendid time
When the mind thinks,
But sometimes you think of things
That make you cry.

For activity 8, move to break silence and then orchestrate the sounds of the world turning. These sounds could be a slow, sensitive turning of the earth . . . cosmic sounds. They also could be the sounds that remind a person that everything is still moving right along!

(8)
One must move
To break the silence.
Has the world
Stopped turning?

Activity 9 is perhaps morbid, but it just might be appropriate for an occasion in your group. I've participated in a Creative Dramatics project that was a death process. It was intense and cathartic. When someone who is well known by the group dies, there will be discussion and questions. There may be a need to have closure so you can move on, and activity 9 and help provide it.

(9)
We all know
Quiet can mean death.
The tears
Fill the ground.

(10[3])
Loud resounding slap,
Falling finally to earth.
A wandering seed.

Activity 11 easily could have been included in Chapter 11 because it deals with psychosocial dynamics.

(11)
I fear
Your silence.
What could it mean?
I suspect
Your silence.
What could it mean?
Silence could mean _____ .

(12)
My constant words
Make you my friend.
My silence means
I accept you already
As a friend.

(13)
If I keep you talking,
I know what you're thinking.
We could make music
And just relate!

Hugh Prather, author of *Notes to Myself: My Struggle to Become a Person*,[4] influenced these next three activities about silence.

(14)
Be still . . .
And let the wind speak.
Hush . . .
A world is talking.

---

[3]Hackett, J. (1969). In *Haiku poetry* (p. 151). Tokyo: Japan Publishers.
[4]Prather, H. (1990). *Notes to myself: My struggle to become a person.* New York: Bantam Books.

(15)
When the wind blows,
The quiet things speak.

(16)
Shhh—silence.
Splash—the sound of seagulls.
The sea rocks itself to sleep.

I explore sounds of the body, the sounds of the environment, soft sounds, and loud sounds, but I enjoy most exploring silent sounds. Below you'll find a list of silent sounds that I've pulled together; I've left space for you to add to the list. Tune in to the silent sounds— maybe making an enjoyable evening of it with friends.

Have You Heard . . .

Sugar melt in a coffee cup?

A cat lick its face?

A flower stem break?

An ice cream cone being licked?

Grass grow in the sun?

Time pass?

A spider coax its victim into its web?

The stillness of graves?

Dust move?

The world turn?

Microwaves cook?

A baby breathe?

A seed crash to earth?

A star fall?

A feather float?

Wet worms wiggle in the grass?

The tiniest whisper?

A toadstool turn?

A giraffe giggle?

A bunny call for help?

Soda pop froth?

A turtle snap?

Someone age?

Teeth decay?

Hurt feelings?

Seedlings break through the black earth?

Fear?
Anticipation?
Surprise?

Silent applause?
Tears of joy?

Tears of sorrow?
A butterfly pop, split, and crackle out of a cocoon?
A pimple pop?
Sun lotion sizzle?

Mosquitoes suck blood?
Blood pressure rise?

Jasmine send out its fragrance?
A gentle old man look at his grandson?
A caterpillar eat lace patterns into a leaf?
A leaf hit a stream?
Night lurk?
A roach slip under a baseboard?
Light switch to dark?
Eyes search a soul?
Ants march?
Someone hesitate?
Puss ooze?
Eyes flash defiance?

A bruise form?

The sun rise?
A flower die?
A tear slide down a child's cheek?
Sweat drip?
A bird suck out the juice of a flower?
The sun bake skin?
Mites chew?

The earth tremble?
Sand fly from dancing feet?
Butterflies show off their wings?
A bird bump a cloud as it passes?
A spider spin a web?

Moss gather on rocks?
A snail leave a track?

Chops being licked?
Moon rays dance?
A moth munch cloth?

Fingernails grow?
Old skin crinkle?
An apricot rot?
Ice melt?
Smog smooch?
A needle coming out of cloth?
A blush?

The following excerpt from *The Phantom Tollbooth*, by Norton Juster, illustrates the importance of silence:

"... Isn't that lovely?" she signed. "It's my favorite program—fifteen minutes of silence—and after that there's a half hour of quiet and then an interlude of lull. Why, did you know that there are almost as many kinds of stillness as there are sounds? But sadly enough, no one pays any attention to them these days.

"Have you heard the wonderful silence just before the dawn?" she inquired. "Or the quiet and calm just as a storm ends? Or perhaps you know the silence when you haven't the answer to a question you've been asked, or the hush of a country road at night, or the expectant pause in a room full of people when someone is about to speak, or, most beautiful of all, the moment after the door closes and you're all alone in the whole house? Each one is different and all vary if you listen carefully."[5]

Silence is what allows phrasing and accent. Silence is the pause. Sometimes the pause is too long and is ineffective. Silence is a tool a leader can use either effectively or poorly. The timing of an activity is vital. How long do you wait? How long can the silence hold attention before becoming confusion? As the leader, you must decide all these things, just as you decide how fast or slow the pace of an activity will be, what mood will be presented with an activity, and what effect you will use in the total presentation of an activity. Besides, if you don't listen to the silence of an individual participant, you won't know what you'll miss:

You probably don't think
I'm listening.
But I am.
I'd be embarrassed to tell you.
But I hear you.
Please don't turn away from me.
I really am
Listening.[6]

[5]Juster, N. (1961). *The phantom tollbooth* (p. 151). New York: Epstein & Carroll.
[6]Herbert, C. (1973). The quiet one. In *I see a child*. Garden City, NY: Anchor Press.

Activity 17 can be a simple, dramatic presentation with the instruments presenting the clatter and then the strange stillness.

(17)

When Father says
"I've had my fill
Of so much noise and clatter,"
Then Mother says,
"You sit so still . . .
Can something be the matter?"[7]

(18)

My stomach growls.
My throat gurgles.
My teeth click.
My fingers crack.
My toes thump.
My nose sniffs.
My lips pop.
Even my blinks make a sound.
I'm really very noisy,
In a quiet way.[8]

---

[7]Fisher, A. (1969). I see a child. In *In one door and out the other* (p. 29). New York: Crowell.

[8]Margolis, R. J. (1969). In *Only the moon and me* (p. 12). Philadelphia: Lippincott.

Chapter 19

THE SEA

There are many images and surprises at the seashore. I feel very poetic when at the seashore, particularly if I'm alone and no one can hear me singing . . . or thinking. Writing messages in the sand with bare feet is one of my favorite pastimes. When you take your group to the seashore—and I hope you're fortunate enough to be located near an ocean—start messages and get others to build on them, using shells, feathers, seaweed, and so on, along with signs and arrows to indicate how the messages move. When the collage is complete, travel the complete course of the messages and art. Early-morning joggers don't always notice what's going on, so if you're out early, try to keep out of their way. They're set on jogging and most likely won't stop to participate in creating artwork.

It's strange, but many of the thoughts I have beside the ocean slip from my consciousness when I leave that environment. The continuous beating of the waves on the shore almost seems to be beating on my mind, sharpening images—vital images, not unlike the vitality of breathing.

For activity 1, have the group stand or lie in a circle and listen to the rhythms of breathing. Indicate separate movements related to *in* breaths and to *out* breaths, such as arms up, arms down, or bending down and pulling up. Each person responds to his or her own breathing. A few instruments, such as a glockenspiel or a metallophone, can provide effective accompaniment, particularly when glissandos are used. If participants are overactive, their breathing will become more frantic and they may get dizzy.

(1)
The sea,
Like my body,
Breathes in . . .
Pauses . . .
And breathes out.

The sounds of the sea can be further developed with different movements depicting objects in the water and on the sand. A metal tube with sand in it or an African bamboo shaker with seeds in the center can be used to make the wave sounds. The sand and seeds roll back and forth as the instruments are tipped. Add to the drama by miming the activity of waders suddenly caught by a wave or grabbed by some sea creature; this can be accompanied by instruments.

Some of the items gathered for activity 2 may not be too pleasant, particularly if young children are involved. Nothing keeps you from taking a few sea items to the ocean with you if you want to guide a particular activity. When the feathers, shells, and long strips of seaweed all arrive, have a show-and-tell, building on the ideas offered. Some items found at the ocean can be taken back to a classroom for future activities that may expand on the initial stimuli of the sea. Reviewing and reexploring later, away from the sea, will produce even more ideas. Periodically, an adventuresome field trip away from the regular group setting is inspiring.

(2)
Down to the seashore,
Down to the sand—
Quickly gather
Whatever you can.

Here are some other fun activities:

- Developing two-part movement with long seaweed
- Jumping rope with seaweed
- Making angels in the sand (instead of in snow): lie down on your back and wave your arms against the sand to form the wings
- Making seascapes out of material found on the beach and framing them with sand
- Listening to repetitive sounds and putting them into the pockets of the mind for future use when developing ostinati on sea themes
- Covering parts of the body with sand
- Making sand faces
- Casting plaster of Paris footprints and handprints in the sand
- Making sand candles, cast in the sand
- Following footsteps already made in the sand

- Building designs made from sand flowing through a clenched fist
- Playing tag or whip with the sea, with the group in a long line and holding hands
- Filling treasure sacks or boxes and sharing the findings later (Put names on the containers.)
- Taunting the sea with ugly faces and then running from the sea's grasp

The seashore provides great learning opportunities: The messiness of sand allows a lot of freedom. The wide-open sea just begs for someone to throw things into it. The plentiful sounds encourage visitors to take a listening walk—no talking, just listening. The tidal changes and the influence of the moon are wonderful resources for projects focusing on science, movement, poetry, art, orchestration, and creative writing.

With your group, form a circle, hold hands, and then move around in the water, daring the waves to catch a few of the participants. Then help pull the wave's captives back into the circle, only to taunt the sea again. Up and down, in and out, skipping, hopping, "flying," jumping, and rolling all are natural and become exaggerated among the waves.[1]

Whether activity 3 is done at a classroom sand table or at the ocean, it's helpful to establish each person's territory. If you don't do this, participants will waste a lot of time and energy worrying whether someone else will bother or destroy a project. Ownership of the castle is momentary anyway when you're at the beach, so make it a little easier by establishing a territory that will be touched by only the creator and the waves. Encourage the addition of feathers, shells, food containers, and other junk found on the beach to help establish visual and tactile uniqueness.

---

[1]Make sure your facility's insurance covers trips to the beach; fear of accidents detracts from the joy of seaside activities.

(3)
Little drops of water,
Little grains of sand—
Can you make a castle
With only your hands?

For activity 4, orchestrate and dramatize the teasing and intimidation of the wave.

(4)
If a wave had its way,
It could scare me—but it doesn't.
But if the ocean gathered its force,
I would be terribly scared, of course.

For activity 5 also, orchestrate and dramatize. Have each member of the group add to the description of what grabbed the foot.

(5)
A wave came grabbing at me.
Something in the wave
Grabbed my foot!
I was afraid to look.

There are clear plastic toys that hold fine sand in various shades; when the toy is moved, the sand builds pretty designs. Such toys could be included in a session for orchestration or merely to stimulate responses. You can use a bottle containing oil and colored water to get somewhat the same effect.

For activity 6, choose a friend, then set out on a fantasy journey, which can include a few instruments. Verbalization may or may not accompany the journey or may occur afterward. As you well know by now, verbalization is not always necessary. Movement in fantasy is enough. Remember, many activities can incorporate both verbal and nonverbal individuals. Perhaps movement will be the only response. That's fine! What are you trying to accomplish?

(6)
Let's plan,
You and I,
To take a journey to
The bottom of the sea.

You can get a most impressive effect by placing water and oil in an oven-safe glass dish, which sits on the projection rack of an overhead projector, and reflecting it on a screen. Ron, a teacher on my staff, used this effect to represent the moon in a play produced at Fairview. The shadow of one of the clients dressed as an astronaut with a flag in his hand was projected onto the simulated moon surface. Colors can be added to the oil and water, and when the dish is gently rocked, the forms change.

(7)
Down, down
Into the ocean blue—
I see many strange things.
How about you?

Cheryl, Bonnie Bickerstaff, Dawn, and I went to Georgia to teach, where Bonnie's mother was interested in having us work with her classroom of students. We did not need a second invitation. The theme in the classroom was fish. There were all kinds of art projects, books, and other resources on fish in the room. We worked on names and other activities using some instruments and then moved to fish faces. It was great! We enjoyed meeting the children. They were charming. Their Southern accent was quite different to Cheryl, Dawn, and me, but it made Bonnie feel right at home because she is from Georgia.

(8)
Bubbles, bubbles
From the deep blue sea—
Make a fish face
That we can see.

(9)
Fish, fish—
For goodness' sake!
What kind of music
[Or: *What kind of movement*]
Do you make?

In activity 9, movement and music could be combined after each has been reviewed separately.

Here's a playful, similar game of teasing and catching:

(10)
Fishie, fishie
In the brook—
Grab ahold of
_____[Name]_____*'s hook.*

You can develop a creative drama project with activity 11 using movement, storytelling, and music. Puppets could tell the story while the fish (with fish faces, of course!) swim in the lake and the fisher develops a whale of a "tale to tell."

(11)
Listen, oh listen
So very well,
For I have a great
Fish tale to tell.

The instruments representing *cry* and *sigh* in activity 12 will add to the composition, and then an instrument such as a tambour can be the moon playing secrets to "the wild sky." Using the rondo form, each person could take turns being the moon playing secrets to the sky or whispering secrets to the group. Musical secrets should provide interesting responses. The closure might be a *shhhhh* after each person is finished, and then everyone goes back to the *A* part of the rondo.

(12, Part I)
Deep in a seashell
You will hear
The wind, the waves,
And the moon, my dear.

(12, Part II)
The winds, they cry [Select instrument for *cry*];
The waves, they sigh [Select instrument for *sigh*];
And the moon tells her secrets
To the wild sky [Orchestrate].

You may face a group that has never experienced an ocean. I've tried ocean activities in locales where the ocean was so far away that many students had never seen an ocean, and the participants found it hard to expand on an idea that they had not experienced. Learning is through discovery. The initial experience of a concept must be concrete if it is to be expanded on and explored, investigated, and integrated. The mysteries, the sounds, and the feeling of hot, cool, wet, or dry sands would certainly contribute to the expansion of the concept of the sea. Recorded wave sounds are available when the ocean isn't nearby; they can add to orchestration as well as to sounds and movements.

(13)
Ocean, ocean,
Such a roar.
Play the sound
When it hits the shore.

I have a giant seashell that I pass around the group for activity 14. Each person listens to the shell, then chooses an instrument to orchestrate what secrets the shell has told. It is an interesting development to combine the music of the different instruments that have told what the shell has to say. The music is usually very soft, delicate, and exciting. Have a rest period, composed just of silence, while listening to the "waves within the body." Listen to the quiet sounds. After everyone is relaxed and you are ready to move on, bring in body waves, with a moon (tambour) coming to each resting participant and beckoning each person to rise, one at a time, and move. When the movement is ended, the moon returns the wave to the resting spot.

(14)
Listen, listen—
Don't you tell!
Listen, listen
To the seashell.

A book I particularly enjoy is *Something Special* by Beatrice Schenk de Regniers and Irene Haas. One section called "If You Find a Little Feather" depicts a sea activity, with a small boy finding a feather lying near his sand castle. The theme of the verse is this:

(15)
A feather is a letter
From a bird,
And it says,
"Think of me."[2]

The variety of feathers usually found on a beach is great, and when they are all pulled together in the form of a letter from birds, the letter could be most interesting. Perhaps the letter will become a group mural or a part of a creative writing project. An expansion can easily follow in the form of a story that participants build and then orchestrated and develop into a creative drama project.

I loaned my book to Julia, a student in one of my classes at the University of California, Irvine, and when I opened it to pull out a reference for this writing, I found a feather neatly tucked between two pages. It was a special feather—and Julia was a special student.

---

[2]From de Regniers, B. S., and Haas, I. (1958). If you find a little feather . . . . . In *Something special*. New York: Harcourt, Brace & World.

(16)
As leaves blow along the beach and
The bleached starfish are washed up on the shore . . .
Sometimes I put a seashell to my ear . . .
And it all comes back.[3]

I would probably shorten this activity to this:

Sometimes I put
A seashell to my ear
And it all comes back.

(17)
I went to the ocean
And what did I see?
A big wooden box floating into me.
I pulled it in close
And opened it up
And looked inside.
Guess what I found?

(18)
Ocean, ocean,
Dance to and fro.
Dance for us
The way the oceans flow.

(19)
Until I saw the sea
I did not know that wind could wrinkle water.
I never knew that sun could splinter a whole sea of blue
Nor did I know before
A sea breathes in and out upon a shore.[4]

---

[3]McKuen, R. (1967). In *Listen to the warm* (p. 31). New York: Random House.
[4]By Lillian Moore.

(20)

The devil's discarded cloak on the
Sand's damp, hard surface, taunted by
The sun which dries it out of
Existence.[5]

(21)

As I stood alone in the dark blue sea,
A wave sprang up from behind me.
My heart missed a beat as I shielded my eyes.
My ears were throbbing
And my hands were shaking.
It seemed to be waiting for me to run.
But I stood there rooted to the ground,
Then suddenly I sank down with it.[6]

Bubbles are a good resource for blowing, attending, and playing. I have added them to this chapter on the sea because they work so well with the fish resources. But bubbles succeed beautifully on their own, too, away from the sea.

Bubble activities can create some problems because some people blow either too softly or too hard. If you assist the participant in blowing bubbles, it's not always clear where the bubbles have come from, and failure is not defined. Have the participants wave a bubble wand with a circle on the end. This is an easy way to produce bubbles if one does not have the breath control to blow bubbles.

There are a variety of recommended mixtures of glycerin and soap to make bubbles bigger and stronger. Ask a preschool teacher what mixture he or she uses for bubbles and you'll probably get good advice. Carole, who worked on my staff, used the plastic holders from soft-drink six-packs. She swirled them into the soap and then swung them in the air—the bubbles flew everywhere!

You can hardly avoid getting at least one bubble on your body during bubble activities. Be careful; sometimes the bubbles pop in the eyes, which is a bit painful. You ca remedy the problem with a washcloth soaked in cool water and a hug of love.

---

[5]Lewis, R. (1969). Seaweed. In *Journeys: Prose by children of the English-speaking world* (p. 198). New York: Simon & Schuster.
[6]Lewis, R. (1969). Seawares. In *Journeys: Prose by children of the English-speaking world* (p. 197). New York: Simon & Schuster.

Remember, bubbles are messy. The first—and last—time I used them at a convalescent home, I realized that the old folks were having a great time but that they were also walking around in puddles of slippery soap. I had created a hazard. Passing the bubbles around the circle can be very messy. The floor or a lap can easily get filled with soapy water. Have a spare bottle or two of the liquid so the activity can move on even if there are accidents—and there most likely will be accidents.

Bubbles can be introduced while instruments are being played; let the bubbles float around the room while the music accompanies them. You can blow bubbles over a projected light and onto a screen during work with shadows and movement, adding to dramatic presentations.

There are alternative liquids with which to make bubbles. Blowing bubbles in a drink through a straw creates froth that can be consumed once the bubbles disappear. Blowing paint through a straw and onto a piece of finger-paint paper can create some interesting designs, but there's always the possibility of ingesting paint, so be careful.

Here are a few bubble activities. Other blowing activities appear in Chapter 8. I'm sure you can come up with many more, so get going!

(22)
Bubbles, bubbles,
Everywhere!
Blow some bubbles into the air.

Have the participants watch the bubbles in activity 22. When they pop, have them snap their fingers, bang a drum, or strike claves together. If instruments are not available, just use popping sounds made with the mouth. The inclusion of such instruments as glockenspiels, triangles, finger cymbals, and kalimbas accentuates the flowing movement of the bubbles as they glisten in the light. The popping sounds announce the departure of the bubbles, and new bubbles can be introduced by other sounds. The instruments provide a quiet activity building on the animation of the bubbles, with all the participants waiting to be the first to announce a *pop!*

(23)
Bubbles, bubbles
Everywhere,
Floating, popping
In the air.
[Pause while bubbles are blown.]
Look through them.
Grasp them quickly
Before they disappear.

Activity 24 is simple and might require only a strike of a drum or a tambour. The sound *boooooom!* could be the response elicited from each participant, or the sound of clapping hands would provide the sound for popping bubbles.

(24)
Big bubbles,
Little bubbles
All around the room.
Some float up
And others go boooooom!

Activity 25 reminds me of Blanca, a teacher who worked at Fairview with severely physically handicapped persons. She changed some of the activities I use so that she was comfortable with them. Her delightful Czechoslovakian syntax, such as "pop for me one," evoked responses even from individuals so disabled that one wouldn't have expected any response. She adapted and developed very basic resources and presented them with such energy and animation that her work provided me with a tremendous lift. I love to watch a child, bent and apparently nonattending, suddenly lifting a hand to play a tambour, strike a ball, or shake a bell. Around Blanca, eyes twinkle and dimples appear because all the children are working so hard to please her that they please themselves in the process. Blanca has trained a number of assistants who model her presentation and become obviously turned on to what they are doing. At the end of the activity, they all are—or should be—exhausted . . . and pleased. As you have probably gathered, Blanca is very special to me.

(25)
The bubbles fly high,
High in the sky.

Activity 26 can be a nonverbal one of pointing to parts of the body or places in the room where participants suppose the bubble goes.

(26)
Where the bubble goes,
No one knows.
Can you suppose?
Can you suppose?

Use activity 27 to identify parts of the body, clothing, or another person's name. If you are using strong bubbles, you can place them on parts of the body and then have the members of the group pop their own bubble on a specific part of their body. You can use plastic bubbles or balloons taped to a part of a body. Choose carefully what tool will pop the balloons; for safety, you may have to be the person who does the popping.   Following a bubble with a flashlight beam can build on the movement of the bubble as it dances around. The flashlight needs to be controlled so that it isn't shined into others' eyes; the bright light can hurt the eyes.

(27)
Move like a bubble;
Groove like a bubble.
Moooooove,
Groooooove!
[Pause.]
Pop!

Chapter 20

FOOD

The processes involved in making and experiencing food are naturals for Orff-Schulwerk. Some of the activities in Chapter 15, among other chapters, involve food; I have not repeated these activities in this chapter. Manners, sequential tasks involved in following a recipe, setting a table, and decorating are all skills that can be included in developing food activities.

Because food is a primary reinforcer, you can be sure it will be a success in Orff-Schulwerk activities. Some leaders choose to give a treat at the end of an activity. Others have to use food bribes to get participants to volunteer to join a group. (I've seen this particularly with the mentally disabled.) I think food reinforcement can easily be overused, thought, because Orff-Schulwerk activities are themselves enough of a reinforcement.

Passing a bowl of fresh strawberries around the circle, each person taking one—or being handed one—and tasting that one food, removed from other food stimuli, is a sensual experience. Smelling and tasting a slice of orange, a small tomato, a fresh carrot, or soup the group has made in a Crock-Pot can be a wonderful part of the group process. Make every effort to stimulate the senses.

Excuse me—I suddenly feel the need for something to eat!

If activities are scheduled right after mealtime, one easy activity would be for each person to tell what he or she ate at the meal. Here are some very simple activities related to recent food experiences:

(1)
Munch, oh munch, and
Crunch, oh crunch,
What did we have for lunch?

(2)
Tell us your
Favorite,
Most favorite food.

(3)
Snap, pop, cer – e – al,
　1　　1　　5　　5　　5

Snap, pop, cer – e – al,
　1　　1　　5　　5　　5

Snap, pop, cer – e – al.
　1　　1　　5　　5　　5

Let's hear some!
　3　　2　　1

The response to activity 3 can be various snaps and pops made by instruments and/or bodies. Move on with the process by putting a few participants into a box, opening it ceremoniously—or secretively, and having the popping cereals come out of the box with movement and orchestration. Pour on the milk and eat the cereal for closure, if it seems appropriate, with the popping dramatically diminishing. Suddenly, nothing is left . . . and the only thing to do is maybe wipe the mouth or—heaven forbid!—burp.

Activities 4 through 6 can be combined or used separately.

(4)
My throat is dry;
I want a drink.
What kind of soda?
[Or: What kind of drink?]
Let me think!

(5)
Soda pop bottles—
Pop, pop, pop!
When the bottle's empty,
Stop, stop, stop!

Pantomime the drinking in activity 5 with dramatic sounds, then finally sigh for closure. Are you ready? Enter the bubbles into the belly!

(6)
Soda pop bottles—
Pop, pop, pop!
Bubbles in the belly—
Stop, stop, stop!

With activity 6, make the sounds of the bubbles in the belly while the person who has indulged in libation holds his or her tummy and walks or rolls around. It's silly, but you know what? It's fun!

In activity 7, orchestrate and/or verbalize what Tommy or Sally Tucker has earned for supper by his or her singing or playing. The group sings the first two lines, and then Tucker sings or plays for a supper. Then either one person or a group of persons decides what to feed Tucker. The group can chant foods in random singing, or Tucker, as a conductor, can bring different people in to determine what he or she will eat. The different people can sing foods or play foods by using pantomime and movement.

(7, Part I)
Lit – tle Tom – my[1] *Tuck – er*
  5   5   5   6   5   3

Sings for his sup – per.
  5   5   6   5   3

[Or: *Plays for his supper.*]

(7, Part II)
[Pause]
_____[Name]_____ *sings* [Or: *plays*] *for sup – per.*
  5   5   6   5   3

(7, Part III)
What will we feed him?
  5   5   6   5   3

---

[1]*Tommy* can become *Sally* (and *him* and *his* can become *her* and *hers*, respectively) if appropriate to the gender of the participants.

(7, Part IV [2])
Lit – tle Tom – my Tuck – ers
5   5   5   6   5   3

Ate all their sup – pers.
5   5   6   5   3

Hush, Tom – my Tuck – ers—shhhhhh!
5   5   6   5   3

The mice want some!
3   3   2   1

I wrote the closure in the plural because there will have been a number of Tuckers by the end of the activity.

(8)
Nothin' says lovin'
Like somethin' from the oven.[3]
What do you think
Says it best?

(9[4])
Mmm-mmm good,
5   3   1

Mmm-mmm good.
4   2   7

Tell us what you think is
5   5   5   5   5   4

Mmm-mmm good!
3   2   1

---

[2]This part brings closure.
[3]This should remind you of the Pillsbury TV commercial.
[4]Sing this to the tune of the Campbell Soup song.

Food values, fattening foods, and food combinations are lively discussion materials for activity 9.

(10)

When my stomach gurgles
With a very loud *sound,*
[Pause for everyone around the circle
to quickly make a gurgling sound.]
I hope for my sake
Special food is around.

What special foods would a stomach be asking for?

(11)

Yummy tummy
Full of that
Makes you fat—
You know that!

With activity 11, develop accompanying movements and rhythms with shaking, scolding fingers while stomachs bulge out and all lick their chops and rub their tummies. The activity can be done in a canon/round form in four parts, with each group coming in after *Yummy tummy.* When developing rounds, you repeat the verse as many times as the number of groups participating. If there are four groups, you will go through the verse four times. The movement and the quickness of the verse should make the canon fun.

When a simple answer, such as one fattening food, is given as a response, go back to the beginning of the circle and have each person repeat his or her response so that the group builds a total listing of the "fat foods."

Get the group "walking fat" or rubbing their tummies. Close with a gradual fading of *Makes you fat—You know that!* until it is very quiet, then a loud *You know that! Clang!*

With activity 12, encourage singing or stating what the meal will be. Have instruments playing the foods or individuals singing foods. The creator of the meal might ask different people to contribute to the meal. Suggest an item like spaghetti. Have spaghetti orchestrated and then add garlic bread. Orchestrate the bread, then move on to salad, coffee, cream, sugar, and so on.

(12)
Company is coming.
What a treat!
Let me plan [play] a meal
We might eat.

With all the activities in this book, I make suggestions that you might want to use. You may want to think up some of your own, though, or stick with a simple response, which might be more appropriate for your group. There is no need to clutter an activity. It takes skill to do things simply but not simplistically; it takes skill to get others to do things simply. Here are some instructions I found on writing haiku:

> Remember Blyth's admonition that Haiku is a finger pointing at the moon, and if the hand is bejeweled, we no longer see that to which it points. . . .[5]

Deliver the goods straight and pure. The combination of the goods will add sophistication to the composition.

Here's an activity that uses various TV food commercials:

(13)
Watch – ing TV ads,
Watch – ing people eat,
Watch – ing TV ads—
Which treat shall I eat?

Make up some good motions with a good ostinato for the bass. Use finger cymbals for accenting the word *ads*. Get a timpani going on the word *eat*, and it becomes a playful activity. Encourage singing, motions for expression, and questioning what to eat. Draw on a ready resource—TV.

Come on leader, risk it! Get your face warmed up and try dividing the groups and presenting them with a challenge. Come on, leader, risk it!

Help your participants think of TV ads. Perhaps divide your group into a few smaller groups and have the smaller groups bring

---

[5]Hackett, J. (1969). In *The way of haiku: An anthology of haiku poems* (p. 252). Tokyo: Japan Publications.

their projects to the main group. Leadership skills will be difficult at first for the smaller groups; you may have to help leadership emerge. The groups will be dependent on you at first. You may want to give the group an opportunity to present something and then finish the activity with an open-ended closure. Then the participants will work on the materials away from the session. They will watch TV and get new ideas, and when it is time for another session of Orff-Schulwerk, let the groups get together again and extend their success. Help them expand and discover!

With activity 14, develop a stirring sound prior to a response.

(14)

Stirring, stirring
Round in the pan.
What, oh what
Comes out of a can?

You could use the following activity before a shopping trip:

(15)

A tisket, a tasket,
I've got a grocery basket.
Listen to the grocery sounds
I have found.

This same activity repeated after a shopping trip might bring new sounds to the session that were discovered while shopping. Again, this would be a product of open-ended closure. The plans for a trip initiate thoughts and sounds, and the experience of shopping expands on them.

(16)

Some foods are good—
Yeah, good!
[Raise arms up in the air in praise.]
Some foods are bad—
Yeah, bad!
[Hold arms down in disapproval.]
What kind of foods
Should your body have?

(17)
Pounds, pounds,
The scale responds.
I want to lose weight—
Tomorrow is too late!

With activity 18, get dramatic. Talk about how people feel when they don't look the way they want to. Talk about movement limitation, difficulty in bending, and general health. What makes you feel better physically and mentally?

(18)
Oh my—ugh—tight!
My clothes hardly fit!
Oh my—ugh—tight!
Whatever should I do?

I've used activity 19 many times. It was developed by a teacher in Bakersfield, California. The motions she used were very good for coordination activities. I've expanded it into a circle ostinati activity. A simple statement or sound that goes into a soup would contribute well to co-authorship.

(19)
Sweet potato,
Sweet potato,
Oop, oop, oop!
What did the cook
Put into the soup?

On the first *Sweet potato*, the right fist pounds the left fist, then vice-versa on the second *Sweet potato*. The right and left feet slide forward and back, changing position on the *Oop, oop, oop!* (like in the Mexican hat dance). Then place the hands on the hips and say, "What did the cook put into the soup?" to finish the action.

Each person decides what he or she will put into the soup and makes motions or gives an impression of what is being put into the soup. When everyone has taken a turn, I start building, from the first person, an ostinato of what was put into the soup. Sustain that ostinato and keep building on each contribution to the soup until the full circle has action and sound developed and a circle ostinati is in process. I close the activity a variety of ways. I might have the group move into the center, chanting "The soup, the soup," and end with either a loud shout from everyone—"That's what the cook put into the soup!"—or with the participants intermingling their soup sounds, gradually coming back to the circle as the sounds fade away. It often seems appropriate to start some rhythm patterns to be imitated at the closure. I think there has to be a gradual unwinding from an activity, and the rhythm exercises draw the group back together and provide relaxed control. The activity is fun and "high" and needs a good closure. Don't kill it!

When you are working with this soup theme, you may need to remember what everyone put in the soup. If you are working with participants who need extra help, as you start around the circle they may well have forgotten what they put in the soup. Give them help and move on. There is no expected response for this activity, only the general idea of what it is the cook put in the soup. That idea can expand in many ways and take many forms. Going back around the circle and restating what each person put into the soup emphasizes what co-authorship is. The end product is a joyous celebration in a group process. Each person, regardless of disability or limitation, can successfully contribute. When I'm teaching, I usually place this activity at the end of a unit, so there is a break and an opportunity to unwind.

The circle ostinati is an excellent party game. It can involve building a machine with motions. Silly sound developments or an emotion composition, such as ostinati of laughter, fear, or crying, can evolve, too, but this will depend on the sensitivity of the group. When a group has worked together for a period of time, their emotional and verbal relationships develop and so does their music. As each person becomes sensitive and responsive to other group members, the group dynamics expand. Each person realizes both his or her own personal worth within the group and the personal worth of the other group members. All the components of Orff-Schulwerk—music, art, movement, dramatics, poetry, mime, and voice—become responsive to the group. The products of co-authorship grow rapidly through exploration, development, discovery, and expansion.

Another activity I use is one I developed after an experience with my daughter Shari. She was a child then and tended to have grimy little hands reflecting play. I was in the bathroom one morning. She came to me with her hands behind her back and said:

(20)

Open your mouth
And close your eyes,
And I will give you
A tasty surprise!

No way was I going to open my mouth and close my eyes, because I could imagine all the horrible things that might be offered to me. I realized immediately what a high level of trust people need when they're asked to open their mouth without their knowing what will be popped into it. I had my reasons to doubt Shari: when I forced the issue, guessing what was behind her back, I didn't succeed. What she had, in fact, was an old, mushy marshmallow Easter egg that she'd found in her treasures in her room, and it was late summer that day. Her hands were encrusted with her gift, and she was delighted to move on when I refused to open my mouth; she'd had no intention of tasting the gift herself.

The next day, I used the activity at Pacific State Hospital (now Laterman Developmental Center) in a workshop I was teaching. Each person lay on the floor, with their feet in the center of the circle. I had one person help me put a morsel of either pineapple, peanut butter, lemon, or honey in each person's mouth, using a fresh spoon with each taste. Everyone was instructed not to discuss each taste but to lie back and just experience it. I assured them each item was clean, safe, and liked by most. When everyone had tasted one of the foods, I had the group sit up and I asked that the various flavors participants had tasted be matched with an instrument, still without discussion. I called out a flavor and those who had eaten that flavor orchestrated it. There were pineapple, honey, lemon, and peanut butter compositions played. Some of the tastes were combined so that two- and three-part developments emerged. It was interesting to find that some of the members of the group did not recognize the taste of pineapple.

Another time, I had clients who were verbal and cooperative join a training group at Laterman. When I passed out the food bites, one of the women complained loudly, "Is that all we get?"

Here are more fun food activities:

(21)
Fee, fi, fo, fum—
What tastes good in your
Tum, tum, tum?

(22)
Cooking, steaming,
Bubbly goo—
What will you throw
Into our stew?

I love tacos. Clay, flour, fantasy, and instruments can all can be part of the taco man in activity 23. A hot buttered taco sure would be good!

(23)
Taco, taco,
Taco man,
Make me a taco and
Put it in my hand.

(24)
You scream,
I scream,
We all scream
For ice cream.

Activity 25 is a good outdoor activity. The blowing and spitting can be great exercise. Choose different surfaces and listen to the sounds each makes when hit by seeds. Aha, is that me?

(25)
Watermelon seeds
Spit from the mouth
Make a funny sound
When they bounce!

Chapter 21

COLORS

The Colors live
Between black and white
In a land that we
Know best by sight.
But knowing best
Isn't everything,
For colors dance
And colors sing
And colors laugh
And colors cry—
Turn off the light
And colors die,
And they make you feel
Every feeling there is
From the grumpiest grump
To the fuzziest fizz.
And you and I
Know well
Each has a taste
And each has a smell
And each has a wonderful
Story to tell . . .[1]

I've included part of the *Hailstones and Halibut Bones* verse on color because it's such a great introduction! I received a copy of the book from an elderly woman who visited a class I was teaching at the University of the Pacific. She observed a unit I was teaching on color, and then she sent the book through a mutual friend. I really have appreciated it. Many of you are familiar with the book, but oftentimes because I am not always teaching, I am not exposed to neat books that are popular in the school system. *Each has a wonderful story to tell* sticks in my mind in so many instances.

---

[1]O'Neill, M. L. (1961). The colors live. In *Hailstones and halibut bones: adventures in color* (p. 59). Garden City, NY: Doubleday.

(1)
Colors live!
Each has
A tale to tell!

For activity 1, have participants select instruments to represent colors and tell a tale. (Use instruments anytime they expand ideas!) You can use color impressions or free-thought colors.

(2)
Everywhere
Choose a color you see
Somewhere!

For activity 3, choose colors and relate them to moods. Then build a story. As the story is told, have someone throw different pieces of colored paper toward the person telling or writing the story while the storyteller incorporates the preestablished mood of the color into the story. Add orchestration with instruments assigned to colors; for example, the color brown is assigned to one person, who chooses the bass xylophone. When the mood color is thrown out, the storyteller uses the mood in story content while the instrument accompanies the mood color. Artwork, such as a large mural, or movement also could be used to illustrate the colors of moods.

(3)
Colors are happy;
Colors are sad.
They make me feel gloomy
Or they make me feel glad.

In activity 4, use bright scarves of color that can swish and shout. One or more color combinations can move together with musical accompaniment. Long, brightly colored ribbons flying from sticks are terrific for introducing movement. Phyllis, a teacher of the deaf and blind at Fairview, brought in wood chopsticks, separated with ribbons stuck between the prongs. They feel very good, and they swish.

(4)
Swish brushes of color;
Twirl and shout!
Reveal what you're all about.

(5)
Colors have moods.
When I feel ____[mood]____ ,
My color is _____[color]_____ .

Activity 6 is a fantasy that provokes identity with color. A story may develop about a wish influenced by color.

(6)
My wishes are colors
That may come true.

For activity 7, narrate a scene with colors perhaps while everyone is still lying down after activity 6, or have the color sounds splashed on to big sheets of paper. So that the paint sticks well, use finger paint with starch added to make it extra thick.

(7)
Color dream—
Lie back and listen.
What colors do you hear?

I developed the following color activity and used it in a video and at a conference of the National Association for Music Therapy, Inc. (now the American Music Therapy Association). At the conference, I had attendees knock around weather balloons. It worked well, except for some loud bangs when the balloons hit the overhead lights and a few of them popped. Oh, well—what's a little extra noise?

(8[2])
Dreams are colors.
Dare to dream,
Dare to dream.
Dreams are colors.
Risk a rainbow,
A rainbow,
A rainbow.

In activity 9, assign colors to instruments, and when participants move, have the colors being worn by the dancer orchestrated. For example, if Suzy is wearing blue shorts and a white blouse, the instruments assigned the colors blue and white accompany or direct her movement.

(9)
Who has ____ [color] ____ clothes?
[Pause to search.]
Stand up and show us those!
Who will play a ____ [color] ____ sound
[Pause to select one or more people.]
So ____ [color] ____ clothes can move around?

Encourage descriptive words, not sentences, relating to each color in activity 10. Colors of fine texture might be shared by participants. These could be explored and orchestrated.

(10)
Colors—
How do they taste?
How do they smell?
How do they feel?
How do they look?
How do they sound?

I use colored transparent Plexiglas palettes in activity 11, passing them around so each person can select a color. The colors can be mixed or used singularly as a primary color. When each person chooses a color, he or she also chooses an instrument to match that color. After

---

[2]Make up a tune to go with the song; encourage harmony.

all have chosen a color, I have the same colors grouped together and develop a color composition. Sometimes it's necessary to ask some participants in one color group to choose a different instrument than the one they originally picked, because there is only one of that type of instrument. If this happens, explain that using another instrument will contribute a greater variety of sound.

(11)

The sky is blue;
The grass is green.
Which of these colors
Makes you dream?

The Phantom Tollbooth,[3] by Norton Juster, has a delightful chapter on color called "A Colorful Symphony." I wish I could share it with you here, but it is too lengthy for this book. Read that chapter and the one called "Discord and Dynne," which continues with colors.

One evening at a creative practices class at the University of California, Los Angeles, Martha Wampler and Mara Sanders informed everyone before mealtime that we would be making movies after dinner. We all combed our hair, the women checked their makeup, and then we all entered a room atypical of a movie set. Newspapers were spread out, felt-tip pens were scattered everywhere, and people were leaning over long rolls of film, drawing away. Some were adding to others' work and some were guarding their work so others would not infringe on their territory. Well, I got in on the action, hair tousled (which is not unusual for me), bottom in the air (which means I was really into it), doing my part in the movie-making. Then the film, which was the clear lead film used at the beginning of every movie shown and is available a low cost from camera stores, was rolled onto a reel and we saw our work A slow-motion switch on the projector made the film easier to work. The newspapers had been used to determine the minimum length of film needed to establish a pattern that could be orchestrated with ostinati and accents. I don't remember if we actually orchestrated the film that night; the group was very large and so took a great deal of time to complete the film. Since then, I've used the project and I've had the instruments selected to represent colors after the first showing. The film conducts the entrance and exit of instruments assigned to colors as the movie rolls away. I've taped the

[3]Juster, N. (1961). *The phantom tollbooth*. New York: Epstein & Carroll.

music and then shown the film again, playing the recorded music while each person moved to one of the colors. With this project, sometimes a single color appears and sometimes three or four patterns of color are projected at one time. It really is a fun time, and it's easy to do. Marks can be made on either side of the film. There's a lot of socialization and while everyone is on the floor working, and there is the joy of discovery.

> Live acrobats on a trapeze,
> The colors pose and bend their knees,
> Twist and turn and leap and blend
> Into shapes and feelings without end . . .[4]

---

[4]O'Neill, M. L. (1961). My dog Clementine. In *Hailstones and halibut bones: adventures in color*. Garden City, NY: Doubleday.

Chapter 22

ART

GLITTER, PAINT,
AND SHAVING CREAM

Art in Orff-Schulwerk has many possibilities. Bonnie Bickerstaff, the special friend of mine who lives in Georgia and about whom I told you in Chapter 19, initiated some of the activities in this chapter. "Swish Blue," activity 1 here, was introduced in a session at Fairview. Bonnie loves glitter, so of course she began the activity by going to different people and sprinkling blue glitter on them in the mystical manner that only she could do. Then she asked those so glittered to follow her. She had them sit at a large piece of butcher paper on the floor and presented each person with a can of blue tempera paint and a wide paintbrush. As the group sat on the paper, they chanted:

(1, Part I)
Swish blue,
Brush blue [Stretching out body],
Big or bitty [Pulling in body].
What is your blue?
What is your blue?

Each participant swished and brushed with delight. Then Bonnie moved on:

(1, Part II)
Swish blue,
Brush blue,
Big or bitty.
Play us your blue.
Play us your blue.

The participants then selected an instrument and played the sounds of their blue. You may well imagine the glitter that was in hair, between teeth, and on the bottoms of dirty bare feet. No spectator—and later, no hallway or car—went untouched by the mystical glow filling the room! I only wish I could swish Bonnie's blue glitter on this page!

Another activity on the blue theme, which also appears in Chapter 6, is this:

(2)
Touch blue,
Touch new—
Touch you!

Use blue paint to mark the part of the body that will be used to touch the person sitting next to the "toucher" and then touch blue paint on the spot where the "toucher" has touched the other person. Be prepared to hear from those who are responsible for providing the clothes for the participants. Try to protect clothing by emphasizing limbs and facial parts. Instead of paint, you can use blue sticky note paper or a blue felt-tip pen.

Try body painting while outdoors and wearing swimsuits or sloppy play clothes. Have a hose near by to rinse off; of course, the activity will end with everyone drenched. If possible, do the painting near a mirror or a window that will reflect participants' colors. This is a social activity, and it requires trust to allow others to paint designs on one's body parts. Mix some body lotion into the paint so it will come off easily and not be so abrasive. Watch the eyes: the paint–lotion combination can smart.

Paint can draw out clients in ways you'd never suspect. I remember Sammy, who would never look in a mirror in Orff-Schulwerk sessions. Suddenly one Fourth of July, he appeared at the makeup booth that was set up as part of the festivities and had his face made up. It was admired by bystanders, so he went directly to the mirror. He was so fascinated that he could not move away from it. He commented approvingly on his body. Sammy, with the right stimulation, sought out the mirror on his own, without the aid of Schulwerk!

On another occasion, paint, with a boost from shaving cream, worked wonders for a therapist. Nice-smelling shaving cream is used in a variety of activities by developmental specialists at Fairview; putting the cream on mirrors and having participants track the cream is a typical activity. One hot summer day, I was directing a class at the University of the Pacific, using felt-tip pens in an art activity. I had a blind music therapist as a student in the class. She was not realizing success with the activity (for obvious reasons). I got out a can of menthol shaving cream and stacked the foam high on a large piece of butcher paper. (I should have used finger paint paper; butcher paper is too absorbent.) I added dry orange tempera to the foam. The student couldn't see the orange, but it helped others see clearly what she was producing. She worked with the foam, whatever she touched turning orange. Finally, after painstaking work, she completed a foam sculpture of two interlocking hands. The artwork was neat . . . but then the fun! Everyone wanted to feel the bright foam. There was orange everywhere and hands grasping other hands, slipping, pulling, playing. The paint was easily washed off with a squirt from a hose, but not until there were orange hand marks on trash cans, bathroom doors, sidewalks, bare thighs, bottoms, and anywhere imaginable. The activity was joyous and spontaneous. The housekeeper did not have the same experience, however.

One of the first art activities I used was on a large piece of butcher paper, rolled out on the floor, on which participants used paint or felt-tip pens. I encouraged everyone to draw with these words:

(3)
Who will scribble
And who will draw?
Who will scribble
And who will draw?

Sometimes with this activity, I've gone around to each person while he or she draws, using the rondo form. The activity moves more quickly when each person draws at the same time. The rondo form emphasizes individual, simple contributions, which I honestly prefer to elaborate works, but it tends to rush those artists who want to spend time selecting colors and extending their design. I've found that the frustration of the participants makes it not worth pursuing that preference. I also have found that it helps to go around to each participant and draw a line on the paper defining specific territory so each person can work without interference and trespassers. I usually draw different shapes on the butcher paper and put each person's name at the bottom.

The activity can expand so that each artist selects an instrument with which to orchestrate his or her drawing. I do use the rondo form for this part of the activity. After each person has orchestrated his or her art product, I have the group move around the butcher paper, orchestrating others' drawings. The music changes as the different instruments orchestrate each drawing. Sometimes it is effective to have one person select other drawings that go with his or her own, and then have those artists join in a composition of "alike" artwork.

I use individual pieces of paper with felt-tip pens, pastels, crayons, or textured substances such as liquid sand or flour with color and enough liquid to be fluid. If you're using wet substances, it's best to use finger paint paper, because newsprint and butcher paper get soggy. Have each person write a message to the group or to one person or tell a simple story on the piece of paper. Hang each picture with tape, then have it orchestrated by the artist while others look at the artwork.

SPIDERS AND BOXES

One student at the University of California, Irvine (UCI) brought in a cigar box and put a piece of paper inside the box, on the bottom. She added some tempera, using one color at a time. She then placed a marble in the box, closed the box, and shook it, which produced surprising spiderweb designs. This is the chant she used with the cigar box spider:

(4)
Spider, spider
In the tree,
Show us what
Your web will be.

Here's another activity with the spider in the box:

(5)
Spider in the box,
Leave us a message . . .
Your own special message.

There is a neat record available that two students introduced in one of my classes at UCI. It's called *Spin, Spider, Spin* and was done by Patty Zeitlin and Marcia Berman. The record has other excellent animal resources, too. The same students introduced spinning a web and playing "Spider Catch Fly" in the web, drawing webs, beautiful wax-and-dye work with spiders drawn by children, and a human spider web, formed by bodies lying on the floor. The presentation was outstanding. I told them I'd already written a spider section and wished I'd waited.

Activity 6 will make spiders of everyone. The movement suggested in weaving a web and then snaring a catch is very dramatic.

(6)
If I were the spider walking there
On a thread of silk in a world of air
Above all blue and beneath all brown,
I'd get so dizzy, I'd fall right down.[1]

Here's a good, purposeful shaking activity:

(7)
Shake to the left [Clap, clap].
Shake to the right [Stamp, stamp].
Shake up high [Lift arms high, then: Snap, snap].
Shake down low [Drop arms to the floor, then: Clap, clap].
Where did ____[Name]____ 's
Marble go?

Each person taking a turn chooses a piece of colored paper and puts it in a cigar box, along with a marble and some liquid paint. The box is then taken to the center of the circle, and while the group chants, the performer shakes the box. Something else that you can use, and that would please Bonnie, is Weldwood Hobby & Craft Glue in place of the paint; you can mix tempera with it. When the box is opened, glitter is thrown onto the gluey paper. When the excess glitter is shaken off, there is a dazzling design made by the marble and the performer. Many of the participants will not want to dirty their hands, because they've been trained to believe they must always looking neat and clean, particularly if they appear different from others. People seem to pay more attention to others' irregularities, including a messy appearance, when a person is physically different. Developmentally disabled women seem to have the most difficulty allowing themselves

[1]Fisher, A. (1969). Tightrope walker. In *In one door and out the other* (p. 17). New York: Crowell.

to get messy. Encourage wearing play clothes and have paper towels and a wet cloth nearby when no sink is available. Soothing, good-smelling lotion can be a reward for cleaning up. It can also be part of another great activity, like this one:

(8)

Teacher: *Hands fresh and clean;*
Lotion is your treat.
[Teacher squirts lotion into each person's hands,
then checks the hands before filling them with lotion.
Some participants may have to return to wash better.
When they return:]
Hands fresh and clean;
Lotion is your treat.
[Teacher squirts lotion into the now clean hands.
After all hands have been squirted with lotion:]
Rub it,
Push it,
Make it disappear!
[The teacher models accentuated wringing
and rubbing of his or her hands,
looking at his or her hands,
and rubbing hands with the participants.
In closure, teacher and group say together:]
The smell lingers
Softly on our fingers.

All participants sniff their hands, and the activity closes quietly.

OTHER ART SUPPLIES

When I've attended various Orff-Schulwerk art sessions, I have been impressed and turned on to a wide range of supplies available for my every need. Lore Grove, an art teacher with the Downey Museum of Art in California, provided more resources from junk items than I ever imagined existed. I can't imagine what her work area at home is like. She brings in such things as bones, boxes, strings, bottle tops, rug samples, sticks, and scraps with unique sounds, and they are all available while she works in the background, encouraging and assisting in strengthening a project so it will not be demolished by being touched. She never interferes with what one is trying to do. She encourages and applauds everyone's efforts. *What fun!*

My friend Bonnie uses a lot of paper plates for faces and hats. They are handy and stiff enough to hold a lot of materials. She's had a group make Halloween masks, space faces, Easter hats, and Christmas decorations. She's also used paper bags for puppets and hats. Here's an activity that goes with her Halloween masks:

(9)

Ghosts and goblins,
Witches and ghouls—
What scares you?

The participants all delight in one another's unique uses of an everyday paper plate, a little glue, a little paper, and some bright colors to make a special mask. Each person shows his or her scary face in rondo form. Clean-up can be the closure. The paint supplies are messy and should be used away from the instruments. Take out the instruments everything is dry and cleaned up and add to the experience.

Clay, another wonderful art medium, is just waiting to be pounded, shaped, dried, and placed in the kiln for firing. There is so much excitement in working the clay that when finally the kiln is opened and the ceramics have cooled, the glazed objects fairly leap out, each expressive, some fooling the viewer, some disappointing, some thrilling, some surprising. Someone always denies having made a particular object, because it has changed so from the dull paint placed on the bisque prior to firing. I make extra pieces, or encourage participants to make more than one piece, in case of accidents in the kiln.

My own initiation into working with clay was in Gatlinburg, Tennessee. I worked with a teacher who approached the clay organically. I excelled in such an environment. My hands, my strength, my stillness, and my active motions controlled and tempered the clay, each wedge of clay becoming part of me. I learned when the clay would fall, when it would assume a leatherlike texture, when it needed to be turned, and what rough edges needed smoothing. Finally, I had the thrill of watching the projects exit the kiln. The teacher's success became as apparent as the student's.

One of the pieces I'd made was my pride—and the teacher's. The teacher accidentally knocked it from the cooling shelf where it was tinkling and cracking as it cooled, bragging of its emergence. (This bragging goes on for hours). The teacher was so disappointed and felt much worse than I did. The color was beautiful, the form a part of me, and the whole was a culmination of my experience. I took the pieces home with me in my suitcase, along with my other projects, because I wanted to share the colors and the ideas in the shape with my family. John, my husband, never let me forget my proudly removing a bunch of broken pieces from a bag in the suitcase, after he had dragged my luggage into the car at the airport, barely able to lift it. The pieces really were nothing to me or the family; their life had ended. I was moving on. That's how it is!

ENABLING SUCCESS
AND OWNERSHIP

In some art sessions, participants will not be able to grasp the brush and hold it upright. Get behind them and put their hands and arms through the motions, gradually removing your assistance, if you can, so that part of the work is their success in approximation of completing the task.

Please don't go around and correct or improve the artwork. Don't add your cute ideas or insist on the addition of lines or colors. You might encourage expansion, but let each person decide and explore on his or her own. I been frustrated by art teachers who infringe on the work of others. In Orff-Schulwerk, diversity is reinforced, so please keep your grimy hands off the participants' work! We are interested in process, not product. Again, the product certainly is of value, but because we are talking about clinical and educational process, the product may never be complete.

My daughter, who was in a program for the mentally gifted, brought home a beautiful acrylic painting that surprised us all. As we discussed it with Shari, it became apparent that the art teacher who came into her class and worked with four children at a time (what nice staffing) had made corrections to Shari's work so that it was more "finished." Shari had learned from the teacher but wasn't that proud of her work, because it changed when just a few "trained" lines were added. She knew that it was not her accomplishment alone. Since that time, she brought home other work that she clearly defined as to whether she had done the work or the instructor had helped her. The assistance seemed to decrease as the school year progressed. I think the students, verbal as sixth-grade preteens can be, took care of the problem. (In fact, sometimes their self-righteousness can be a bit obnoxious!)

It is hard not to strive for perfection if you know how to get there. But the process of exploration and discovery should not be denied the student. A few of my peers who were studying to be a music therapists felt great disappointment in their clinical work because they were striving for accomplishment. Their own needs were more for music performance and accomplishment than for meeting the needs of those they were treating. It was difficult for them to accept the fact that some of those they were working with would never move beyond the most elemental accomplishments. I accept their feelings, but I also think that they had chosen the wrong profession.

Be sure to put each person's name on his or her work and try to display the work on the wall, or take it back to a residence if you are working in an institutional setting. Once the artwork is open to observation, *I am* is clearly defined, as is co-authorship. When all the work is observed, *I am a part of, I am worthy*, and *I am aware of others* are defined. Sharing with the total group encourages observation, possible imitation, and eventual expansion. One learns to judge one's own work as well as deal with the judgment of others, allowing the confidence in one's worth and abilities to develop.

Dr. Ronald Kogler, a practicing psychiatrist in the Los Angeles area, wrote an article for *The Circle,* a publication included by the Creative Practices Council, Inc. in a "Happy Birthday, Carl Orff" issue. In the article, which was entitled "A Selfish Tribute to Carl Orff," Dr. Kogler stated that "the creative person, almost by definition, sees *beyond* the crowd and cannot afford to let himself be swayed by its opinions, since he senses that no one can really understand what he is trying to do. . . ."[2] Perhaps this outlook seems too sophisticated in work with limited, disabled individuals, but if you are truly providing elemental expression and exploration, do not brush aside the creativity of these people. The unique interests, traits, and abilities of the most elemental human beings are worthy of exploration. The splattering of flying paint can be as rewarding to limited individuals as careful line drawings are to those who can do them with skill and intellect.

It is your responsibility to adapt materials so that all participants can be successful. Build up the handles of brushes with tape, Aire-cast,

---

[2]Koelger, R. (1973). A selfish tribute to Carl Orff. *Creative Practices Anthology: What Excites Me* (Bitcon, C., ed.) (p. 6).

or other adaptive materials you've discovered. Short brush handles are easier to use than long handles in most cases, just as heavier brushes are easier to use than lightweight brushes. Experiment with art materials just as you experiment with mallet handles, beaters, and the sticks used on instruments. For the most successful participation, each person must be positioned according to his or her needs. This may mean moving an individual from a chair to a mat, turning someone on his or her side, or even letting a person use his or her toes to hold the brush. As the facilitator, you must be inventive in developing resources that provide a successful, creative experience for all.

ℰⓈⓇ   ℰⓈⓇ   ℰⓈⓇ

Don't you see my rainbow, teacher?
Don't you see all the colors?
I know that you're mad at me.
I know that you said to color the cherries red
        and the leaves green.
I guess I shouldn't have done it backwards.
But teacher, don't you see my rainbow?
Don't you see all the colors?
DON'T YOU SEE ME?[3]

---

[3]From Cullum, A. (1971). *The geranium on the window sill just died, but teacher you went right on* (p. 34). New York: Harlan Quist.

Chapter 23

CREATIVE DRAMATICS

The other chapters in this book contain many examples of creative dramatics resources. I wrote a specific chapter on creative dramatics, however, because fantasy, imagery, and stories require special thought. This chapter doesn't spend much time on mime because there are others who can teach you much more about it than I can. There are many good books available on mime.

Dawn Noll Lemonds usually covers creative dramatics when she teaches with me, and she does an outstanding job. She changes her presentation each time, so I am still attending and excited. Many of her storybooks are ready production material.

When people are challenged to get together, draw on the resources they have, and produce, in a specified amount of time, such as 20 minutes, it is amazing how the creative process works and adapts as the show goes on. Not only are the people in the audience surprised, amused, and pleased but so are the performers. All sorts of unplanned additions are made, even during the show, because the creative process is continuous. It does not stop when you're ready to go on stage!

I think sometimes I've been most free, and most silly, and played roles most unlike myself in the creative storytelling and dramatic sessions I've attended at different conferences and workshops. The process is always mysterious because no one person knows what will happen. If a group is well established, the creation of dramatic roles and the emergence of leadership move swiftly. If the group is incompatible, the joy is not as apparent. When I'm in the audience, I often become aware of the contrast between people's personalities and the roles they selected. Working with contrasts or opposites is how we explore and discover.

In Easy in English, by Mauree Applegate, there are many creative resources in game form for writing creative poetry, stories, and, in some cases, dramatization. Many times, creative dramatics involve the creative use of prose-poetry and flashing words. Applegate wrote that one should "begin with actions, pantomime, and creative play, then proceed to words. Poems at first are only 'talk-offs' of feelings and actions." Applegate is hard on teachers, giving them sole responsibility for turning on students:

> . . . No teacher ever has to teach a child to write poetry; it lies in his interest unborn. The teacher is merely the midwife. A poem is just a picture of feeling and anybody that has feeling can write out his kind of picture; deeper pictures for deeper people and lesser pictures for lesser. . . . Which people are deep and which are shallow? Sometimes a child who seems to be a cup is just a well with a tight lid on. Poetry writing allows a perceptive teacher an occasional look under the lid . . . but he mustn't stand and stare![1]

I think the same thoughts apply to creative dramatics.

Activity 1 encourages seeing beyond surface appearances. The item in activity 1 could be many things—a tambourine, a big bass drum, a bamboo shaker. Whatever is selected, pass it around and explore it. What else could it be? A tambourine is round and has metal shakers and skin pulled across it tautly. But really look at it! What else could it be? Bobbie developed this excellent activity to provide an opportunity to really examine an instrument and to get participants thinking about things that are alike and those that are different. This activity can stimulate participants to come up with resources for subsequent activities.

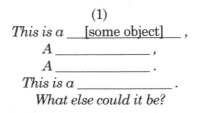

(1)
This is a __[some object]__ ,
A _____ ,
A _____ .
This is a _____ .
What else could it be?

An occupational therapist in a class at the University of California, Irvine (UCI) put a curtain on a box. She put all sorts of items into the box for touch-and-feel experiences. You can do the same for activities 3 and 4, but since I'm dealing with make-believe/fantasy, I would seek items of an imaginary form to be drawn from an imaginary box.

---

[1]Applegate, M. (1960). Fog. In *Easy in English: An imaginative approach to the teaching of the language arts* (p. 235). Evanston, IL: Row, Peterson.

(2)
Clocks and rocks
And fuzzy socks.
Can you guess
What's in this box?

(3)
What's in the box?
What's in the box?
Sweatsocks?
Goldilocks?
What's in the box?

You can use instruments with these activities. Going through them ahead of time might better prepare participants to attempt new instruments and movements.

Staff from Camarillo State Hospital (now closed) in Camarillo, California, developed this with Dawn at a Fairview workshop:

(4)
What's under the rug?
What's under the rug?
Give it a tug—
A tug.

The instruments in activity 5 could be small hand instruments, either imaginary or real.

(5)
Hickelty, picklety,
Snickelty, snag—
What kind of magic
Is in this bag?

Pass the secret, which is of an established size and weight, from one person to another in activity 6. The secret must be handled carefully because it belongs to someone.

(6)

Who has a secret to share?
What size is it?
What shape is it?
Who has a secret to share?

Where the Sidewalk Ends,[2] by Shel Silverstein, has a poem entitled "The Invisible Boy." A blank square is presented with the poem. From this idea comes an activity that could be an art project, mere verbal description, or music and a story:

(7)

Here's an invisible picture
As interesting as can be.
What's in your special picture?
Will you please tell [show] me?

You could split the activity and have the story told and then say:

Oh what a special picture to see!
Will you draw the picture for me?

Or:

Oh what a great picture!
Now, how about drawing it?
We would like to see.

---

[2]Silverstein, S. (1974). *Where the sidewalk ends.* New York: Harper & Row.

After telling the story in activity 8, have it dramatized. Make a production out of it!

(8)
Strange, weird things
Going on around you.
If you were invisible,
What would you do?

These last few activities are quite advanced for many, but they are usable for a few. Remember, you have access to these if you have a group ready to try; alternatively, you can adapt the activities for a less sophisticated group or a group that seems to prefer less structure.

Anyone who has learned "going around the corner" in mime will want to include activity 9 for sure. It might be a good time to teach some mime, have everyone practice, and then include it in the chant.

(9)
Hey, just around the corner,
You might meet _____ .

For the next activity, the question is asked by one person of another. Each asker fills in the blank as he or she chooses:

(10)
Fiddle dee dee,
Diddle dee poo.
If you saw a _____ ,
What would you do?

Activity 11 can involving miming of opening the door, entering it, and looking it.

(11)
Someone's knocking on the door, the door.
Someone's knocking on the door.
Who can it be?
Let's go see.
Someone's knocking on the door, the door.

Cymbals clashing or a gong being struck would work well with activity 12. After the gossip is told (probably made up), then the group says together, "Oh my!"

(12)
Gossip—
He said that she said
That _____ .
[Closure:] *Oh my!*

Activities 13 and 14 will get everyone laughing with shared funny tales.

(13)
A little yellow monkey
Sitting in a tree
One morning got the giggles,
Going "Tee hee hee."

(14)
What's the funniest thing
You can think of?
What's the funniest [*saddest, noisiest, most quiet*, and so on] *thing*
You can share?

Coffee cans filled with different materials deliver different messages in activity 15.

(15)
I have an ear
On each side of my head.
Shaking the can,
I think that it said _____ .

The subject of hibernating might help bring out diverse responses.

(16)
What do you say to a bear
That's waiting,
Just about ready
For hibernating?

Activities 17 and 18 are pure fun.

(17)
And now . . . and now
For dancing pants
Doing—yes, doing—
A fabulous dance!

(18)
One, two, three,
Father caught a flea.
How did he catch him?
Let me see!

Dramatize and build the story in activity 19. Try dividing a group into smaller groups and see what the variations on the story will be. You can make it a very simple storytelling activity if you want—it's a little more simple than even "The Three Little Kittens."

(19)
When the cat's away,
The mice will play.

Let everyone's imagination run wild with activities 20 through 22.

(20)
Heigh hi,
Heigh ho,
Let's all go
To the rodeo.
Heigh hi,
Heigh ho,
Do your thing
At the great big show.

(21)
Circus, circus, everyone;
Bring a friend and have some fun.
Peanuts, popcorn, Crackerjacks,
Who will make a circus act?

(22[3])
I can be anything I want,
So try to guess what I
Am going to be.

Storytelling is always fun. My shuffle nook frequently provides a good break in a day's activity. The book is a group of cards that have simple, colorful pictures, with such statements as "and the walrus said," "the banana ran," or "the police officer climbed." Each person draws a card, and the story begins. Each person has two sides of the card, with specific words that have to be included in the story at any point when telling his or her part of the continuous story. I used the shuffle book recently with teenagers and they didn't want to stop. You can make up your own cards or, if appropriate, give out blank cards to students and have them bring in a collection of their own cards after they've seen the shuffle book. Magazine pictures work well on the cards.

Narrating a story and bringing in instruments and actors as you go along can be both very complex and very simple. Take, for example, the simple scenario of a family coming in from the farm fields to eat dinner. If you include animal sounds, the family walking to the house, the dinner, and so on, the total composition might be very sophisticated.

---

[3]Sung to the tune of the Oscar Mayer Weiner song ("Oh I Wish I Were an Oscar Mayer Weiner"), which first came out in TV commercials in the early 1960s.

Though activity 23 sounds very simple, it, too, can produce sophisticated stories.

(23)

... Old coins
With finger-marks
They tell stories.[4]

Storytelling and creative dramatics many times provide seren-dipity—an unlooked for loveliness in a day that truly warms the heart.

Carlos B. Hagen wrote of Carl Orff, "For Orff, music is born of language and poetry and becomes an inseparable entity with speech delivery, body movement, acting, dance, lights, and so on."[5] This chapter is the extensive "and so on." Lights truly contribute to the storytelling, just as do the curtain, the audience, a stage, and of course masks, makeup, and costumes. How far do you go? Well, what do you and your group members want?

Do you have to perform for the Parent-Teacher Association? Make it less painful by including a few parents; get the story going and develop the scenes and costumes in your Orff-Schulwerk session. Let it happen. Carlos Hagen referred to Orff's works as

> ... In a way sort of 'happenings' onstage, with a well-defined guideline or score. In all the criticisms I've read of Orff's works, one fact stands out clearly: with very few exceptions, most critics fall time and again into the same trap, that is, for them Orff is only a musician, a composer, and must be measured and gauged with the same standard patterns of traditional musical criticism that are applied to Bach, Beethoven, or Stravinsky. The fact that he has gone far beyond the field of music and merged it thoroughly with theater, dance, speech, and even gymnastics is something that is either totally ignored or regarded as absolute heresy.

---

[4]Sandburg, C. (1978). Iron prose street window. In *Early moon* (p. 125). New York: Harcourt Brace Jovanovich.

[5]Author's note: I don't know anything about Carlos Hagen other than that in the 1970s, he was from the University of California, Los Angeles area and was a writer and broadcasted on a radio station. The article of Hagen's from which I took this quote was a photocopy given to me by a student; I don't know its origin.

This is why, in my opinion, Orff's works can only be judged fairly by a critic who is not only well versed in music and opera but also well versed in all of the other arts that Orff makes inseparable from music, a sort of critic of the future (or of the primitive past), a critic that in our compartmentalized Western milieu has yet to be developed.[5]

A student presented a project in Arizona that had Peanuts characters talking to each other in comic strips. She blocked out what was being said and had the story developed about Lucy and what she was saying to Charlie Brown. What a creative way to develop a story!

In Easy in English, Mauree Applegate wrote, "Mood creates the mind-weather of a story. . . . When one wants a humorous effect, one just reverses the process and prepares the reader for the wrong mood."[6]

Dawn used activity 24 in a presentation at a state hospital. Aged grandparents who remembered the times of slavery told stories of black heritage. One woman remembered tales her uncle told her. He had a wooden leg, and she sat on it while he told the stories. The whole process of remembering stories was warm and touching. When we moved on to developing popular fairy tales, the group produced projects that really took me by surprise. They had Red Riding Hood out looking for a fix, and Snow White overdosed. I was taken aback that such scenes followed the warm sharing time. But that was the group process!

(24)
When I was nine,
Storytelling was
My favorite time.

---

[6]Applegate, M. (1960). *Easy in English: An imaginative approach to the teaching of the language arts* (p. 307). Evanston, IL: Row, Peterson.

What happens in creative dramatics is not reflected by the quality of the production, the beauty of the music, or the depth of the story but by what it does to each person creating the drama.

This excerpt from *The Phantom Tollbooth*, by Norton Juster, illustrates the power of imagination:

> . . . In a few more steps, the forest opened before them, and off to the left, a magnificent metropolis appeared. The rooftops shone like mirrors, the walls glistened with thousands of precious stones, and the broad avenues were paved in silver.
>
> "Is that it?" shouted Milo, running toward the shining streets.
>
> "Oh no, that's only Illusions, " said Alec. "The real city is over there."
>
> "What are Illusions?" Milo asked, for it was the loveliest city he'd ever seen.
>
> "Illusions," explained Alec, "are like mirages," and realizing that this didn't help much, he continued. "And mirages are things that aren't really there that you can see very clearly."
>
> "How can you see something that isn't there?" yawned the Humbug, who wasn't fully awake yet.
>
> "Sometimes it's much simpler than seeing things that are," he said. "For instance, if something is there, you can only see it with your eyes open, but if it isn't there, you can see it just as well with your eyes closed. That's why imaginary things are often easier to see than real ones."
>
> "Then where is Reality?" barked Tock.
>
> "Right here," cried Alex, waving his arms. "You're standing in the middle of the Main Street."[7]

Numerous creative dramatics and storytelling resources are listed in the Bibliography, but they represent only the beginning of a collection. Get acquainted with your local bookstores. I've spent hours in bookstores with my daughter, reading and making notes. We always would end up buying a number of books we couldn't part with, so the manager really didn't mind.

---

[7]Juster, N. (1961). *The phantom tollbooth* (p. 115). New York: Epstein & Carroll.

If you are in Great Britain or Canada, be sure to take advantage of the many paperback books there that are sold only as hardbacks in the United States. I really feel annoyed that children's books are so expensive here in the States. They are easier to carry in paperback form, and I am happy to say Shari and I stocked up on a bunch of paperback books we're still enjoying.

Chapter 24

MISCELLANEOUS RESOURCES

When you are initiating a group, you will find that it is most help-ful to have both an established opening and an established closing for each session. In Chapter 6, I gave an opening and closing activity dealing with taking off shoes, going barefoot, and then putting the shoes back on so participants can make feet sounds. Don't forget that particular activity, because if you are taking off shoes at all during a session, it can be very helpful.

Sing or chant each time you do activity 1 so it's always recognized.

(1)
Hello, hello, hello!
It's nice to see you today.
Hello, hello, hello!
Let's have fun, okay?

Give personal attention to each person, touching his or her hair or arms and making direct eye contact. Smile and acknowledge one another.

Use activity 2 when moving from one location to another.

(2[1])
Heigh ho, heigh ho,
It's off to Orff we go.
We sing and dance;
We like to play.
Heigh ho, heigh ho!
[And so on.]

Get train sounds going. Pick up each member of your group by chugging and having them join your line. I've gone around residence

---

[1]Sung to the tune of "Heigh Ho, Heigh Ho, It's Off to Work We Go," the song sung by the seven dwarves in the 1937 animated Walt Disney movie *Snow White and the Seven Dwarves*.

areas and pulled clients from the play yard, the bathroom, or dormitories, having them grab on to the train.

I like the area for Orff-Schulwerk sessions to be somewhere away from a central activity area. As I walk outdoors with the participants to the session, we notice flowers, colors, and smells. Sometimes we discover treasures that can be used in a session.

If you have the right situation, it's fun to wait outside the door and suggest that there will be mysterious and magical things happening behind the door. I sometimes say, "Quickly go into the room, explore the room, and find your own special spot." Have each person grab a spot, "pull in" all that surrounds it, and bring it back to the circle where the session will begin.

Here's a closing activity:

(3)
The time has come to go!
The time has come to go!
Good-bye!
Goodbye!

I try to get the group members to sing "good-bye" back to me. I go to the door and shake hands or hug each person as he or she leaves. If something is lost or misplaced, I can assist while continuing the singing. I do not want to encourage any manipulation. The message is that the session is over until another day. But there is always a stay-behind. I try to ignore that person until he or she makes a step toward the door, and then I quickly smile and encourage the movement out the door. If the person stays longer, I start cleaning up and ignore him or her. Eventually I am at the door singing good-bye. I know—it doesn't always work! I've also had to forcefully remove a limp body. It's difficult to be joyful in such a situation.

Here are more closure activities:

(4)
Good-bye, good-bye!
The clock says we're done.
Good-bye, good-bye,
Good-bye, everyone.

(5[2])
Heigh ho, heigh ho,
The time has come to go.
We'll meet again.
We'll see you then.
Heigh ho, heigh ho.
[And so on.]

Here's a time activity developed by Alice at Porterville State Hospital in California:

(6)
Time, time, telling time.
Time, time, telling time.
What time,
What time,
What time are you?

Get the group moving in a circle going backward, with everyone swinging arms. Use a clock or body movement on the floor to determine time. Or, if you want "to be a-teachin'," use a clock and ask what time it is. All the group members can count off the hours with movement.

Here are a few grooming activities, many of which are functional and can be coordinated with other duties, that are effective if done routinely as a check on how each person looks:

(7)
Who combed their hair,
And who brushed their teeth?
Who combed their hair,
And who brushed their teeth?

---

[2]This activity, like an earlier one, is sung to the tune of "Heigh Ho, Heigh Ho, It's Off to Work We Go," the song sung by the seven dwarves in the 1937 animated Walt Disney movie *Snow White and the Seven Dwarves*.

(8)
This is my body;
This is me.
Look in the mirror,
And what do I see?

Bring in some hand instruments to accentuate parts of the body and for approval/applause.

(9)
Show us how you brush your hair;
Show us that you really care.

If you can get a set of those large teeth with a brush that are used for teaching dental hygiene, you can pass them around and go through the motions of brushing teeth with activity 10.

(10)
My teeth look great
When they're clean and white.
This is my way of keeping them
Clean and bright.

The new and old sounds in activity 11 could take on an added dimension with a group that has knowledge of both songs of the past and those of the present.

(11)
New and old,
New and old—
What is new
And what is old?

Activity 12 needs more of an introduction so people will not be named unless it is appropriate.

(12)
Look all around,
On the ground and in the air.
You will find round things
Everywhere.
What did you find?

Activity 13 can be serious or silly.

(13)
Chow, chow,
It's time to eat.
Tell [show] us how
You stay so neat!

Have everyone make hiccup sounds for activity 14, and then count off the drinks from the cup. You could add more drinks if it takes more to get rid of the hiccups. Have a stash of paper cups and paper towels and a container of water.

(14)
Hiccup, snickup,
Rise up, kick up!
Three drinks in the cup
Are good for a hiccup!

Elaborate on activity 15 by thinking of all the things a doctor is needed for.

(15)
Aaachoo!
Bless you!
Doctor, doctor,
We need you!

Use dramatics and sounds with activity 16.

(16)
Aaachoo, aaachoo!
Bless you!
When you aaachoo,
What should you do?

If you're working in a school or institution, find out what the rules there are so you can use them in activity 17. Combine instruments and verbalization, accenting feelings and encouraging movement. The familiar "Keep calm," "Watch your step," and "Look before you leap" are a typical set of rules. Some colleagues and I did this group of rules with clients one time. When asked what movements went with "Keep calm," one of the boys kept hitting his chest. I couldn't understand until I realized he was saying "King Kong!" We just kept the movement because it came from the group. The group that was supposed to chant "Look before you leap" was saying, "Look before you leave." I only wish I'd written down all the different adaptations of words and titles I've heard through my years as a music therapist. A three-part development is waiting to happen with this activity.

(17)
Safety first
Is an important rule.
At home, at play,
And in your school.

Many of these activities may be age inappropriate for your group. Make changes!

(18)
Piggle wiggle, piggle wiggle,
Piggle wiggle say.
We can learn manners in a fun way.
What's a way to be polite
Every single day?

(19)
Coffeepot, coffeepot,
Blip, blip, blip.
Where would you go
If you went on a trip?

With activity 21, develop a story, a trip, or a place and orchestrate it. If you're really going somewhere after this activity, build on where you're going or have group members determine where they really would like to go. Repeat the activity after the trip, encouraging responses that bring back what was seen or what happened. A field trip becomes more valuable if it is used in activities afterward.

(21)
Let's go someplace—
What do you say? [Clap, clap]
Let's go someplace,
Okay? [Snap, snap]
Does anybody know
Where we shall go?
Let's go someplace [Clap, clap],
Okay?

(22)
Went to the zoo the other day,
Watched the animals run and play.
Some talked soft and some talked loud;
Some of them sat and looked at the crowd.

Instruments and dramatics enter the scene with activity 23.

(23)
Look at the sky;
Look at the stars.
What do you think
Lives on Mars?

Here's another space-related activity that can result in great group development:

(24)
Bloop, bleep,
Bloop, bloop, blah.
How do they talk
In the land of Mars?

The group is divided into a number of small groups, each of which decides what word and what action will be used. The word would not be shared until the movement is shared, and after the movement is shared by the groups, the words with movement are shared by the groups. This activity will end up with active laughter

Activity 25 can use movement, music, art, or just simple statements.

(25)
There are lots of things
That go together:
Shoes and socks,
Bread and butter.
What else
Goes together?

Nancy developed swimming activities for her project in Bakersfield, California, when she first started Orff-Schulwerk. Now she is very wise and, I hope, is doing her work in Hawaii.

(26, Part I: Entering Water)
Who will come to my party?
Who will splash with me?

(26, Part II: Confidence)
Squiggle, squiggle,
Fish in the net.
No place on my body that
I can't get wet.

(26, Part III: Bubbles)
Blow bubbles,
Blow bubbles,
Blow troubles away!

Many activities can be adapted for use in a pool and are fun for getting everyone relaxed and trusting.

For activity 27, get the children who love to make motor sounds putting and purring. Use some instruments if you want, but they won't really be noticed amidst all the noise from the human cars.

(27)
The road was hilly
So the car bounced silly.

Build up train sounds with instruments and then do this next activity:

(28)
Clickity clack
Over the track—
Beautiful things to see
When I look back.

Expand on what is seen from a train. Perhaps develop train sound ostinati and have the "beautiful things" played on an instrument as the melody.

A UCI student brought this to class as a project:

(29)
Pyro-symplastic-infantibulum[3]
Is a word from the world of make-believe.
Pyro-symplastic-infantibulum—
Whatever could it mean?

You'll get lots of noise with this activity:

(30)
Cock-a-doodle-do!
The rooster shouts for you.
Cock-a-doodle-do!
You shout, too.

---

[3]You can use other words, whether found or developed.

QUESTIONS COMMONLY ASKED

1. Where do you find all of these activities?

I haunt bookstores. I think about open-ended statements when I should be thinking about other things. I talk with people. I share with peers. I work with students in developing resources. I attend workshops. I work with other specialists whenever I can. It helps if you are a little bit—just a little bit—crazy!

2. Where do I get training in Orff-Schulwerk?

Internationally there are Orff-Schulwerk specialists. The Orff Institute[1] is in Salzburg, Austria.

When I meet people who work in Orff-Schulwerk or other creative practices, I usually have found a new source for information about exciting and innovating developments in the community. I also find that attending conferences for special-needs groups or for different professional groups provides many opportunities for sharing.

Allow yourself the experience of working with a variety of teachers and specialists. Each has a tale to tell and a uniqueness to share. Eventually, as you filter through your experiences, your unique qualities will become apparent to you and others. You will find yourself giving as much, if not more, than you take.

Four of my favorite teachers were Martha Wampler, Gertrud Orff, Grace Nash, and Avon Gillespie. There are many teachers I have not worked with, but these four were co-authors in a composition—Orff-Schulwerk.

---

[1] Orff Institute, 5010S Salsburg, Frohmburgweg 55, Austria.

3. Where is Orff-Schulwerk used clinically?

Schulwerk is used in a number of state facilities, schools, and private facilities across the United States as well as internationally.

I have trained others in hospitals and educational systems out of California, but I do not know which facilities in other states are using Orff-Schulwerk. There are other clinicians who provide training, so you might try contacting the American Orff-Schulwerk Association[2] to inquire about clinical programs.

When I teach, I have as many teachers as I have clinicians in my classes. There is little difference between working with adults and children in that the skill of the teacher or clinician determines the value of the program. Orff-Schulwerk is used clinically with all ages and with people of all needs. Sometimes it is used in business seminars. There is a lot to be explored, and age-appropriate activities can be developed with different functions. Don't think any particular activity can't be used; it can, if you adapt it. You have to hang loose, find or remember your resources, and attempt and explore. Try it—you'll like it. You'll experience success and perhaps find a new specialty.

4. How do you determine who should be in Orff-Schulwerk?

Your abilities and the needs of those for whom you are providing services should establish some guidelines for you as to who should be in which group. I think it's necessary for an individual to be able to respond to basic commands:

- "Look at me!"
- "Come to me!"
- "Sit down!"
- "Stand up!"
- "Give me your hand!"

---

[2]American Orff-Schulwerk Association, Department of Music, Cleveland State University, P.O. Box 391089, Cleveland, OH 44189-8089.

If an individual is can respond to these five commands, it's likely he or she can start participating in a group situation.

When establishing a group for Orff-Schulwerk, I frequently include nonverbal people and verbal people in the same group and physically disabled people and people without physical disabilities in the same group. I include one or two acting-out behavior problems, until the behavior is under control, and then add a few more when establishing a group. Social levels, ages, and interests all are considered when making up a group.

5. How large should a group be?

I like to have between 8 and 12 participants in a group that has people who need a lot of assistance and have developmental potential. A staff of 3 to 4 people is appropriate in a group this size because of the seriousness of problem behaviors. The social process does not easily flow if there are too few people in the group. The leaders in a group participate just as like other members of the group. Models are very necessary, and they should be trained.

6. How long are the sessions and how frequently are they held?

This varies according to the needs of the participants and the purpose of the sessions. Some sessions might be once or twice a week for an hour's duration, whereas another group might have 20-minute sessions five times a week because of hyperactivity, limited attention span, and conflict of schedules and personal life plans. Remember, there are activities in addition to Orff-Schulwerk that all are vying for time in the schedule. Let others who work with your clients know the benefits of Orff-Schulwerk so you can combine efforts and share.

7. Why is a circle used, and why do sessions frequently occur on the floor?

The circle is a natural group form. In a circle, each person can see the others in the group and a feeling of unity is created. Movements can be easily seen and shared. Why sit in rows and look at the back of someone else's head? I have used chairs in a circle because many participants have problems getting down to the floor, but this may result in sliding and scooting around and use of legs to interfere or get more attention. This is manageable once the rules of taking turns are understood and when you remember to reinforce good sitting behavior. A rolling bedside table can be used to move instruments around. Staff are more likely to join in when they're sitting on a chair like the rest of the group.

In the circle, one can go around, up and down, in and out. The circle provides a natural stage—the center of the circle, a sacred area where ideas are shared. The floor provides a structural limit. It helps maintain the group, in the form of a physical barrier. When one is on the floor, one can go no further down. Body movements relate to the floor and space. It takes the floor to establish balance and territory, and space to expand and explore that territory. When chairs are used, movement in space is inhibited. Sitting on the floor prevents swinging feet from hitting a target and prevents participants from falling over or knocking a chair over, causing interference. In some situations, though, chairs are appropriate.

The leader gets on the floor with everyone else. There is bound to be interaction when everyone is in each others' face. When a teacher sits on a chair and the students watch, there is much less togetherness than I desire in an Orff-Schulwerk session.

Who will the participant please and why? Don't give more attention to those who seem to be sitting or walking in the right space. When instruments are on the floor, bodies can more readily adapt their position and balance. Sounds can more freely be explored when everyone is on the floor.

Adapt the shape of the circle when appropriate. The circle could be extended to lines, random movement, small clusters of forms, semicircles, triangles, or squares. When the group is starting and closing an activity, though, it's likely that the activities will again take place in a circle.

8. I've noticed that many times I'm the only one chanting. Am I doing something wrong?

Not necessarily. If you are using a simple chant, one with few words and a voice range appropriate to the abilities of the participants, you probably are on your way. Have you repeated the chant enough times? Are you singing too loudly? Is the group—or part of the group—nonverbal?

If you are getting at least one word, mumbling, or maybe some body movements that accompany the chants, then you're moving right along. The level of participation depends on who's in the circle. If the participants are quiet and listening, you might be working miracles.

9. Why are sessions sometimes great and sometimes horrible?

We all experience ups and downs. It's part of the group process. Don't always expect an exciting, rewarding experience. Let it happen! Don't miss it when it provides the "ahas" of Orff-Schulwerk. When you place too many expectations on the sessions, you are really being too controlling. You might well prevent diversity or miss what is happening. It might feel safe at first, but it quickly becomes a bore to always know what's going to happen. Let your group experience those ups and downs. Realizing that there are different moods and feelings is part of the growth process.

10. What about behavior problems? How do you manage them?

Those who are providing the leadership to the group must have their act together! If one person can manipulate the group so he or she gets all the attention, then there is trouble. Have different behavior problems assigned to specific staff members. Each staff member should know what the plan is when a specific behavior occurs. One might remove the individual who is acting out from the circle, explain to that person that his or her behavior is not acceptable, deny that individual a turn, or ignore the behavior and praise someone else demonstrating the desired behavior.

I do not want to get into a behavior management discussion, because that's someone else's book. I think those working in Orff-Schulwerk with individuals with behavior problems should be very knowledgeable in managing behavior. Orff-Schulwerk provides an excellent opportunity to observe cause and effect. A skilled leader will be able to change behavior. If the leader stops, the activity stops and the undesirable behavior is rewarded. All the other members of the group learn that quickly!

Sitting on the floor makes it easy to turn someone away from the group, particularly if that someone is sitting on a carpet square and the floor is waxed. Sitting in a circle makes it easy to deny eye contact and gives the leaders the chance to quickly reinforce any approximation of appropriate behavior, by giving eye contact, facial approval, and verbal praise. I use my legs to block movement into the circle or to turn my body to "time out" while reinforcing another person. On occasion, I will place a small person between my legs on the floor and reinforce any appropriate behavior demonstrated with body touch and praise. I've seen tire inner tubes and paper cartons used with little people, around the circle, each having his or her own spot to sit in. The carton and inner tubes keep each person in place and are comfortable if adapted.

The leader's attitude is very important. Will the use of time-out materials be considered punishment or a possible success? It is necessary to determine when an individual is shy and when an individual is merely manipulating his or her turn. Don't put yourself in the position of reinforcing the slow response. Sometimes I use a countdown if someone delays his or her response for too long a time. I ask the group to count down with me from 10 to 1. If there is no response, we "blast off" to the next person. Sometimes it seems a bit mean to move on when it looks like an answer is forthcoming; if you haven't adequately analyzed the situation, it might be mean! If someone is painfully shy, you can be more helpful if you assist that person with striking an instrument or providing a response and then gradually fade out your assistance. However, it is interesting to observe how quickly a response is made after there have been a few countdowns and a few turns have been missed.

Occasionally, a participant will leave the circle altogether. If the person isn't disturbing the rest of the group, let the person go and return by him- or herself. Some people have been known to leave the circle every session for as long as 3 months and then gradually remain in the circle a bit longer each time. Leave a place in the circle for the "wandering Orffer." Reinforce that person whenever he or she returns to the circle and ignore the departure.

Sometimes wanderers manage to walk right through the circle at the time that is most manipulative. Evaluate that behavior and develop a plan for dealing with it. I use my leg to block entrance if we're sitting on the floor, or I use my back when the group is standing, moving around the circle as the activity progresses. If someone is not in the circle with the group, that person should be denied a turn. The instruments usually bring a wanderer quickly back to his or her spot.

The room ideally will not have entertaining distractions. A wanderer can destroy art projects, find noisy toys, or decide to put on a tape or CD if the room provides such an opportunity. Sometimes, when working with someone at an instrument, I'll suddenly become aware of kicking feet pushing the instrument or tapping a performer's leg. I try to position myself in front of that person. Sometimes I get my leg tapped, too.

11. What props do you carry?

I have a Mary Poppins–type bag. In it, I usually carry

- A circular, nonbreakable mirror
- A few puppets
- Bubbles
- Shaving cream
- An inflatable beach ball
- Texture tools, such as a sponge or brush
- Color pallets
- A room deodorizer
- Facial tissues
- A floppy hat

- A scarf
- A bit of masking tape
- Cotton
- Felt-tip pens
- Paper
- A few safety pins
- A few shoelaces
- A bunch of little instruments

I add a seashell, an Appalachian Dancing Man (see Chapter 3 for instructions for making one), a kaleidoscope, lead film, tempera paint, paintbrushes, paper towels, and aspirin when I'm planning art projects.

12. Why are some of the notes missing on the instruments?

The pentatonic scale is used extensively in Orff-Schulwerk. It is elemental. The dissonant notes are removed. The pentatonic scale provides a simple framework for melodic improvisation. There are no harmonic demands; thus, the melody is free to soar. The fourth and seventh steps of a scale are removed to form the pentatonic scale. The keys of C and G are the most commonly used on the tone-bar instruments. There are many scales used in Orff-Schulwerk.

Remember:

- Listen to content, not just words.
- Do not place expectations on an activity or person.
- "Boudoirize." In the privacy of your own boudoir, develop your own image and explore that with which you are comfortable.
- If you think your students are turning off, shake yourself and get new resources organized. You that control their "switch."
- Simplify, simplify, simplify!
- Seek out resource people and materials. Put ideas away for another day.

- Take care in monitoring your voice inflection and facial affect. Pace yourself in activities and don't overuse the motions with which you've become comfortable. Otherwise, you might fall into a rut.
- Orff-Schulwerk is preintellectual and intuitive.
- Don't overlook humor.
- Let things happen.
- We are seeking child*like* images, not child*ish* images.
- You may be criticized for having so much fun, sitting on the floor "all by yourself in the moonlight." Hang in there and give others the chance to explore and discover. The first time is the hardest. All you need is some success.
- Instruments are not crucial when you're initiating Orff-Schulwerk.
- Enjoy!

ℰℛ   ℰℛ   ℰℛ

God bless you
You grew
You learned hard lessons
How to exist
But the children you were are still waiting
For you to go back for them[3]

---

[3]Pintauro, J. (1970). *A box of sun*. New York: Harper & Row.

ORFF-SCHULWERK
BEHAVIOR CHECKLIST

This is a copy of a behavior checklist that was developed at Fairview when we first started using Schulwerk. This can be a good resource for developing other assessment tools, because it offers a number of ideas of what can be observed and worked with in Orff-Schulwerk. Modify it as you desire.

I. Measurement of Creativity
    A. Development of Independent Responses

        Scale 1, *Content of Contributions* (frequency of
        self-initiated responses):
           0—Makes no contribution
           1—Responds by copying others
           2—Response includes some individual
              contribution
           3—Initiates total contribution

        Scale 2, *Frequency of Patterned Responses:*
           0—Does not respond
           1—Repeats same patterns always
           2—Varies pattern of responses somewhat
           3—Nearly always changes response patterns

        Scale 3, *Completion of Unfinished Expression:*
           0—Never completes expression
           1—Sometimes completes expression
           2—Usually completes expression
           3—Always completes expression

    B. Development of the Use of Descriptive Resources

        Scale 1, *Verbal Use of Resources Response:*
           1—Unintelligible verbalization
           2—Minimal intelligible verbalization (single-word
              responses)
           3—Simple description with little elaboration
           4—Considerable elaboration of experiences

Scale 2, *Nonverbal Use of Resources:*
0—No response or inappropriate responses
(includes physical, musical, or facial)
1—Minimal response
2—Appropriate response with some elaboration
3—Appropriate response with considerable
elaboration

II. UNDERSTANDING OF INSTRUMENTS

	Never	Sometimes	Usually	Always	Comment
1. Correct force applied					
2. Holds instrument correctly					
3. Assumes correct posture when required					
4. Recognizes physical properties (e.g., wood, glass, metal)					

III. MEASUREMENT OF ATTENTION SPAN

	Never	Sometimes	Usually	Always	Comment
1. Eye contact with leaders					
2. Eye contact with peers					
3. Waits attentively in group formation while others perform					
4. Involvement with group activity					

IV. MEASUREMENT OF RETENTION

	Never	Sometimes	Usually	Always	Comment
1. Takes turns within rondo form					
2. Joins in group re-sponse					
3. Forms circle upon enter-ing room					
4. Stays within circle during routine					
5. As-sumes appro-priate body po-sition for activi-ties					
6. Returns to appro-priate posi-tion in circle after turn					

	Never	Sometimes	Usually	Always	Comment
7. Remembers appropriate use of equipment					
8. Remembers chants					
9. Can choose other members of the group by name					

V. MEASUREMENT OF ATTITUDES

	Never	Sometimes	Usually	Always	Comment
1. Anticipates activity with pleasure					
2. Willingly participates (without coaxing)					
3. Conforms to activity					
4. Exhibits confidence in ability to participate					
5. Accepts directions from peers (any attempt to follow directions)					
6. Accepts directions from leaders (any attempt to follow directions)					
7. Volunteers to lead activities					
8. Volunteers to assist with equipment					
9. Volunteers to perform in activities					
10. Aware of self					
11. Accepts others' behavior					
12. Accepts visitors					

	Never	Sometimes	Usually	Always	Comment
13. Accepts new materials					
14. Accepts unusual situations					
15. Handles instruments carefully					
16. Respects personal possessions and others' gifts					
17. Cares for personal belongings					
18. Relinquishes belongings inappropriate to activity					

VI. UNDERSTANDING OF BASIC CONCEPTS

	Never	Sometimes	Usually	Always	Comment
1. Uses appropriate accompaniment with name					
2. Verbalizes own name during chant					
3. Names group members					
4. Responds to own name					

VII. LEARNING BASIC CONCEPTS OF COLORS

	Red	Blue	Yellow	Green	Brown	White	Black	Total
1. Matches colors								
2. Identifies colors by name								
3. Responds to verbal directions to a specific color								

Instructions:

Item 1—Arrange color packet on table in a straight line. Place one color from another packet on table and say, "Can you find this color?"

Item 2—Rater holds up one color card and says, "What color is this?"

Item 3—Arrange one color packet on table in a straight line. Rater says, "Show me the color."

VIII. BASIC CONCEPTS OF NUMBERS 1–10

	1	2	3	4	5	6	7	8	9	10
1. Identifies printed symbol by pointing or selecting										
2. Names printed symbol										
3. Says numbers 1–10 in sequence										
4. Responds to verbal directions regarding numbers										

Instructions:

Item 1—Arrange number cards as shown below on table in a straight line. Ask, "Where is number one?" Indicate in appropriate box whether answer is correct.

Item 2—Rater selects the first number card and says, "What number is this?" Indicate in box whether correct response was made.

Item 3—Ask person to count from 1 to 10 in sequence and indicate in box the numbers given in sequence.

Item 4—Rater arranges 10 empty spools (or any similar item) on table in a straight line. Rater says, "Hand me one spool." Record in appropriate box the number of successful performances. Sequence of numbers presented in Items 1, 2, and 4:

1	9	7	10	5	4	2	3	6	8

IX. CONCEPTS OF BODY PARTS ON SELF AND OTHERS:

Item 1

Where is your _____?	Yes	No
1. Head		
2. Face		
3. Nose		
4. Ears		
5. Eyes		
6. Mouth		
7. Teeth		
8. Arms		
9. Hands		
10. Stomach (belly, tummy)		
11. Back		
12. Legs		

Where is your _____?	Yes	No
13. Feet		
14. Eyebrows		
15. Eyelashes		
16. Tongue		
17. Neck		
18. Cheeks		
19. Chest		
20. Elbow		
21. Wrist		
22. Shoulder		
23. Navel (belly button)		
24. Knees		
25. Rear end (fanny, butt, and so on)		

Item 2

Where is your _____?	Yes	No
1. Head		
2. Face		
3. Face		
4. Ears		
5. Eyes		
6. Mouth		
7. Teeth		
8. Arms		
9. Hands		
10. Stomach (belly, tummy)		
11. Back		
12. Legs		

Where is your _____?	Yes	No
13. Feet		
14. Eyebrows		
15. Eyelashes		
16. Tongue		
17. Neck		
18. Cheeks		
19. Chest		
20. Elbow		
21. Wrist		
22. Shoulder		
23. Navel (belly button)		
24. Knees		
25. Rear end (fanny, butt, and so on)		

Instructions:

> Item 1—Ask person, "Where is your _____ ?"
>> Person indicates by pointing to or moving body parts. Complete all items.
>
> Item 2—Ask, "Where is my _____ ?"
>> Person is to point to location. Complete all items.
>
> (*Note:* For a physically handicapped person, the rater should ask "Is this your _____ ?" and then randomly point to three parts on the person's body and have him or her nod yes or no for a response. The rater should ask, "Is this my _____ ?" and point to three body parts on him- or herself, each time asking for a yes or no response.)

Appendix 3

A BRIEF ON THE CLINICAL USE
OF ORFF-SCHULWERK

Carl Orff, contemporary Bavarian composer-conductor, developed Schulwerk (German for schoolwork) initially in Munich, Germany, and Schulwerk is now used in many nations and languages.

Schulwerk is the use of elemental music in learning through discovery. Elemental music is one's own contribution using music, rhythm, movement, voice, speech, and silence.

Schulwerk is composed of four phases: the idea, its development, its exploration, and closure. The forms are simple, commonly including rondos, ostinati, inventions, call–response and games, allowing experience, learning, and success in co-authorship.

In the clinical use of Orff-Schulwerk, the group process integrates music, movement, language, poetry, art, mime, and creative dramatics. It provides an environment of success in the development of communication skills, sensorimotor skills, social skills, behavioral control, modeling, a sense of personal worth, an understanding of cause and effect, and of an understanding of feelings and affect. It teaches basic concepts and promotes self-help.

Each participant contributes to the group process (the contribution is accepted regardless of the level of sophistication) and is encouraged to further develop his or her ideas.

A variety of instruments that are success oriented are used and other teaching tools are adapted as resources. The quality and skill of leadership in Orff-Schulwerk in clinical practice determines its success. Orff-Schulwerk is lifelong learning and is a joyful celebration!

I'M GETTING INVOLVED![1]

I was touched, unknowingly.
Touched by play,
Disguised as therapy, "used"
With others.
The touch lingered, never
Quite leaving, festering and
Sometimes channeled,
Aware of parts of me that I still
Possessed but had long since cherished
As childhood.
I shuddered to think of the labels of
"Senile," "childlike," and "immature" I'd
Freely used to describe divergence when
Perhaps it was, too, a festering unchanneled.
Critical, laborious relationships replaced
By relationships of trust, acceptance,
Experimentation and wonderment,
An adult—not yet molded?
Not a solid model of expectations
Long ago established,
With "success"?
Others confused, but entertained, gradually
Turning to me for stimuli, exploration, growth, and
Freedom.
Together we soar, diverse beings, without
Fear of diversity.

In the workshop or classroom setting, teachers, clinicians, and others who work with children and adults provide an opportunity to sharing ideas, alluding to accomplishments, referring to the "others" or "they" when speaking of clients/patients/students who are being served, always with the qualification of clinical purpose rather than a natural process.

---

[1]Modified from Bitcon, C. H. (1973). I'm getting involved. *The Orff Echo*.

In the initial phases of instructing a workshop in the clinical application of Orff-Schulwerk, there is a gradual fading, a gradual diminishing of relating participation to "they" and "others." There is, less often, the refusal of eye contact with the instructor, accompanied by nervous giggles and overreaction to diverse responses. Gradually, the gasp of concern when participation is requested diminishes, the clumsy phrasing is less often intellectualized, and the participant less fervently hopes not to be noticed. Constantly, solidly, the group involvement grows, unnoticed, touching us all. We are a group! We've come together to learn to relate to others, away from the group, others who are unique individuals. Instead, we are relating through diverse responses. Spontaneity is rewarded. We are successful; those who seem shy and lingering are given reinforcement for every effort they make, by peers who are suddenly energized by their own success in opening up, by their eagerness to participate and share. Yes, we are still relating the new concepts explored to the clinical application of Orff-Schulwerk. The clinical objectives are reviewed . . . but the process of learning is through the process of participation. We are changing, we the clinicians. How easy it is to wear the title, fit the description, and be safe in establishing methods and using them unswervingly. To suddenly be grouped with others and sitting on the floor, attempting new instruments, sounds, rhythms, movements, and calling into a gong, we enter the second phase of the Orff-Schulwerk workshop process—enjoying what we're doing. We hope no one happens by, because we are not sure what we are doing is right . . . fun, but not necessarily right.

We review some of the components of the clinical application of Orff-Schulwerk, realizing that the components were necessary for our group process, our growth and expansion:

1. **Establish the uniqueness each of us possesses. Perhaps when working with the limited, the initial uniqueness might be in who you are, just by name.**

"I have a name and it sounds like this! I am someone!" Reinforce diversity and help each member seek out the uniqueness he or she possesses, blending it into co-authorship. It is a different experience for disabled individuals to have uniqueness emphasized when usually abnormalities are demeaning and a focus.

Alike and different,

Alike and different,
We are both alike
And different.

I frequently find myself referring to my daughter, who voiced concern to me when she realized her front tooth (a silver shield) would soon be coming out and she would no longer be the only one in the class with a silver tooth. What was her substitute for uniqueness going to be? She now is a very successful lawyer, and she did understand the issue when or just after it came up. I guess I did it right, helping her develop comfort with her uniqueness.

2. **Frame a clear presentation of oneself, stating, "I am beginning; I have something to say; this is my part of the composition," and clearly state closure: "I am through; I readily relinquish my instrument, stick, time and am now ready to attend to others."**

How very difficult it is to relinquish a possession, and how rewarding to the clinician when the participant suddenly establishes closure and relinquishes a turn, knowing that he or she will again be a contributing co-author. The modeling is generalized, and learning is in process, all implied in the structure.

Who will come to my table?
Who will talk with me?
Listen, speak, or look at me?

I have communicated without the need for intellectualization.

3. Focus on success.

Success is an attitude, as is failure. Failure, coming from within the participant, is difficult to identify or modify. The standards for success are established by the group; the standards for failure are a part of the individual's own intellectualized expectations. Place the emphasis on relating, with various forms of communication, and take care in selecting topics of discussion and exploration so all activities relate to everyone in some form. Use material with commonality, basic enough to be retained. Truly, the skill of keeping things simple is worthy of praise as the process matures. Beware communication barriers, such as frills, expansive use of language skills, unrelated material, poor listening, and poor closure.

Listen, listen,
Listen to the sounds I make!

There are many sounds we hear.
Play your sounds for us.
Choose a friend to play with you;
Choose a friend by name!

When themes are kept simple, any participant can expand on them and ideas and sounds will flow from them while others listen and some relate. Personal worth is realized through selection and identification as all listen, wait, and provide reinforcement. Time, dynamics, silence, accent, and length all work together to create a unique response, perhaps an unexpected one.

As the workshop draws to a close, there comes a general feeling of letdown and anxiety. "How will I continue? What happens when we leave this self-stimulating group?" These concerns are real and come from having been exposed to the unexpected—involvement. The spark is there, but how to kindle the flame? The students have soared, but can they maintain flight? They will return to established clinical environments with the responsibility of creating change. This responsibility can easily out weigh the joy of participating in Orff-Schulwerk. Others, not having participated in the group, will question and perhaps belittle because of lack of understanding and an unwillingness to be open. The students must cling to the workshop experience for support. Some students will establish themselves as successful models, whereas others will succumb to tradition, with Orff-Schulwerk being but a small part of their repertoire. But it is still there, perhaps making those students a bit uncomfortable that it is not set free. The "ahas" of Orff-Schulwerk will linger, pushing for involvement.

> I once was touched unknowingly,
> Then touched and touched again,
> The stimuli enabling me the clinician
> To touch others, and touch again,
> For I know I am a part of many compositions.
> I can create change; I *am* change.
> I accept, support, and contribute to
> Diversity.

BIBLIOGRAPHY

CHILDREN'S LITERATURE

Anglund, Joan Walsh (1967). *A cup of sun*. New York: Harcourt, Brace & World.

Austin, Mary C., Mills, Queenie (1963). *The sound of poetry*. Boston: Allyn & Bacon.

Baring-Gould, William S., Baring-Gould, Ceil (1967). *The annotated Mother Goose*. New York: Meridian Books World Publishing.

Baylor, Byrd (1971). *Plink, plink, plink*. Boston: Houghton Mifflin.

Fisher, Aileen (1960). *Going barefoot*. New York: Thomas Y. Crowell.

Jacobs, Leland B. (1964). *Just around the corner*. New York: Holt, Rinehart, and Winston.

Livingston, Myra Chon (1958). *Whispers and other poems*. New York: Harcourt, Brace & World.

Margolis, Richard J. (1969). *Only the moon and me*. New York: J. B. Lippincott.

Newell, William Wells (1963). *Games and songs of American children*. New York: Dover Publications.

O'Neill, Mary (1962). *Fingers always bring me news*. New York: Doubleday.

O'Neill, Mary (1961). *Hailstones and halibut bones: adventures in color*. New York: Doubleday

Scheer, Julian, Bileck, Marvin (1964). *Rain makes applesauce*. New York: Holiday House.

Seagal, Edith (1952). *Be my friend, and other poems for boys and girls*. New York: Citadel Press.

Showers, Paul (1961). *The listening walk: let's-read-and-find-out science book*. New York: Thomas Y. Crowell.

Silverstein, Shel (1974). *Where the sidewalk ends*. New York: Harper & Row.

Withers, Carl (1948). *A rocket in my pocket: the rhymes and chants of young Americans.* New York: H. Holt

POEMS AND PROSE FOR ADULTS

Applegate, Mauree (1960). *Easy in English: an imaginative approach to the teaching of the language arts.* New York: Harper & Row.

Bitcon, Carol Hampton (1989). *Risk it express* (New Horizons series). Kansas City: MMB.

Cullum, A. (1971). *The geranium on the window sill just died, but teacher you went right on.* New York: Harlan Quist.

Hackett, J. (1969). *The way of haiku: An anthology of haiku poems.* Tokyo: Japan Publications.
Herbert, Cindy (1974). *See a child.* New York: Doubleday Anchor Books.

Lewis, Richard (1966). *Miracles: Poems by children of the English-speaking world.* New York: Simon & Schuster.
Lewis, Richard (1969). *Journeys: Prose by children of the English-speaking world.* New York: Simon & Schuster.
Los Altos Writers Roundtable (1966). *Borrowed water: A book of American haiku.* Rutland, VT: Charles E. Tuttle.

Merriam, Eve (1969). *The inner city Mother Goose.* New York: Simon & Schuster.
Midler, Bette (1983). *The saga of Baby Divine.* New York: Crown Publishers.

Pintauro, Joseph (1970). *A box of sun.* New York: Harper & Row.
Prather, Hugh (1970). *Notes to myself: My struggle to become a person.* Lafayette, CA: Real People Press.

Sandburg, Carl (1960). *Early moon.* New York: Harcourt, Brace & World.

ACTIVITY RESOURCES

American Association for Orff-Schulwerk, Music and Movement Education, Cleveland State University, P.O. Box 391089, Cleveland, OH 44139-8089.

Canfield, Jack, Wells, Harold C. (1976). *100 says to enhance self-concept in the classroom.* Englewood Cliffs, NJ: Prentice-Hall.

Hefter, Richard, Moskof, Martin Stepeh (1970). *Shuffle book, a big Golden Book.* New York: Golden Press, Western Publishing.

Nash, Grace (1974). *Child development with music, language, and movement.* **City**: Alfred Publishing.

Raskam, Kay (in press). *Feelings through music* (2nd ed.). Kansas City: MMB.
Ristad, L. A. (1982). *Soprano on her head.* Moab, UT: Real People Press.

MUSIC

Gillespie, Avon. In workshop with Avon Gillespie: A collection of games and songs designed for vocal improvisation and body movement. Melville, NY: Belwin/Mills Publishing; Columbus, OH: Coronet Recordings.

Zeitlin, Patty, Berman, Maria (1974). *Spin, spider, spin.* Freeport, NY: Educational Activities.

CREATIVE DRAMATICS

Ets, Marie Hall (1969). *Gilberto and the wind.* New York: Viking Press.

Field, Edward (1967). *Songs and stories of the Netsilik Eskimos.* Cambridge, MA: Education Development Center.
Friesel, Uwe (1970). *Tim the peacemaker.* New York: Scott Press.

Keeping, Charles (1969). *Joseph's yard.* New York: Franklin Watts.
Klagsbrun, Francine (1974). *Free to be you and me.* New York: McGraw-Hill.

McDermott, Gerald (1974). *Arrow to the sun: A Pueblo Indian tale.* New York: Viking Press. [This book won the Caldecott Award in 1975.]

Saroyan, William (1963). *Me: A modern masters book for children.* New York: Crowell-Collier Press.

Sendak, Maurice (1970). *In the night kitchen.* Middlesex, England: Puffin Books.

Sendak, Maurice (1970). *Where the wild things are.* Middlesex, England: Puffin Books.

Shulevitz, Vri. (1974). *Dawn.* New York: Farrar, Straus Giroux.

Silverstein, Shel (1970). *The giving tree.* New York: Harper & Row.

Tennyson, Alfred Lord (1964). *The charge of the light brigade.* New York: Golden Press.

Way, Brian (1998). *Development through drama.* Amherst, NY: Humanity Books.

MOVEMENT

Barlin, Anne, Barlin, Paul (1971). *The art of learning through movement.* Los Angeles: Ward Ritchie Press.

Bradley, Geraldin Konicki, Leedy, Catherine (1968). *Daily sensori-motor training activities: A handbook for teacher and parents of pre-school children.* Freeport, NY: Educational Activities.

Canner, Norma, Klebanoff, Harriet (1968). *And a time to dance: A sensitive exposition of the use of creative movement with retarded children.* Boston: Beacon Press.

Cherry, Clare (1971). *Creative movement for the developing child: A nursery school handbook for non-musicians* (Rev. ed.). Belmont, CA: Fearon Publishers.

Findlay, Elsa (1971). *Rhythm and movement; applications of Dacroze eurhythmics.* Evanston, IL: Summy-Birchard.

Lowndes, Betty (1971). *Movement and creative drama for children.* Boston: Plays.

Mason, Kathleen Criddly (Ed.) (1974). *Dance therapy, focus on dance VII.* Washington, D.C.: Ampher Publications (American Health,

Physical Education, and Recreation, 1201 Sixteenth Street, N.W.,
Washington, D.C., 20036).
Mettler, Barbara (1960). *Materials of dance as a creative art activity.*
Tucson: Mettler Studios (Box 4456, University Station, Tucson,
AZ 85722).

Schoop, Trudi (1974). *Won't you join the dance?: A dancer's essay into
the treatment of psychosis.* Palo Alto, CA: National Press Books.
Stecher, Miriam, McElheny, Hugh, Greenwood, Marion (1971).
*Threshold early learning library: Vol. 4. Music and movement
improvisations.* New York: Macmillan.

RELATED TOPICS

American Music Therapy Association, 8455 Colesville Road, suite
1000, Silver Springs, MD 20910.

Ball, T. S., Bitcon, Carol H. (1974). Generalized imitation and
Orff-Schulwerk. *Mental Retardation, 12(3).*
Ball, Thomas S. (1971). *Itard, Seguin, and Kephart sensory
education—a learning interpretation.* Columbus, OH: Merrill.

Chaney, Clara M., Kephart, Newell C. (1968). *Motoric aids to per-
ceptual training.* Columbus, OH: Charles E. Merill Publishing.
Cratty, Bryant J. (1967). *Movement behavior and motor learning.*
Philadelphia: Lea & Febiger.

Fast, Julius (1970). *Body language.* Philadelphia: J. B. Lippincott.
Freed, Alvyn M., *T.A. for Tots.* Sacramento: Jalmar Press.
Fruelich, Mary Ann R. (1966). *Music therapy with hospitalized
children.* Cherry Hill, NJ: Jeffrey Books.

Gaston, E. Thayer (1968). *Music in therapy.* New York: Macmillan.

Jones, Bessie Hawes, Lomax, Bess (1972). *Step it down.* New York:
Harper & Row.

Montessori, Maria (1970). *The child in the family.* (Nancy Rockmore
Cirillo, Trans.) Chicago: H. Regnery.

Nash, Grace C. (1974). *Creative approaches to child development with
music, language and movement.* Sherman Oaks, CA: Alfred
Publishing.

Piaget, Jean (1951). *Play, dreams and imitation in childhood.* (C. Gattegno and F. M. Hodgson, Trans.) New York: W. W. Norton.

Ponath, Louise Hauck, Bitcon, Carol H. (1972). Behavioral analysis of Orff-Schulwerk. *Journal of Music Therapy, 9(2),* 56–63.

Sark (1984). *Living juicy.* Berkeley, CA: Celestial Arts.

Schott's Orff-Institute (1963). *Yearbook, 1962.* Manz, Germany: Werner Thomas.

Wampler, Martha Maybury (1973). *And early sing.* Far Rockaway, NY: Peripole Music.

Music curriculum guide for teaching gifted children music in grades four through six. Bellflower, CA: Division of Special Education, California State Department of Education, 1973.

A VERY SPECIAL THANKS

Special thanks for getting this edition together goes to

- Pam Healy, for artwork
- Michel MacKillpop, for computer assistance
- Addie Sorenson, for enduring it *all* and assistance with ZOOM Tect, an adaptive computer
- Shari, for getting me through problems as my daughter and lawyer

ᔕᯋᲠ᎒   ᔕᯋᲠ᎒   ᔕᯋᲠ᎒

One can be creative;
One can expand.
Without friendship,
Teamwork,
Love, and care,
It all would just
Never land.
This book just keeps growing,
And those to be thanked have been . . .
So just keep trying
And make up your own activities;
Trade and share.
Have fun!
Try it—and rock!